Cowboy Christians

Cowboy Christians

MARIE W. DALLAM

OXFORD
UNIVERSITY PRESS

OXFORD
UNIVERSITY PRESS

Oxford University Press is a department of the University of Oxford. It furthers
the University's objective of excellence in research, scholarship, and education
by publishing worldwide. Oxford is a registered trade mark of Oxford University
Press in the UK and certain other countries.

Published in the United States of America by Oxford University Press
198 Madison Avenue, New York, NY 10016, United States of America.

CIP data is on file at the Library of Congress
ISBN 978–0–19–085656–4

9 8 7 6 5 4 3 2 1

Printed by Sheridan Books, Inc., United States of America

This book is about people who are both strong and kind,
and so I dedicate it to
Jean Marie Longo,
the strongest and kindest person I have ever known.

Contents

Acknowledgments

IN 2010, I was having a drink with a colleague at a conference when we ran out of things to talk about. Struggling to keep the conversation going, I pulled something from the back of my brain: cowboy church. It was a thing I had become aware of in Oklahoma, I told him, and I was vaguely considering doing some research on it. He was intrigued, and pushed me to tell him what little I knew. The following day he told someone else about it, and before I knew it, word got around that I was writing a book about cowboy church.

And so I did.

Thank you, Doug Cowan, for the drink, the conversation, and the enthusiasm. It is amazing how that one moment changed my path.

One of the best things in life is getting to know new people. Because this project forced me out of my comfort zone, I was able to meet, talk with, and befriend a huge range of people whom I never would have even encountered before. I have come to appreciate so many of them, especially because they were often very welcoming, generous with their time, and warm of spirit. In many cases we laughed a lot. For their kindness in speaking with me, I thank all of the following: Lee Alphen, Ira Antoine, Richard Boyanton, Michelle Carson, Jon Coe, Jeff and Sherry Copenhaver, Carl Crisswell, Cody Custer, Dave Harvey, Ginger Hayes, Terry and Evelyn Hill, Paul and Donna Lutz, Charky Marquis, Jake McAdams, Scott McAfee, Rob McDonald, Mike Meeks, Larry Miller, Rodney Mitchell, Todd Mitchell, Gary Morgan, Mike Morrow, Ron and Jane Nolen, Dan O'Daniel, Todd Pierce, Randy Reasoner, Bunny Reid, Lynne Schricker, Jake Shue, Sam Ed Spence, Sonny and Cindy Spurger, Jason and Christie Taylor, Chap Thomas, Lynn Walker, Russ Weaver, Tuck Whitaker, Stacy Wiley, Shane Winters, and Steve Womack. I also thank those people who spoke with me only on the condition of anonymity, who were no less a part of the process.

I am also grateful for the cooperation of both the American Fellowship of Cowboy Churches and the Nazarene Cowboy Church Network.

In this book I have repeatedly pulled snippets out of long interviews in order to provide examples or substantiate assertions. In doing so, there is a risk that I decontextualized the speaker such that he or she will feel misrepresented. It has always been my intent to accurately present what people have said to me; therefore if any mistaken interpretations have crept in, I most certainly apologize. On the whole, I do not expect that cowboy Christians will like or even agree with all of my assessments, but I hope they will find something to appreciate in the text, and I hope they will see that individuals have been portrayed with respect and fairness. As an academic, I always approached the world of cowboy Christians very differently from the way believers do. Many people I met seemed to assume this book would be about God, or about a personal faith journey, although I repeatedly explained that it would not be. This book may not be what they expected me to write, and with disappointment many cowboy Christians will conclude that I didn't "get it." On this we will just have to agree to disagree.

I want to extend extraspecial gratitude to a few interviewees with whom I had personally meaningful conversations that continue to resonate with me: Jeff Copenhaver, Rob McDonald, Ron Nolen, and Shane Winters. Thank you for those conversations.

I am grateful for the encouragement I received from many colleagues at the University of Oklahoma. All of my fellow faculty members in the Honors College, as well as in the Religious Studies program, were supportive throughout the research and writing processes, and I feel very lucky to count myself among them. In particular, Julia Ehrhardt provided ongoing pep talks as well as significant advice about the manuscript for which I am quite appreciative. And, although he did not realize it, David Ray spoke pivotal words to me about this project over lunch one day, and I am thankful for his honesty. I also appreciate the many Honors students who expressed interest in my work and asked about it as it unfolded, which was incredibly encouraging. Two particularly excellent students, Elizabeth Abell and Hailey Neubauer, worked as research assistants for parts of this project and contributed in meaningful ways.

Additionally, I want to thank colleagues outside of OU who provided advice and encouragement at different points of the project: David Watt at Temple University; Beth Stroud at Princeton University; Rick Moore at the University of Chicago; Tim Miller at the University of Kansas; and

Gordon Melton and Carey Newman, both at Baylor University. Special thanks goes to Dan Gallagher at the University of Maryland who was a shining star for me, being the trusted friend to whom I could show first drafts without fear. I am also grateful to my friend Benjamin Zeller at Lake Forest College, who generously offered eleventh-hour feedback on the entire manuscript.

I am particularly appreciative to those who loaned, gave, or otherwise helped me acquire research materials: Dave Harvey, Gary Morgan, Larry Miller, Becca Cox Schilinski, Sam Ed Spence, Sonny Spurger, the AFCC, and the Nazarene Cowboy Church Network. Cody Custer gave me a behind-the-scenes tour of the PBR that I will not forget, and Carl Crisswell generously allowed me to shadow him at Remington Park Racetrack. Several librarians and archivists went out of their way to assist me with particular questions, and so I thank Laura Harris (Iliff), Brenda Hawley (FUMC-CS), Laurie Scrivener (OU), and Ariana Ross (Denver Public Library).

I am grateful for funding from entities at the University of Oklahoma that supported portions of the research, including the Walton Family Endowed Professorship; the Junior Faculty Summer Research Program; the VPR Faculty Travel Assistance Fund; and the Honors Research Assistant Program.

Finally, I am lucky to have so many friends, family members, and acquaintances who have been enthusiastic supporters during the course of the project. I wish I had space to list every one of you by name. Please know how much I appreciate your encouragement! It has propelled me forward and given me confidence through the most challenging parts of this work.

Cowboy Christians

1

Introduction

THE COWBOY CHURCH is not easy to find.[1] It does not have a website or a dedicated telephone line, and it has taken some perseverance to find out the exact location and meeting time. I am glad when I see a canvas sign tied to a fence post, indicating I am almost there. Down a bumpy gravel road, I reach a clearing where pickups have organized themselves into jagged rows, and I park my foreign subcompact car among them.

A group of men sits smoking and laughing on a bench outside of a large corrugated metal building, and I walk through their cluster to enter via an opening big enough for a truck to pass through. To my right are empty pens, and up ahead I see the arena. As my eyes adjust from the glaring sunlight and my nose adjusts to the smell of manure, I follow the noise to find where people are congregating. A small section of bleacher seats, installed decades ago when people were more petite, is where the action is. The seats face the arena, and a mobile stage has been pulled up inside the pen, right up against the fence. Climbing into the bleachers, I find an empty spot among the regular churchgoers, who are happily talking and getting up and down to greet each other. They are dressed in jeans and boots, some of them scrubby and others pristine, and the men wear cowboy hats or baseball caps. They are all ages, and they are almost all white.

On stage, men are playing instruments—several guitars, a bass, a fiddle, and drums. The music is loud and energetic, and people socializing in the bleachers have to shout to be heard over it. A man takes the lead on singing, supported by two women, and they harmonize on familiar Christian gospel tunes arranged with country-western flair. Though they make vague enticements for people to join in, most do not. For one song, a woman well over sixty accompanies them with a mean harmonica solo.

It is difficult to pinpoint the moment the service officially begins, because so much of what happens is fluid, and the order of things seems irrelevant. There are announcements, and prayers, a testimony, and there is some banter among the various people onstage and members of the congregation. For much of the service, it is not clear to me who the pastor is. There is a special song sung to everyone having a birthday that week. There is "the Howdy," a period of several minutes during which people walk around saying hello to each other. People welcome me, and shake my hand, but because I do not actually know anyone, it feels like the Howdy lasts much too long. At some point during all of this, a small group of men huddles up in a corner, praying. There is more music, this time clearly performed rather than participatory. People continue to come into the arena and climb over each other to get seats. One man, who has pulled a stray chair off to the side, appears to have brought his dog.

The uniform of the cowboy pastor is a snap-front plaid dress shirt, jeans and boots, a cowboy hat, and a headset mic; it is this last component that most clearly distinguishes him from the rest of the men present. His sermon is the one organized element that emerges from the flurry of activity that is cowboy church. When he takes the stage, everything else stops. All the assistants and band members leave their special posts and people quiet down. By now, the service may have been going on for an hour or more, but his sermon is its central moment to which everyone pays attention.

The pastor opens with a joke, then speaks for about thirty minutes, rarely consulting the notes he has prepared. His sermon has a simple and straightforward thesis that can be articulated in one sentence. He tells everyone the bottom line up front, then starts back at the basics, utilizing a short list of Bible verses to build the argument, illustrate it, and prove its truth. He reiterates the main point numerous times so that no one in the room will miss it; later, he will tell me in confidence that many people miss it nonetheless. In and around his message, he inserts humor. He moves off the stage and walks around near the front rows. He lets his personality shine through. He uses examples from his own life, such as a story about something that happened at the sale barn last week, to tease out points. His sermon deliberately focuses on positive messages about Jesus and humanity rather than dire warnings of hell.

The pastor ends with a brief final prayer. It is noticeably anticlimactic. Everyone chimes in on "Amen," then in a flash, the arena clears. People are up, headed for the door, hopping into their pickups and creating clouds of dust as they pull onto the road.

This is cowboy church. There has been no altar call, no passing of the plate, no choir or singing of antique hymns. No one has flipped open a Bible or prayer book the entire time. Everyone has laughed, and most have tapped their toes to the music. I leave feeling good and wanting to return for more.

Identifying Western Heritage Culture

This book takes as its subject "cowboy Christians." These are people whose religious identity is Christian, and who closely identify with a North American subculture revolving around a matrix of concepts that can include cowboys, ranch work, rodeos, rural life, and nostalgia for aspects of the "Old West." This subculture is often called western heritage culture by its members; others prefer the term "cowboy culture." Many use the shorthand of simply describing things as "cowboy," treating the singular form of the word as an adjective. While some people describe themselves as Christian cowboys, that is a more specific term; my emphasis here is on a wider group of Christian people who personally identify with the cowboy culture, but who are not necessarily cowboys by trade or by lineage: cowboy Christians.[2]

Cowboy Christianity and the cowboy church have grown to become a movement. In the past several decades, cowboy Christians began to organize among themselves, recognizing that they wanted religious spaces that would be contoured by western heritage culture and that would speak to them as a particular subgroup of people. They started forming what are called cowboy churches, a name that is at once simplistic and complex. A cowboy church may be described as an evangelical Protestant Christian church in which everything is western heritage flavor, almost like a cowboy-themed church. But this description fails to capture the depths of what "cowboy" can signify within these spaces, and the levels of meaning church organizers imply by invoking the word. As I have learned about them little by little, I have seen that cowboy churches are not easily summed up with a few words, because they involve layers of structure, ideology, method, values, and expectations.

Furthermore, the world of cowboy Christians goes beyond church congregations and institutions. It involves members' social and intellectual spheres, because the cowboy culture reaches into their homes and private lives and potentially affects how they spend their time, what they discuss, how they see the world, what media they consume, and what they value most. Because I am a scholar who is intrigued by new interactions of religion and American culture, my attention was first drawn to the cowboy church itself. But as I engaged in the first steps of research by attending a few cowboy churches, talking to pastors, and trying to understand the crux of it all, I began to find all manner of cowboy Christian formations, and a long developmental history that had not been systematically retained anywhere. I made it my job to understand and write the history of cowboy Christians and to connect it, as much as possible, with present developments in cowboy Christianity.

I did not come by this subject readily. I spent the first thirty-eight years of my life living in urban centers on the eastern seaboard. Most of my exposure to cowboy culture had come through media representations and distortions, like the television show *Dallas*, the movie *Urban Cowboy*, and the messages of any country singer in a cowboy hat. From these limited sources it seemed to me—if I ever gave it any thought at all—that cowboys were a thing of the past, and people who used this term for themselves were just quaintly referencing a culture that was long gone. When I moved to Oklahoma in 2009, I was surprised to discover many people who consider themselves active members of a thriving cowboy culture, and who readily distinguish between "real" and "fake" cowboys of the present day. I realized that I had a lot to learn.

For instance, what is the difference between English riding and western riding? When I began this project, I did not even know that this *was* a question, because to me horse riding is simply horse riding: an activity that "city people" like myself do not do. But now I can comfortably explain that there are mechanical, functional, and social differences in these two styles. For starters, the tack and saddles are different. Riders wear different styles of clothing and protective gear, and even at the level of language small differences emerge, with English riders more often referring to equestrian centers and western riders talking about arenas. Skilled events in English riding include things like jumping, dressage, and polo, whereas western riders might participate and compete in cutting, reining, or roping. English-style riding and competitions are certainly found in the American West, and in fact I even attended a small Christian fellowship at an Oklahoma equestrian center.[3] However, western-style riding tends to be more dominant in this part of the country, and more importantly, the world of western riding is the cultural home of cowboy Christians. Before arriving in Oklahoma, questions like this had never occurred to me, just as I had never thought about the difference between a ranch cowboy and a rodeo cowboy, nor had I noticed that there are different styles of cowboy hats for summer and winter. This project allowed me learn all sorts of new things, both tiny and large, and conquer all manner of fears. It provided me the opportunity to have long, personal conversations with people I had never previously had the chance to encounter. It was exhilarating to immerse myself in an entirely new milieu and to find that I was still socially and intellectually adaptable, and able to step out of my cozy academic lifestyle that was identifiable by—as one cowboy pastor put it—the softness of my hands.

Certainly, my learning curve about cowboy culture was steep. I was a true greenhorn, and, despite several years participating in aspects of cowboy Christianity, I am barely more than that today. But whether in cowboy church or attending a rodeo or arena event, I have never tried to pretend that I am a part of the western heritage culture. My self-admitted naiveté has often worked in my favor, as I eagerly allowed people to explain things to me and found that most cowboy culture people were happy to oblige. I believe my inexperience with this culture has also allowed me to see it with fresh eyes, able to observe things that insiders might fail to notice. Furthermore, I am more keenly aware of the level of explanation outsiders may need, so I consider myself to be a kind of cultural translator between cowboy Christians and the academic world of religious studies.

Early on in the research, many people told me that the cowboy church movement started in the year 2000 when a Texan named Ron Nolen founded a couple of new churches. As a historian and general skeptic, this story gave me more questions than answers. Foremost, without a specific precipitating event, an actual *movement* is unlikely to begin so quickly. A movement takes time to attract attention and gain steam before people can recognize that something is going on. Secondly, the idea of cowboy church seemed so unusual that I was certain it must have had predecessors or antecedents of some kind, especially considering the long history of western heritage culture. Taking a cue from historian Patricia Nelson Limerick, I always approached the concept of cowboy church as something that probably had deep roots, even if most people were not aware of them. The aim of much of my work has been to figure out the bigger picture of cowboy Christianity so that I could understand not only what it constitutes today, but where it has come from and what might be discerned about its potential future.[4]

To understand that long history, then, I had to begin with "the West." In historical writings, some have used geographical designations to talk about the West, while others consider it a combination of place and activity; some equate the West with ideologies about the American frontier or manifest destiny, while others conceive of it as the rugged spirit of hardscrabble people trying to farm, ranch, or dig for gold on a vast and tricky landscape. Shelves and shelves of books have attempted to solve the issue of defining what the West is and what it has been, and this book is not intended to extend that conversation in new ways. Rather, I seek to pinpoint a definition of the West that reflects what is envisioned and articulated by my subject community in order to explore the ways it shapes their religious identity. However, existing in tension with that statement is the fact that this study is, for practical reasons, geographically limited. Although cowboy Christianity is found all across the United States as well as in other countries, most of its historical "firsts," as well as the majority of its present adherents, have been in Texas and Oklahoma. I have therefore tried to mirror this in my data-gathering, focusing mainly on developments in the Southern Great Plains with occasional glimpses at other locales as they have proven relevant, but also keeping in mind the ways that the West can function as a concept and not just a place.

In the past several decades, scholars have moved away from treating the West as a monolith, increasingly distinguishing its subregions, and the Southern Great Plains might be considered one such area.[5] Distinctive cultural identities specific to subregions sometimes form based on structural factors, such as the physical environment, economics, politics, and vernacular culture. At times, the identity may be shaped by more subjective forces, such as artistic interpretations or propaganda aimed at tourism or investment. A regional identity can even be a rejection of something. As historians Michael Steiner and David Wrobel have lamented, since the postbellum years, "American regions have been battered by successive waves of nationalism, metropolitanism, capitalism, commercialism, and cyberspace. After a century and a half of incessant pounding, New England, the Midwest, the South, and finally the West have been leveled into a smooth expanse covered with interchangeable cities where Americans will always find what they left behind."[6] Perhaps in reaction against this leveling, they suggest, some subregions indulge in aspects of uniqueness that can be highlighted over and against the mind-numbing stasis of the American cultural landscape. Regional identities, then, become deliberate creative endeavors, even while most people come to embrace them without much conscious thought. One way to understand western heritage culture is to think of it as a subregional identity of the Great Plains that celebrates the legacy, both real and imagined, of the Old West cowboy. While this makes logical sense, even a very quick survey demonstrates that cowboy culture today falls outside of regional identity models because its adherents are spread across the globe. Therefore, while it may have started as a subregional identity, cowboy culture today transcends region and thus cannot be effectively explained through that lens.

In fact, because my subject group conceives of a culturally defined community that can stretch far and wide to any place that "horse people" might be found, defining the West—geographically or conceptually—is not of particular importance to them.[7] They are also not necessarily concerned with distinguishing western history from western mythos, because their cultural identity is about the sum total in the present day. The core of cowboy culture relates to an imagined history of white, able-bodied men riding horses across a pristine landscape, assuming authority as caretakers of land and animals, and interacting with each other in noble ways. The cowboy image represents ideals such as honor, individualism, freedom, independence, and bravery. In addition to smoothing and romanticizing actual historical circumstances, this version of western heritage pays scant attention to the influence of Native Americans, Mexican Americans, or African Americans, and women exist only as peripheral figures. Nonetheless, cowboy culture functions as a historical narrative, and members may conceive of themselves as carrying on a tradition, or at least some portion of a tradition. They dress in ways to show they are in that tradition, they show appreciation for art forms that represent it, and they socialize in ways that are attendant to it. It is a culture that makes people feel they are part of a common worldview, a set of social practices, and possibly even a political perspective, regardless of where they live. It is also a culture flexible enough to allow outsiders to dabble or indulge in it. And, because it is not geographically limited, the cowboy culture may be alive and meaningful in the life of one person but be utterly absent from the life of the person who lives right next door.

Certainly, there are exceptions that challenge my generalizations about how understandings of "the West" and "cowboy culture" operate. There are people whose idea of western heritage culture is narrowly based on practices of ranching and pastoralism; there are those who have substantive things to say about distinct regional differences in cowboy cultures; and there are those who are very conscious of the constructed image of the Anglo cowboy and problems that follow from that. There was also a time when I was speaking with a church member in Texas and he mentioned the values "they hold in the United States—"; I interrupted with laughter, thinking he was making a joke, but he did not return my smile. Then, uncertain, I said, "Texas is part of the United States, of course." He stared at me and simply started his sentence again, completing his thought this time. On some level, this man apparently does think of Texas as an entirely different country where they hold different values from Americans, and that was the point he wished to make. Despite these sorts of exceptions, rather than delineating every possible substream of thought on the matter, my aim here is to find commonalities in the way people expressed what western heritage/cowboy culture means to them, and how it connects people who are geographically dispersed.

Cowboys

At the center of western heritage culture is the figure of the cowboy, who may be equally difficult to satisfactorily pin down. Popular culture has supplied Americans with concrete images of cowboys that have evolved over time, albeit always dominated by white male representations. Variations on that image include the outlaw with a quick-draw; the man tending cattle on the open range; the guitar-playing crooner who serves as a role model for children; the simple-minded bumpkin; the steer-wrestling rodeo man; and the two-stepping, truck-driving urban cowboy, among many others. This plethora of different ideas about the cowboy is the result of a century and a half of changing imagery, with each emergent idea about the cowboy being rolled into the previous image rather than replacing it. The reality of the cowboy profession changed dramatically during this period, and in addition, the American populace has had ebbs and flows in its fascination with him. The definition of "cowboy" is a moving target, and individual assumptions about cowboy characteristics are influenced not only by history but by a person's age and the places where they have lived. Historian William Savage has astutely observed that the problem of truly understanding the historical cowboy of the late 1800s boils down to a lack of sources. Because we lack sources, we will forever be limited in what we can know about the lives of working cowboys beyond basic information about the job itself. But that lack of concrete information has also allowed the cowboy to become the subject of fantasy, recreated a thousand times over for different audiences and purposes. For that reason, Savage says it is more useful to study the pop culture versions of "cowboy" and how they have affected segments of the population, rather than trying to figure out how the various images relate to the actual cowboy of range-riding history.[8]

As he has been described to me in idealized form, the cowboy Christian is a rugged family man who is both conservative and independent. He may not be very educated, but he is sincere, having learned from his own rough past. There is a chance he works in agriculture or the cattle industry, but even if he does not, he spends some of his leisure time fooling with horses. He teaches his children to ride and occasionally competes in ranch rodeos. In the present, he may just be a man who has an unspoken belief in a creator God and no interest in church involvement. But if the cowboy churches are successful in reaching him, in the long run he will believe in Jesus Christ as his personal Lord and Savior. He will humble himself in prayer each day, setting the example for his wife and children; following a biblical path, he will also become the spiritual head of his family such that he has the final say in all things as a servant of God. And he will become an active and enthusiastic member of a cowboy church, unafraid to proclaim his faith at every opportunity.

Regardless of whether this cowboy exists or not, the belief that he does shapes cowboy church ideology, and he is front and center for today's cowboy church pastors and other leaders as they envision their potential audience. When they talk about their target, they are very specific, and yet they are also cognizant that, like any organization, cowboy churches will attract different spheres of people.[9] The American Fellowship of Cowboy Churches (AFCC), a nondenominational association with which many cowboy churches are affiliated, delineates seven tiers of cowboy subculture that may be represented in the church. They visualize the groups as the concentric rings on a target, and they also express a hierarchy: the center of the target is the primary audience, and the outer ring the least important group, with varying degrees in between. As their handbook advises, "The bulls-eye is the 'working cowboy.'. . . Aim for the bulls-eye and hit the target. Shoot for the outer edge . . . [and you] might miss the target of who [sic] God has called cowboy church to reach with the Gospel." The rings of people moving out from that center arc as follows: "pro-rodeo contestants, arena cowboys and cowgirls, cattle people, horse people, cowboys at heart, and cowboy mentality people."[10] "Cowboys at heart" might be further understood as people who were once part of the cowboy world in some way but are now urban dwellers; in another instance, they were described to me as people who simply "love the idea of the cowboy" and the accoutrements of cowboy culture, such as the music or the boots. "Cowboy mentality people" essentially refers to those who have an appreciation for cowboy culture but are not necessarily trying to be a part of it; they tend to be "roughnecks and rednecks" who are "similar in mentality" to cowboy culture people, but you will not see them wearing cowboy hats. Thus, the goal is to reach working cowboys, but anyone from these various cowboy subcultures is also desirable as a member.

In practical terms, the identification of a hierarchy among these groups does not mean that some people are actually more important in the church than others. Rather, what it means for AFCC churches is that every element of functional church structure is designed with the center of the target—the working cowboy—in mind, which includes modes of evangelism. The preferences of arena cowboys, for example, might be slightly different from what appeals to the working cowboy, but nonetheless everything in church should be focused on the latter group. As one pastor advised in a training seminar, there are always going to be "lots of posers" in the cowboy church, including the oft-disparaged "urban cowboys." Nonetheless, the focus should remain on the needs of "the man on horseback tending stock," who is the "true cowboy."[11]

The Nazarene church, which oversees a separate denominational cowboy church association, has a list of target audience groups that is similar, though not identical, to that of the AFCC. However, in training seminars and conversations with pastors, they more commonly emphasize their target in terms of religiosity, rather than by cowboy subculture. With the implied understanding that they are reaching out to a range of people within cowboy culture, the Nazarenes have three target audiences: unchurched unbelievers, unchurched believers, and churched unbelievers, in that order of preference. As it was clarified to me during a seminar, the third group, churched unbelievers, are those who have "wrong ideas about what it really means to be a Christian," and so in a sense they are false Christians even though they are active or semiactive in a church. This also implies that the Nazarenes' primary category, unchurched unbelievers, probably includes people who think they are Christian but not in the way that Nazarenes conceive of authentic Christianity; this helps make sense of the fact that they also typically refer to this person as "the lost cowboy."

What is intriguing is that leaders are fully aware that the working cowboy will only ever represent a tiny portion of their actual church population. Numerically, there are very few working cowboys, which makes locating them for outreach and evangelism a complicated undertaking. "We can't fill a church with them," elder Stacy Wiley readily admitted.[12] Very approximate statistics have been offered by different pastors: one in a hundred members is a working cowboy, said one interviewee; perhaps one could hope for as much as 20 percent of the membership, said another. Nazarene pastor Jon Coe said that his church of several hundred mostly has an assortment of arena cowboys and western heritage affinity people, and that maybe four or five members truly earn their living as working cowboys. "Because we are able to attract that hardcore guy, I know we're doing it right," Coe said with satisfaction.[13] Gary Morgan, the pastor of an influential cowboy church in Texas, said, "If you're defining a cowboy as a person that goes out here and makes his living working cows, there's not six in Ellis County! Not anymore." He generalized that most members of his church, which sits only forty miles from the Dallas-Fort Worth metroplex, are a little bit "more urban in flavor" than those found in rural cowboy churches.[14] The real target audience, then, is so small and potentially unfindable as to leave an outside observer like myself scratching her head in wonder at this religious enterprise constructed around a person who may not actually be there.

For some, the relevance of the religious work goes beyond the "lost cowboy," and Morgan expressed this view. He recalled that, as a young man, he heard a conference speaker posit that the Baptist church was becoming so white-collar that poor people were being left behind. "And he said, 'Gentlemen, I have a prediction to make: you're not going to do anything about it.'" In our interview, Morgan became choked up at the memory. He paused for a minute to gather his thoughts, and then added, in a barely audible voice, "I think the cowboy church is doing something about it." For Morgan, the importance of having working cowboys in the crowd appears to be less of a priority than simply reaching people who are not being exposed to the gospel, particularly those from a low socioeconomic stratum. He added that western heritage people "still have that desire to worship the Lord, and they still have that desire to be connected and have community, but somehow, they just got left behind as the church moved on."[15] Morgan seems to feel that the responsibility for unsaved souls sits squarely on the shoulders of anyone aware enough to notice, and he has noticed. His life path has put him in a place to evangelize among cowboy culture people, but the working cowboy is just one among many people he might hope to reach.

However, Morgan's democratized perspective was not generally representative of the pastors I interviewed. Most are instead firmly focused on a narrow, culturally defined audience, and people outside of that are somewhat extraneous. For instance, one elder mentioned that his church attracts a high number of bikers, and although they believe God has sent the bikers there, leaders have to consciously keep the church culturally relevant for working cowboys rather than "allowing it to become biker church."[16] When I asked Todd Mitchell, executive director of the AFCC, about this issue, he expressed some concern about cowboy churches being opened in areas where cowboys are unlikely to live, and suggested it can lead to problems in church focus. He emphasized the mission of the organization, saying, "If you reversed the AFCC's initials, our purpose is Christ, the Cowboy, Fellowship, and then America," and he considers that to be a hierarchy in what pastors should focus on. So, although he adroitly dodged answering questions about what he thinks of cowboy churches that are populated by noncowboys, many of his statements suggested that he considers them problematic.[17]

In the course of my research, I was party to numerous conversations about a given church being dominated by a particular type of cowboy Christian; for some, this is just a neutral observation, while for others it can become a concern, or even the basis of negative judgment. Many cowboy pastors are surprisingly forthright about passing judgment, particularly regarding the "authenticity" of other churches or pastors. For instance, a church that is mostly populated by people who are dabblers in cowboy culture may be regarded as inauthentic. It is not uncommon to hear people refer to "a church with boots on," "a hat church," "a suit and tie cowboy church," or other variations on this theme, all disparaging terms that suggest members and leaders are not "real" cowboys. Others, though, embrace this as cowboy diversity and consider it a valid mission field within the purview of cowboy church goals, especially since working cowboys are so few in number. For instance, one Oklahoma pastor working to get his cowboy church off the ground described his attendees: "We get a lot of curious people, but we don't get a lot of cowboys . . . . We're a cowboy church wannabe at the moment." He attributed much of this to the church location, which was not ideally situated to attract the target group, but he was optimistic that both of these would eventually change.[18] In a similarly good-natured way, pastor Lynn Walker commented that his cowboy church did not have any "real" cowboy members, just "country people who identify with the western culture." Many cowboy churches, he added, wind up attracting a niche audience that distinguishes them.[19] And as pastor Jon Coe commented, "I think every cowboy church is going to be a little different, and it's going to be according to the guy in the pulpit . . . . If he's not a cowboy then it's gonna be hard for him to embrace and use cowboy stuff." Nevertheless, Coe does not think such a situation entirely invalidates a man's potential in the cowboy ministry, adding, "I'm not gonna judge 'em."[20] Thus, while some vocal leaders hammer home the point that working cowboys must always be at the center of cowboy church, in reality there are different views on the issue and different practices being enacted.

A related distinction that often comes up is when a church contains more rodeo cowboys than ranch cowboys, and to what degree that should be allowed to impact the social structure of the church—or if it even does so. The conversation about whether rodeo cowboys are the same as ranch cowboys has been rehearsed numerous times in both popular and academic circles, without a conclusion on which everyone can agree. Some rodeo competitors have come from working ranches, with their skills first perfected there. There has also been a long tradition of ranch rodeos in which men have honed their skills; these are amateur rodeos that pit teams of ranch workers against each other in a variety of events. But there have also been men with no ranching background who became rodeo competitors by training in the requisite skills, sometimes through college programs. Many would argue that rodeo is a unique sport-entertainment environment with its own set of cultural norms that stand apart from what are classed as ranch cowboy values. However, I am most convinced by those who argue that despite the differences there remains tremendous overlap in the cultural contexts of rodeo cowboys and working cowboys, and by extension—and perhaps even more importantly—with the people who identify with either or both of these groups. As researcher of rodeo Elizabeth Atwood Lawrence has written, rodeo as a leisure activity is integral in many parts of the West, and it is deeply tied to people's sense of place, belonging, and meaning.[21] Trying to separate the cultures of rodeo cowboys and ranch cowboys and their respective constituents may be useful in some endeavors, such as in discussing work challenges or family patterns. However, in the case of religious outreach and the nature of cowboy churches, it is not particularly fruitful. And, as the history will show, religious overtures to the cowboy have always included multiple types of cowboys; thus there is little reason to delineate them as separate audiences.

Denominational ties can also serve as a marker of difference in cowboy Christian circles. Although all cowboy churches are Protestant (thus far) and can be further classified as evangelical, they are not the product of a single denomination. Many cowboy churches are overtly and deliberately nondenominational, often seeking to avoid the trappings of a big organization. Of the others, a large number are affiliated with Baptists; some pastors indicated that they consider this affiliation to be on paper only, primarily for the sake of gaining tax-exempt status. There is also a growing hub of cowboy outreach within the Church of the Nazarene, which includes some churches in the Lone Star "franchise" and some outside of it.[22] There are a handful of cowboy churches that are part of the Assemblies of God, another small number in the Seventh-day Adventist Church, and it is likely that there are some affiliated with other denominations that I simply have not come across. Beyond denominational differences, another way that churches group themselves—or divide themselves, depending on one's perspective—includes institutional membership in one of various cowboy church network groups, such as the AFCC, the International Cowboy Church Alliance Network (ICCAN), or the Cowboy Church Network of North America (CCN). Such membership can potentially, though not necessarily, affect the internal structure of a church, as well as whom it considers ecumenical partners.

There are those who will consider it misguided that, in this book, I treat all cowboy churches as a single group. Some would have me eliminate from discussion those regarded as "hat churches"; others would have me separate urban and rural cowboy churches; still others would distinguish churches that have arenas from those that do not. Many would argue that cowboy churches of different denominations should be discussed in separate conversations. On a microlevel, all of these distinctions (and others) make sense, and so objections to my broad comparisons will be understandable. However, the bigger picture that I seek to examine is about the cowboy church movement as a whole, and as a movement it includes a vast array of churches both large and small that have self-identified as "cowboy." While insiders may frequently differentiate themselves from one another based on gradations of perceived authenticity, I try not to take sides in these identity politics. In fact, I firmly believe that if a given body identifies itself as a cowboy church, then it should not merely be counted in that group, but its presence must also be allowed to shape and define what that category is, even against the protestations of other group members.

Demographic Challenges

It is impossible to say how many cowboy churches exist on any given day. Based on my knowledge of the field, I estimate that in the United States today there are more than five hundred churches, and possibly close to one thousand.[23] The fact that so many are independent, rather than denominationally affiliated, means they cannot all be tracked through formal channels. It is not uncommon to find a church that has no permanent location, nor any web presence. Some open and shut down within a year or two, but their names may continue appearing in church listings online or elsewhere.[24] Several times, I tried to follow up with a pastor I had spoken with or church I had visited a couple years earlier, and found that it no longer seemed to exist—or at least, not in the same location, or with the same contact information. I have been to cowboy churches where I was one of two dozen in attendance, and I have been to cowboy churches with close to a thousand full seats. Some cowboy churches are very careful about tracking active members, but many do not keep any kind of permanent records, and therefore they can only estimate about membership, stability, and attrition; this seemed particularly characteristic of the larger churches. In fact, for some, maintaining anonymous attendance is considered part of what makes the concept work, because people can be present without feeling any pressure to identify themselves.

All of this makes it even more difficult to determine who actually attends cowboy church. Going beyond questions about what subcultures of horse people attend, in a single breath cowboy church leaders frequently announce that they are attracting "unchurched" people who are "new Christians." That is, they do not seek to compete with other churches and draw members away. Instead, there is an emphasis on finding people who are not presently involved with any church, and preferably people who do not even consider themselves religious. Pastor Terry Hill, for instance, said about potential new members, "I tell 'em, you know, if you're happy with your church, stay there. We don't need you. And I don't mean it in a mean way . . . . That's our goal, is to bring in people *not* going to church. It's not about growing our church from other churches." Or, as succinctly phrased in the cowboy idiom by pastor John Spencer, "We ain't rustling nobody else's cattle."[25]

It is problematic that many leaders casually equate "unchurched" with "new Christians," because the first term appears to describe behavioral history, while the second describes the state of one's faith. In deeper conversation, I found most pastors were attuned to this distinction. Nonetheless, across the board, the adjective "unchurched" is used to describe new members and target members, with a variety of definitions actually in play. Some pastors use it to refer to people who have never been involved with a church institution, at least not as adults making a choice to participate, thus indicating that the cowboy church milieu marks their first real experience with organized religion. But many other pastors describe unchurched people as those who have fallen away from church because they lost interest or found it unsatisfactory, not that they actually have no experience with it. Pastor Dan O'Daniel, for example, described his members as predominantly "unchurched," elaborating that most had been turned off by church in the distant past and had never gone back. He added that they are "tough old men who've fallen through the cracks."[26] More complex was the multilayered way one pastor's wife explained their member base: "It's the unchurched. Whether they're a sinner, or just hadn't found their niche, hadn't found a church they liked, or those who had never gone to a church before. We're trying to reach the lost, of course, but everyone needs fellowship. And we're trying to reach those that didn't fit in, or didn't feel at home in the other churches."[27] In her explanation, an unchurched person seems to be anyone who wants to be part of a church but is uncomfortable with the options, for any reason. This is not unlike the way a small number of pastors use the word "unchurched" as an antonym for "church people," the latter being a derogatory phrase for those who are content with the predictability of more mainstream Protestantism.

After years of speaking with cowboy church pastors, I am confident in generalizing that they all consistently use the word "unchurched" to describe anyone who was not attending a church immediately prior to cowboy church, but a portion of them also use it to make a broader statement about the individual's longer church history. The problem is that this range in the usage blurs categorical boundaries between people who have never been churchgoers and people who are church dropouts, and it does nothing to help distinguish what kind of belief system they enter cowboy church with. In short, it makes it difficult to assess what types of people the church is truly attracting. Cowboy church leaders, however, are by no means unique in using the term "unchurched" in such a vague way.

Social scientists have used this word in a variety of ways, such that is not, objectively, a stable research term. Many have suggested and used more specific words to describe peoples' affiliation experience: estranged, indifferent, and nominal Christians; dropouts; marginal members and mental affiliates; disaffiliates, disidentifiers, and deserters; and nones, including many possible subcategories such as structural nones and marginal nones, or liminal nones and stable nones.[28] Agreeing on more precise terminology to use within the cowboy church would be the first step in accurately assessing the religious background and history of those who come into it. However, this degree of accuracy is unlikely to be a concern within cowboy church leadership circles until it becomes a more stabilized institution, by which time its membership profile may have shifted.

In my own casual conversations with members, I most often encountered people who had come to cowboy church as lapsed or disinterested Christians, rather than as "new" Christians. The most specific data I gathered was from a written survey filled out by women attending a 2014 Cowgirl Get Together.[29] Of those surveyed, who were all cowboy church attendees over the age of eighteen, only 5 percent indicated no prior religiosity before attending cowboy church, which was phrased on the questionnaire as "I did not attend church and was not concerned about religion." An additional 21 percent had not attended church previously but had considered themselves religious. The argument could reasonably be made that both of these groups count as "unchurched" and/or as "new Christians." However, the remaining 74 percent *did* have previous involvement in a church. Some of those indicated their participation had been sporadic, while others indicated it was active, and more than half of those with previous involvement indicated that it was in a Baptist church.[30] It would be impossible to argue that this larger percentage of people are categorically "new Christians" or "unchurched," which challenges leaders' claims about their statistical dominance among members.[31] On the other hand, the survey numbers still support leaders' more basic assertions: at 26 percent, the cowboy church is drawing a disproportionately high number of previously unaffiliated women, because according to Pew Forum statistics from 2014, just over 7 percent of Texas women claimed no religious affiliation.[32]

Certainly, pastors do consistently claim that cowboy churches are attracting significant numbers of people who have little or no prior church experience and who were not previously religious. Because demographic data is not being systematically collected within the churches, and because of the murkiness of terminology, there can be no certainty about even approximate numbers, which they occasionally offer. However, assuming their anecdotal assessments of members are within the realm of truth, I did note one interesting pattern about membership that emerged through interviews. Many pastors said that in the earliest years, their churches attracted a high number of unchurched people, but over time the ratio has dropped and a greater number of new members now come from other churches. Thus, regardless of how they defined "unchurched" people, many identified that this audience is now dwindling and instead they are becoming a competitor in the wider evangelical religious marketplace. If this remains true, it will surely have an impact on their internal dynamics, as well as reverberations among more mainstream churches in their communities.

Paradoxes of Cowboy Identity

Several questions related to cowboy identity run throughout this book, at times being discussed explicitly and other times serving as subtext. One that has already made itself evident is the question of "authenticity," which pervades discussions of who cowboys are as well as how religion is practiced. As thoughtfully delineated by the AFCC, cowboy culture involves people from a variety of horse-related subcultures who mix and mingle. The working cowboy is far outnumbered by cultural interlocutors who are actually peripheral to his specific world; these people might be considered dabblers or even consumers, yet they shape cowboy culture by virtue of their feet, their dollars, and their enthusiasm. This dominance of peripheral people raises important questions about cultural ownership and representation. Who, for example, is consecrated to speak authoritatively about cowboy culture? Conflicting answers to this question reveal underlying tensions regarding perceived degrees of realness, or authenticity, among western heritage subcultures. At times, "realness" appears dependent on one's tie to ranching and rural life, but in other cases it relies on changing ideas about what constitutes cowboy culture. Furthermore, judgments are often contoured by social factors that include regional background, economic status, education, race, and gender. Recent fieldwork by anthropologists reveals that cowboy "authenticity" remains an active concern despite the fact that there are no standardized measures of cowboy-ness on which people are able to agree; my own interviewees also bore this out, as person after person casually referred to "real" and "fake" cowboys in conversation.[33] Some disparaged other churches that they perceived as inauthentic because of the pastor's lack of cowboy cred or because of the type of cowboy culture people who attend, but only a very few ever suggested that they consider "authenticity" really just an issue of perspective or opinion.

Relevant to these questions, Justin Williams has written about the idea of historical authenticity, in which a specific earlier form of culture is considered "more authentic and of greater value" than present innovations. People imagine the earlier iteration to have been pristine and unmediated, and thus subsequent changes to the culture may be considered corruptions, rather than normal and fruitful adaptations.[34] This is certainly the case in the western heritage world where, as anthropologist Terri C. Aihoshi notes, "The epic proportions of the legacy of the cowboy, both mythological and historical, have been carried forward and amplified by the people who have participated, and continue to participate . . . in that occupation."[35] And as Williams points out, as a result, "the past becomes an authority figure, [and] the 'true starting' becomes a utopian space and an archetype."[36] This is often what can be observed when people talk about cowboy authenticity, because they alight on particular attributes associated with a cowboy image from long ago, rather than recognizing that in the present day people who fully consider themselves cowboys may live in the city and work in an office, and they may strongly favor written contracts over handshakes. Nonetheless, those with the loudest voices insist that a small echelon of people carries on the values and practices of an unbroken and stable cowboy tradition.[37]

The cultural authenticity of pastors is a topic that, in my experience, people express concern about more often than their ministerial credentials or overall leadership style. Because pastors can be important figureheads in attracting or repelling people from a church, most leaders say that it is preferential to have preachers who have been immersed in the cowboy cultural milieu. As church member Sonny Spurger said, "The joke used to be whether it was easier to take a traditional pastor out of seminary and put boots and a hat on him and make him a cowboy pastor, though he didn't know the north from the south end of a horse. Or, take one of these warm-hearted cowboys who had really come to the Lord, had his life changed, and didn't know the difference between Genesis and Revelation." Spurger's conclusion was that it could be done either way, but that the latter was likely to be more effective in a cowboy church.[38] This view was echoed by pastor Mike Morrow, who said, "We've had some

Baptist preachers think [cowboy church] was the solution to their ministry collapse. So they've come over, and they went down to the western store and bought them a hat and bought them some boots, and they wanted to put in a cowboy church. I mean, they wasn't even interested in horses or cattle or rodeoing, they didn't use the arena, and many of them still don't . . . to me, that's not even a cowboy church."[39] Of course, between the imagined polar opposites of authentic and fake there is a wide, flexible area that perhaps most cowboy culture people occupy. Yet questions of who and what is real always seem to bubble just beneath the surface in the cowboy Christian world as an important marker of identity, and readers can expect to see this theme present in the chapters that follow.

Another issue that flows throughout the text is a tension between independence and control. The idealized cowboy is a paragon of individualism, and his autonomy is often framed as a by-product of a life lived alone on the range. This attribute is also generally accepted as a truism in the present day, and most pastors include the word "independent" when asked to describe cowboy culture people. As leaders explain it, it is because of this individualism that predictable programs and rigid expectations found in mainstream churches do not appeal to a cowboy culture audience. Pastor Ron Nolen commented that "cowboys are pretty well known for that independent spirit . . . . They are bred this way in the western culture, to be pretty independent. 'We can ride our horse, I don't need your help. I can get my horse saddled. I ride with the best of 'em.' I got a lot of that. So, to form a team out of that . . ." Nolen trailed off, suggesting that building cooperation among them in the church context is a big challenge.[40] Thus, one of the ways that cowboy church promotes itself is as an entity that offers something different, by recognizing and appreciating people's disinterest in doing what everyone else does, and respecting their independence. And yet, in the cowboy Christian rejection of denominations and comfortable church structures, they wind up embracing new forms of control through the much-touted cowboy church "model," which delineates aspects of hierarchy, theology, structure, social rules, and consensus decision-making. At times cowboy church appears so controlled as to entirely thwart the goal of honoring independence and individualism. One unaffiliated pastor said that although he's not opposed to cowboy church associations, "I think when you get into that they almost make you a cookie cutter church, this is how we do everything . . . . Sometimes you've gotta get out of what makes you comfortable."[41] Even Todd Mitchell of the AFCC suggested that "independence" may not always be an admirable trait either for individuals or for institutions, and instead may just indicate immaturity; therefore, some elements of structure are absolutely necessary in order to distinguish and unify cowboy churches.[42] Yet, this tension between independence and uniformity often goes unspoken and unresolved in the world of cowboy Christians.

The Religious Context

Depending on whether one is thinking of development, theology, structure, or some other specific characteristic, there are a variety of ways to contextualize cowboy Christianity. Readers will see that I employ different religious frames as they become useful for deepening understanding, rather than as an attempt to permanently box in and categorize the movement. Both because of its age and its marginality, the cowboy church appears to me as a kind of new religious movement (NRM). Most cowboy churches are quite young—two decades at the oldest, and often less than half of that age; therefore members today are part of its first generation. As a result, analytical frameworks used to study new and developing religions may be helpful in the case of the cowboy church, especially in anticipating its institutional evolution. If typologies hold true, members today are likely to be enthusiastic about their faith while also vulnerable to falling away from it; and while the cowboy church can anticipate some eventual demographic stabilization, because of its target audience, financial instability is likely to remain characteristic for years to come. Additionally, schismatic groups that already exist within it may become increasingly polarized.[43] The other factor aligning the cowboy church with NRMs is its socio-religious marginality. Although the argument can be made that cowboy church is just an iteration of Christianity without any theological innovation, its practices are creative and sometimes cause outsiders to be skeptical about its integrity. Similarly, NRMs are often treated with hostility from people outside their group, especially from members of dominant religions who are suspicious of anything that goes against the mainstream, fearing that the new group could "undermine the very fabric of society."[44] Many cowboy pastors say they have experienced this kind of "external antagonism" from traditional church people and institutions, and in educational seminars leaders speak openly about remaining strong in the face of such criticism. As sociologist Eileen Barker has indicated, disputes between NRMs and the wider society can play out in a variety of ways, from mild disregard to active persecution, and everything in between. From what I have observed, at worst, the negative judgments from outsiders give some cowboy preachers a persecution complex that allows them to exaggerate the degree of hostility aimed at their endeavors. I have found no reason to suspect that any anticowboy church hostility would actually lead to deliberate persecution, and it is very likely that external suspicion will decrease naturally over time.[45] In these ways, then, NRM modeling is relatively promising for the future of cowboy churches.

Putting aside its newness and its marginalization, cowboy Christianity can also be framed within the larger body of American evangelicalism. Based on both theology and motivation, cowboy Christians fall within the parameters of evangelicalism used by most scholars of religious studies: Biblicism, conversionism, activism, and crucicentrism.[46] That being the case, several trends within evangelicalism already recognized by historians can provide a context for this emerging religious movement: particularly, ministries for men in the tradition of muscular Christianity, as well as forms of modern revivalism like that seen in the Jesus movement and new paradigm churches. Cowboy church is a new spin on all of these developments, and by its existence and proliferation provides one more piece of evidence that American evangelicals remain adept at reinventing their religion to keep it relevant for a changing world.

Ministries overtly tailored to men have existed among Protestant Christians in the United States for well over a century, and these ministries have typically included essentialist notions about the nature and character of the sexes. From a theological perspective, the cowboy church is a new version of men's ministry, despite the fact that women make up approximately half of its adherents. One ideological predecessor of the cowboy church is muscular Christianity, which came to America from England in the second half of the nineteenth century and wielded a great deal of influence among Protestants at that time. As Clifford Putney has written, muscular Christianity was a social teaching that linked ideals of masculinity and athleticism with religiously based morality and patriotism. It sought to make "manly" Christian men, who would be physically strong and robust as "true Christians" should be. Within institutional religion, the goals of muscular Christianity included "'defeminizing' the clergy, 'masculinizing' religious imagery, and getting more men involved in the churches"; the first and third of these points are major concerns within cowboy Christianity today.[47] After a period of decline, a new generation of muscular Christians emerged in the mid-twentieth century through a variety of evangelical sports ministries, including the Fellowship of Christian

Athletes and the Race Track Chaplaincy of America, both of which have direct genealogical links to the cowboy church movement as well as more general ideological parallels. For those cowboy Christians who consider the arena to be the focal point of the entire cowboy church movement, there is no more apt way to typologize them than as muscular Christians.[48]

The Promise Keepers, a nondenominational ministry to men founded in 1990, serves as another ideological predecessor of the cowboy church movement. It too lies within the muscular Christian tradition, and like other more recent versions, it includes a heightened emphasis on individual morality.[49] Promise Keepers asserts that social upheaval has been caused by humans thwarting their God-given roles, so one ministry goal has been cleansing and restoring society by encouraging men to reclaim their place as upstanding leaders, which "allows" women to take more subservient roles. Inherent to that leadership is an assumption that men and women have differing natures, and this teaching is predicated on what sociologist Michael Messner has called "biblical essentialism." That is, rather than claiming that biology creates fundamental differences between the sexes, biblical essentialism dismisses biological science and social science altogether, simply relying on scripture to understand the essence of God's plan for the sexes. In doing so, this perspective concludes that men are rational while women are emotional, and social structures function optimally when men control public realms and women control domestic realms. Promise Keepers promotes building nuclear family units in which men are moral leaders as well as breadwinners and decision-makers, much like the idealized family units of white middle-class America circa 1950.[50] Cowboy Christian leaders subscribe to a similar biblical view about the sexes and gender roles, and they too are keen on reinforcing nuclear family units to improve or "restore" society. To all of this, they add a layer of rhetoric about what cowboy culture people are "like," which might appropriately be called "cowboy essentialism." Since the turn of the century, Promise Keepers has declined in membership and influence; the cowboy church movement, as a parallel ripple on this wave of muscular Christianity, concurrently gained momentum and continues to thrive as one of the new faces of ministry for men.

Finally, one other way that cowboy church can be framed religiously is as a revival movement bubbling up from within mainstream evangelicalism, structurally and methodologically aligned with the new paradigm church family. Donald Miller has described new paradigm churches as those that cast aside traditional church norms in favor of an emphasis on contemporary culture in an effort to reach people who are turned off by mainline churches.[51] Its characteristics include pastors who are casual and accessible, a greater focus on the Bible than on doctrine, extensive opportunities for lay leadership, and a strong belief that every aspect of the church must be led by the spirit of God. All told, Miller delineates twelve characteristics of the new paradigm church, ten of which are generally applicable to cowboy churches.[52] While Miller favors the term "new paradigm" partly because he thinks the model cuts across other taxonomies, in the two decades since the publication of his work, it has become increasingly evident that new paradigm churches are most often found in the religious milieu of American evangelicals, and so it might be considered a subcategory of that world. Though Miller was probably overreaching when he called new paradigm churches "a second reformation that is transforming the way Christianity will be experienced in the new millennium," he was accurate in anticipating that this impulse would unleash "new movements, unbounded by denominational bureaucracy and the restraint of tradition."[53] The cowboy church is small-scale in comparison with movements like Great Awakenings or the Jesus movement, but seeing it as a type of new paradigm church allows us to recognize its contextual place as a form of Protestant revivalism for the twenty-first century.

Scope of the Research

This book contributes to the growing area of study about religion of the American West. Until recent decades, most of the publications on this topic were autobiographical writings of missionaries and itinerant preachers, or denominational histories that centered on institution-building. As studies have become more regionally focused, knowledge about the role of religion in particular geographic areas of the West has grown. Since the 1980s, many excellent publications have correlated religious patterns in western locales with factors such as migration and immigration, politics, gender, race and ethnicity, and environment. In recent years, an intellectual meeting place has been created within the American Academy of Religion for scholars whose work is focused on religion of the American West. All of this implies that high-quality research on this subject has a promising future.

Thus far, cowboy Christianity has been relatively absent from this body of scholarship. It lies somewhat outside the boundaries of institutionalized religion and formal denominations, and it is also cross-regional;

thus, it does not fall within traditional research purviews. To sketch out a representative picture of historic cowboy religious life, I have often needed to look at the larger structures of which they were a part. Furthermore, sources are often difficult to pinpoint. Cowboys of the nineteenth century left few writings, and those that exist rarely speak about matters as personal as religion. Memoirs, newspapers, archival sources, and cultural artifacts permit me to piece together evidence of religious life among cowboys while on the ranch, on the trail, and in the towns, and occasionally a more modern source reflects on some of these issues. At the same time, I am cognizant of the biases and agendas potentially present among people who became the knowledge-makers and producers of the records that have been left behind. A century's worth of people have sought to preserve a glorified image of cowboys, rejecting evidence that suggests their jobs were boring instead of thrilling, and trying to whitewash indications that cowboys could have had coarse and undignified behavior.[54] All of that comes into play as I close-read the sources.

To date, the only detailed academic attempts to characterize the religious lives of late nineteenth-century working cowboys come from Clifford P. Westermeier, a history professor who specialized in the American West and wrote influential works on both rodeo and western art. In his two short pieces on the subject of cowboy religion, he posited that cowboys of the 1865–1900 "golden era" were predominantly religious believers but not church attenders. Both essays drew on the same source material, which mostly consisted of brief observations culled from periodicals of the 1880s.[55] Westermeier's intention was good but leaves present researchers with little substance to build upon. The most important work dealing more broadly with religion on the frontier west has come from historian Ferenc Morton Szasz. His two books on western religious history provide an overview of denominational evangelism efforts, and they thematically explore religious developments in the West as variations on larger national trends. However, attention to cowboys in both works is minimal. Most of Szasz's specific references to them are from after 1900, by which time the era of the range-riding cowboy was over. Furthermore, he appeared to depend on artistic source material without criticism, thus accepting as fact the portrayals of cowboy religiosity offered in songs and poetry. Although his work is commendable in many respects, it does not extend the discussion of cowboy religion in any substantive way.[56]

The lack of scholarly attention to more recent forms of organized cowboy Christianity is primarily due to the fact that it is still new and developing; the academic world of systematic study and analysis needs time to catch up. Several master's theses and dissertations have included an aspect of study of the cowboy church, some of them focusing on particular congregations.[57] A plethora of popular articles and television segments highlight the most visually engaging aspects of cowboy Christianity, such as preaching from horseback or baptisms in horse troughs. But there have been no attempts to trace its long history—that is, history that goes back more than twenty years—and no one has conducted a widespread study that permits consideration of its overall trajectory and relationship to other forms of Christianity in America. That gap in the academic literature is part of what drove me to undertake this project and to structure it as I did.

The research for this project combines methods from history and sociology. Part of my work has been archival, involving newspapers and memoirs and documents of various types. Another part of my work has been sociological, including site visits, interviews, and one written survey. Although I engaged in a significant amount of participant-observation, I never tried to immerse myself or become an active part of the cowboy Christian community, and therefore I do not consider my research findings ethnographic in the strict sense of the word. Between 2011–2016, I attended more than fifty services at cowboy churches in Oklahoma and Texas, attempting to have a diverse array of experiences in terms of location, congregation size, and denomination. Other site visits that I made included worship services at rodeos, various church training seminars, Christian horse whispering events, and a Cowgirl Get Together conference.

Initially, I tried to set up an interview with the pastor at each church I attended, but this was not always feasible, especially because I preferred to meet in person rather than speaking by phone. Sometimes, even prearranged interviews were cut short by a pastor who decided he had little interest in assisting me. Most pastors, however, seemed very happy to talk about the world of cowboy church, and they were kind and generous with their time and their thoughts, making it a very pleasant experience. The interviews always began with a standard list of questions but usually deviated from that path as pastors spoke about unique aspects of their ministry or experience. Each person was given the opportunity to make himself anonymous if he so desired, and some took that option. Further insight was provided by members during countless numbers of informal interactions and conversations, and these have certainly helped to shape my understanding.[58] However, I readily admit that this study more heavily depends upon the perspectives of leaders and aspiring leaders in the world of cowboy Christianity, rather than the average members or attendees.

That caveat aside, there is also a way in which pastors can represent more than just a top-down perspective in this particular context. Though some cowboy church pastors are men who have made ministry their vocation, even earning a seminary credential, many others simply shifted out of the membership ranks to become a pastor when it became evident they were the best men to fill a ministerial void. Usually they were chosen because of their connection to the cowboy culture in combination with other traits or abilities, and they often state clearly that they do not consider themselves any more articulate about the significance of cowboy church than other members would be.[59] I found a similarly modest attitude among some rodeo pastors. For instance, one specifically said that he does not even consider himself a minister, but just a person trying to disciple others in Christian faith. "I just love to love people, and inspire them, and teach them the truth," he said, adding, "Never saw myself as a preacher, pastor, nothing like that, and still really don't to tell you the truth."[60] This was echoed by the founding chaplain of the Professional Bull Riders (PBR), Cody Custer, who commented, "Ministry is a strange thing . . . . It gets out of hand if you don't keep people first, because people matter more than anything. People need to feel valued. Needed. Like they mean something." For that reason, Custer's method of ministry—if he would even call it that—is to "just be Christ-like to other people," rather than actively trying to convert every person he meets.[61] This type of humility was representative of a great many cowboy pastors I encountered, and they did not clamor to provide me with authoritative statements about cowboy Christianity. My overall takeaway was that worrying about whether the research might be "too dependent" on leader voices came to feel like a very minor concern.

However, the most practical reason why voices of members are not systematically included in this project is that I realized that obtaining widespread member feedback would require an entirely different project design: one that would have me becoming a regular, known presence in a particular church or two. I often felt that I was perceived as a little bit of a dangerous figure in cowboy church, if not just an oddity. I was a woman attending church alone, with no apparent interest in joining, who did not even slightly look the part of a cowgirl. In most cases that made the average person avoid me, and this was especially true of the men. The fact that I was from the world of academia often added another layer of uncertainty about my presence. Because I had to work to get people to engage with me, and because it is not a culture where people are eager to fill out written forms, I was not able to conceive of a method whereby I could gather a broad, sound sampling of data on member perspectives that would mirror the geographic range of my site visits. Perhaps immersing myself in one or two congregations would have allowed me to build the requisite trust for acquiring member perspectives within limited settings, but that was very different from the broad study in which I was already engaged. Ultimately, I determined that casual conversations with individuals and couples would have to suffice to fill in gaps wherever possible.[62]

On a related note, this study does not include race as a category of analysis, despite its relevance as a lens for examining American religious forms. Certainly, complicated interactions involving race and ethnicity have affected the developmental history of the American West, and explicit racism has been a factor in the evolution of the Anglicized cowboy image and the mythos about his exploits. At present, the cowboy church is predominantly populated by white people, with the occasional Hispanic person, Native American, or, much more rarely, African American, and they attend because they, too, are cowboy Christians. Thus far, these groups are a tiny minority in the movement such that diversity of racial dynamics has not yet arisen as a point of tension on a broad institutional level. That is not to say that no cowboy Christians are experiencing or perpetrating racism; rather, a specialized and focused study would be required to tease out this issue and give it sufficient attention. Such a study needs to include interviews with a large number of minority participants in the cowboy church, as well as emphasizing a critical cultural reading of movement ideology. In my own experience of the cowboy church movement—an experience that I recognize was contoured by my white privilege—I did not observe enough about racial dynamics in the movement to get a real sense of their practical effects. Primarily because my own research design had limited parameters, race and racism as issues are not, therefore, thematically explored in this text.[63]

Nonetheless, I was somewhat surprised that pastors rarely mentioned racial diversity as being a concern, considering that it tends to be at the forefront of many discussions in American society today. The primary exception to this was among leaders in the Church of the Nazarene, where, nationwide, there have been concerted efforts at church planting among various subcultures and with a variety of structural styles. It was in interviews with Nazarene leaders that race and ethnicity would sometimes emerge as a point of discussion. Some outreach has been done with Spanish speakers, who populate many jobs in ranching and farming; as of this writing, at least three Spanish-language cowboy churches have been started and fostered by Jon Coe, who enthusiastically predicted, "We're going to start the *vaquero* movement in the Church of the Nazarene."[64] Among AFCC affiliates, the most defined view I encountered was put forth by Chap Thomas, the pastor of an African American cowboy church in Big Sandy, Texas.[65] Thomas believes that just as a cowboy church must be strategically sensitive to its target audience of cowboys, so too must there be additional layers of cultural connectedness, including visible African American leadership, if a church hopes to reach minority audiences. In his view, cowboy church plants that simply follow standard modeling are unlikely to succeed with minority groups because the model itself is not attuned to racial nuances. Within his own racially mixed congregation, Thomas attempts to forge a path of social change by spending one month a year focusing on open discussion of race relations.[66] But aside from exceptions like these, it is unclear when, if ever, the cowboy church as a broad entity will actively start engaging in racially conscious outreach.

In contrast, conceptions of gender emerged as important for both my analysis of the cowboy church and the mechanics of my research process. The dynamics of cowboy church are such that men and women typically socialize with their own gender group. There is a salient concern about heterosexual impropriety; thus a man is rarely found alone with a woman who is not his wife. Though initially surprising, the presence of the pastor's wife in interviews was something I became accustomed to; sometimes she sat in the room, but off to the side, and at other times she chose to be an active participant. On a few other occasions, the pastor sat alone with me but made sure we were in a very public place.[67] I also gradually realized that women in the movement—whether pastor's wives, administrative assistants, or in some other role—tended to act as strict gatekeepers of men, often suggesting that they could help me with my questions *instead* of passing along my message to the pastor requesting an interview. On a few occasions, after speaking with a woman at length, I had to be insistent that I also wanted to personally reach the pastor.

There is one other way that my gender may have played an unexpected role. Over the years, I observed that cowboy pastors would cry during our interviews; it was quite common for a pastor to get teary at least once while speaking with me, and sometimes more than once. The most striking emotional outpouring was the pastor who teared up eight times in a fifty-three minute interview, such that by the end I even started teasing him about it. I never really gave this much thought, but in passing wondered if the cowboy machismo might actually be balanced by a very delicate emotional nature. However, in 2015 I had the chance to read several interviews conducted by Jake McAdams as part of his master's thesis research, and I saw that the tone of his interactions was quite different.[68] Some of the very same pastors were much more likely to swear or joke around in his presence than cry. In comparing the kinds of questions we asked, I did not see a marked difference in content or approach. My conclusion is that my gender must have affected how pastors responded to me, though I do not know exactly how or why; surely it also impacted the kind of information I was able to gather (and not gather).

As I have spoken to various audiences about this project over the past several years, I realized that people were as interested in hearing about my personal experience of cowboy culture as they were in hearing about my actual findings. I gradually came to think of my adventure—*city girl tries to learn about cowboy Christianity*—as an integral part of my findings, and that is why my voice weaves in and out of the text. One question that I have been asked many times is whether I am afraid when I go to cowboy churches. The answer is yes: I am always afraid. I am a somewhat shy person, and entering a church building for purposes of research rather than personal spiritual seekership is always daunting. Even if I have attended the church before, stepping out of the car and walking up the path has always been accompanied by trepidation. I fear that people will judge me or be unfriendly. I fear that I will have dressed wrong, or that I will sit in the wrong seat. I worry about what the service will involve, and how long it will last. I worry that I am a nuisance.

The surprising thing is how quickly these fears melted away in the vast majority of my cowboy church experiences. Once inside, it was almost always a comfortable environment, even though I have absolutely no connection to nor nostalgia for western heritage culture. The low-key decor was disarming. The lively music was fun. Rarely did a sermon topic make me bristle, and only twice was I pressured to participate in something that made me uncomfortable (both times I refused). Even on a couple of occasions when I was comparatively underdressed in a church that turned out to be more formal, no one seemed to care. In short, I found myself genuinely enjoying cowboy churches of all different types, and retrospectively I would be hard-pressed to choose a favorite. A part of me will miss having an excuse to visit them.

2

Cowboys and Religion before Cowboy Church

THE TWENTIETH CENTURY saw the emergence of a new semifictional American hero: the cowboy. He stepped into public consciousness from the stage of *Buffalo Bill's Wild West* in the 1880s, and from the pages of Owen Wister's novel *The Virginian* in 1902, and he captured the American imagination. Within a couple of decades, he began to show a sensitive side through affection for his horse and his innate ability to sing. He maintained a sexual naiveté, always choosing his horse and his friends over the pretty woman who had fallen in love with him. By the late 1940s, parents trusted incarnations of him to instruct their children. Having fully absorbed representations of the cowboy from radio, film, and television, Americans believed they understood what his character was all about, including his religious values.

During these decades, the cowboy had transformed from an actual laboring man into a paragon of virtue, and onto his image we projected an evolving slate of traits that met our changing needs for a public hero. His imagined legacy was also a moral one. By 1961, historian Ramon F. Adams asserted that a unique cowboy moral tradition had been carried forward through time. The range-era cowboy "had a code of his own of great beauty, and one to which he strictly adhered," Adams explained, describing him as deeply Christian and a staunch upholder of the Golden Rule.[1] The work of Adams is merely one example in which history and mythos have been blended and offered to readers as a factual accounting of cowboy religiosity. Other writers followed his lead and, at times, took it several steps further, suggesting that the historical cowboy was the recipient of a mantle of morality passed down from Jesus himself in an unbroken religious succession to the cowboy of the present day. By unpacking the development of this multilayered image, we can begin to understand the ideological infrastructure of today's cowboy Christianity.

The Cowboy's Work

Vaqueros, the Spanish-language equivalent of *cowboys*, are the predecessors of the "all-American" cowboys who came to dominate the imagination of North Americans in the twentieth century. From the 1500s onward, vaqueros tended the cattle of Spanish colonials who settled in the American West, including areas that today stretch from Texas to California. Vaqueros developed cattle-tending practices, unique terminology, functional tools and attire, and even social diversions that came to demarcate them as a professional group, all of which strongly influenced the practices of their Anglo successors in the latter half of the nineteenth century. Of course, the American cowboy was never solely Anglo; there were certainly many cowboys of Mexican, African, and Native American descent. However, the cowboy culture that came to be the focus of American fascination was dominated by white men. With increased settlement west of the Mississippi as well as the formal acquisition of lands by the United States, vaqueros and their employers were pushed further south and gradually replaced by their white counterparts with US citizenship. The cattle industry in the West was experiencing its first spurts of growth when the Civil War broke out. Politics, the economy, social relationships, and business were all disrupted while the states fought each other for resolution. Cattle, left untended, roamed freely.[2]

The 1860s were a point of change to the cattle business. Prior to that time, cattle profits had primarily come from products made from the hide and other parts, and small livestock markets for consumption were based in the East. Developments in the technology of refrigerated rail cars, however, altered the possibilities for the meat industry. The open range of the West provided free sustenance for raising cattle, and refrigerated trains made long-distance transport of meat viable. As fresh beef became more readily available to Americans at low prices, the demand increased, and a booming western cow market was born. The new industry focused on producing cattle fit for consumption, and one of the key workers in this industry was the cowboy.[3]

Cowboy is a term that has exhibited plasticity, undergoing a variety of permutations over time. In the early and mid-1800s, men sometimes referred to as "cowboys" roamed the West, in search of trouble as much as anything. Such men were gunslinging ruffians who were hard drinkers and, often, thieves. Settlers of western towns typically feared these outlaw cowboys and the disruption they could cause. The evolution from ruffian to cultural hero began during the 1860s, when the growth of the cattle industry created an array of jobs for "cowboys." Cow, in this sense, is an umbrella term, used for bulls and cows of all types. While those who worked with them were lumped together as cowboys, they were also called by more specific job terms, such as herders, drivers/drovers, cowhands, cowpokes, cowpunchers, and waddies.[4] In contrast, ranchers, cattlemen, cowmen, and stockmen were those who owned land and cattle and hired the cowboys, and the extent to which the power holders shared the culture of the men they employed varied greatly.[5] Some ranchmen were locals who had built cattle businesses from small starts, while others were cattle barons, men who traveled from parts East simply to build their fortunes by investing in a growing market. Ranchers, then, were a more culturally diverse group than cowboys.

During the decades following the Civil War, the West was treated as a free range for animals needing to eat, and the essence of the cowboy's job was round-the-clock tending of cattle.[6] The primary tasks were driving cows hundreds of miles as they grazed, with twice-yearly roundups for sorting and branding, as well as trail drives to push the cattle to the nearest large marketplace or railhead for transport. On some days, the work was difficult and even dangerous, as cowboys dealt with navigating river crossings, containing stampedes, or rough weather. On others, it could be immensely boring, with long, solitary stretches of little to do but ride a horse and direct and monitor the animals. There were also peripheral cowboy jobs, such as wrangling the remuda or driving the chuck wagon. The remuda was a stock of work horses that accompanied trail drives so that cowboys could change horses whenever theirs tired, and managing it was typically a job for a young man with little experience. The chuck wagon carried cooking utensils as well as the bedrolls and other gear, and its driver served as the company cook. On some of the largest ranches, other jobs included the line rider, a cowboy who lived alone in a remote area and patrolled the lands of an outpost. Many young men hoped to work their way up through the ranks of cowboying, starting with minimal jobs on the ranch and aspiring to supervisory positions on the trail.

Adding to the complexity was that cowboy work was seasonal, with fewer people required in the winters when cattle tending was minimal. Some men found basic work doing chores on farms and ranches, while others went home and lived meagerly on their earnings until the spring cattle season began.

Meager, in fact, was the lifestyle of most cowboys. Although the pay varied with skill set, experience, location, and demand, cowboys typically earned thirty to fifty dollars in a working month, and most worked nine months a year or fewer. On the surface, this figure places cowboys in the "working class" economic strata, as it was comparable to pay for men who held positions of low skill nationwide. However, for much of the year, cowboys had no expenses for room and board, so in fact their net income was more akin to that of skilled workers. Nonetheless, cowboys as a group are not known for having moved up the economic ladder. One factor that seems to have been relevant was an inability to manage money: these were young men, often teenagers, with few commitments and limited professional experience. It was not uncommon for the cowboy to indulge in a spending spree as soon his pay was in hand, either in a town along the trail or at the end of a drive. Frontier towns referred to as "sin holes" or the "Sodom of the plains," especially those at the ends of rail lines, were places where cowboys could find respite from the herd.[7] In towns like Abilene, Wichita, and Dodge City, men could clean themselves up, buy a new hat or other gear, and spend their money indulging in liquor, gambling, and prostitutes, just as the outlaw cowboys had done in the years before the Civil War.[8]

Cowboy Values and Religiosity

Just as the idea of cowboy changed from "outlaw" to "cattle worker" over the course of the 1800s, new perceptions about the cowboy's persona and values also developed. Realistically speaking, at no time has there been a single type of cowboy, even during the "golden era" of cowboy work on the open range (1865–1895/1900).[9] Like any group of workers, the men differed in their education, family background, beliefs, manners, and other factors. Yet the cowboy of the golden era is repeatedly described—in literature, histories, and popular culture—with a single set of characteristics that are now often referred to as the "romantic cowboy" image.[10] He was strong, quiet, independent, honest, loyal, God-fearing, willing to endure hardship without complaint, likely to mind his own business, true to his word, and always willing to help a person in need. Some will elaborate that the cowboy had a tender heart in a rough package, or that he was gruff yet sensitive, in each case suggesting that one balanced the other. Others add characteristics of a more negative quality, such as that the cowboy was uncouth, a poor speaker, and not well educated. But the extent to which any of these characteristics can be true is limited, especially by time and geography, and blanket statements about eternal cowboy values and beliefs are mostly instances of myth-making. Jacqueline Moore's study of Texas cowboys of the 1865–1900 period has found that there are close parallels between the socio-behavioral descriptions of cowboys and several other working-class groups of that same time period, specifically Northwest loggers, East Coast factory workers, frontier miners, and railroad workers. Moore suggests that the cowboy value set, often romanticized as exceptional and culturally unique, is more likely rooted in the social and economic realities found within closely knit, all-male laboring groups, rather than in a distinctive and eternal cowboy outlook. Even if a historic set of values and descriptive characteristics could be pinpointed, Moore would argue, the same list would not necessarily apply to cowboys today because of changes in their social and economic circumstances.[11]

Consideration of values leads to the question, then, of cowboy religion. Were cowboys religious men? And if they were, in what ways was that religion expressed? In the antebellum years, organized religion in the West was erratic, and a great many people were unchurched. Missionaries and itinerant preachers from different faith groups who worked in Texas during the second half of the nineteenth century often commented on the scarcity of organized religion in frontier towns.[12] The churches most commonly found were Presbyterian, Methodist, and Catholic, though there were other religious pockets here and there, and while Baptists later came to dominate Texas, they did not gain real traction until the 1880s. It is, therefore, entirely possible that a working cowboy could have been genuinely unfamiliar with religion, especially if he had been raised in a far rural area. For example, the diary of a Texas school teacher noted in 1865 that "[t]he first sermon ever preached in Fort Davis was preached here today by Parson Slaughter, and it was the first sermon many of our people ever heard."[13] Even the presence of a church and preacher did not automatically mean that everyone attended services. A newspaper writer in Tascosa, Texas felt the need to defend his community in print, commenting in 1886 that his fellow townspeople were law-abiding folks despite the fact that, by and large, they were not churchgoers.[14] Though social pressures might have influenced church attendance when living at home, the working cowboy was in charge of his own spiritual life, and there is little evidence to suggest that many availed themselves of formal religious structures. As one observer commented in 1888, "The average cowboy does not bother himself about religion. The creeds and isms that worry civilization are a sealed book to the ranger, who is distinctively a fatalist. He believes that when the time comes for him to go over the range nothing can stand death off, and no matter what danger he faces previous to that time no deadly harm can come."[15]

Others have indicated that it was primarily the church setting, rather than belief in God, that was problematic for the cowboy, and that because of their rough lifestyles, cowboys were relatively unwelcome in straight-laced Protestant churches that dotted the plains. In an early example of a challenge to this situation, "cowboy evangelist" George Rosure preached in Kansas City saloons in an attempt to lure the men to his revival services at a nearby church; when local church members learned what he was doing, they shut down his efforts.[16] Though it is difficult to measure, there is little reason to doubt the longstanding bias against "sinful" men in mainstream churches; in fact, the continued presence of this barrier is one reason the modern cowboy church came into existence.

Nonetheless, the majority of modern history sources assert that cowboys of the golden era were familiar with religion, specifically Christianity, and largely indifferent to it.[17] Ramon F. Adams, for example, posited that most cowboys of the golden era were nominally Christian, in that they had been raised within some sort of religious framework, but that they were not usually churchgoers or Bible readers. Stepping into speculation, Adams added that cowboy religion was expressed as praxis: they valued respect, kindness, and generosity, and they enacted these values every day. Whether cowboys themselves would have regarded this behavior as a form of religious expression, however, is an open question. In a similar effort to claim that cowboys were not atheists, historian Clifford P. Westermeier has said that the cowboy's "innumerable spontaneous appeals to God for help" are proof of his belief in God, but Westermeier's documentable evidence of these "innumerable" cowboy prayers is scant, consisting of two anecdotes from funerals and one cowboy-themed prayer printed in a periodical. Ferenc Morton Szasz has asserted that cowboys "scorned formal churchgoing as unnecessary and unmasculine," and Richard W. Slatta has weighed in that "cowboys had little time or use for organized religion or church-going."[18] What we can be certain of is that a basic characteristic of the cowboy's life was that he was on the move most of the year. There may have been a few religious men who cleaned themselves up and returned to local church attendance during the winter season, but, realistically, the number of cowboys regularly participating in organized religious life would have been quite small. It is perhaps only his life on the trail, then, that can reveal the cowboy's tendency toward religious engagement.

For some working cowboys, it appears that religion was simply diversionary entertainment that bordered on farce. Will S. James, a cowboy and self-appointed lay missionary, recalled from his preconversion days that when the religious men were away from camp, the other cowboys sometimes held mock worship services as entertainment, even theatrically re-enacting sermons they had heard or trudging to the river to perform fake baptisms. At other times, the entertainment value was in disruption. When Oklahoma cowboy Isaac Hosey converted and sought to preach to his fellow men, they tried to break up his meetings by shooting off their pistols as he spoke. Hosey, described as "a walking arsenal," eventually started placing his own gun on the pulpit next to his Bible as a warning that he was not to be toyed with. Historian Philip Rollins recalled that a "vicious, stupid, and hopelessly vulgar printed parody on the Bible" was readily passed around among cowboys, almost serving as a litmus test for newcomers. And cowboy Teddy Blue Abbott remembered a time on the Texas Trail when the fellows passed a campfire evening listening to the preaching and singing of a Presbyterian minister and his nineteen-year-old daughter. They had no desire for religious conversion but participated because there was simply nothing better to do. As the evening passed and their interest grew in the daughter, Abbott and his companions agreed to visit the next time they passed near the man's home in Montana, with the daughter the potential prize each cowboy envisioned for himself.[19]

In some instances, religion was imposed upon cowboys, such as when the new management of the XIT Ranch in Texas—famous for being one of the largest ranches ever at approximately three million acres—insisted in 1888 that the men must observe the Sunday Sabbath. But as ranch historian James Evetts Haley commented, "In theory alone was Sunday observed," because cattle tending could not be put aside for a day. Nonetheless, a photograph documents at least one instance when the XIT rule-maker conducted a Sunday service in the Spring Lake section of the ranch, though the twenty attendees were almost all older, well-dressed gentlemen, surely not working cowboys on any day of the week.[20]

Regardless of the potential reception by cowboys, there were many hardworking itinerant preachers riding the West pursuing conversion among them. Some visited the ranches and made their primary appeals to the cattlemen, while others traveled the trails in search of cowboy encampments where they might spend an evening sharing the gospel with men around the fire. One example was Methodist preacher John DeVilbiss, who missionized in Texas from 1865 to 1879 and diligently logged each mile traveled, each sermon preached, each Bible handed out, and each letter written. Another was Baptist preacher Leander Randon Millican, called the "cowboy preacher of west Texas," who was remembered for baptizing a cowboy at the watering hole late one night between the man's shifts on the round-up. And the Reverend Sam P. Jones, a Methodist, deliberately used slang when preaching so as to reach the cowboy in his own language. He was sorely criticized by other pastors for tossing out impertinent phrases like "You grand old rascals" during his preaching.[21] Among these itinerants, and the hundreds more like them, there is little evidence to go on in trying to measure their "success." Perhaps the lack of information implies an answer; missionary memoirs are typically chock full of stories about successful conversions made in all sorts of challenging situations, but the instances of cowboy conversions in these records are few and far between. A greater number of engaging stories emerge from the lives of those men who were deemed *genuine* cowboy preachers: that is, men who were cowboys first, and became Christians later, merging the two as one identity.

The preachers who rose up within the cowboy setting were more likely to experience acceptance because they shared a culture with working cowboys and ranchers. They were men who moved from the pasture to pastorate, and therefore embodied crucial markers of both worlds.[22] They did not have to *try* to connect with cowboys, because they *were* cowboys. Their Christian conversion and training allowed them to minister to the men as any other pastor would, but their rootedness in cowboy life gave them a unique bridge of trust and understanding to men on the range. The record strongly suggests that men on the trail more often considered them genuine or authentic cowboy preachers, distinguishing them from the preaching men whose cultural background was rooted in a different way of life.

John W. Anderson (1855–1923) is an example of this kind of Christian cowboy. Anderson, the son of a Texas rancher, was a religious child, being raised Methodist and even nicknamed the "little preacher." He started work on the range at age ten and was promoted through the ranks during his teen years. Concurrently, though, he became reckless in his personal

life, no longer living up to his Christian ideals as he engaged in the seam-
ier aspects of cowboy living. In his twenties, Anderson took a break from
cowboying to attend Baylor University. Subsequently ordained in the
Baptist faith, he developed a reputation as a fiery preacher who provoked
people in ways both good and bad, and was known for railing against sinful diversions like liquor and dancing. Even after ordination, though, his
work continued to be a mix of cowboying and pastoring, as both were close
to his heart, and across the prairie he came to be known as "the cowboy
preacher." In story after story, Anderson's memoir attests to the reticence
of many cowboys when it came to religion. As he phrased it, the "stiff,
cold formality" of most preachers was off-putting, but cowboys were more
likely to respond to religious overtures from someone with whom they
could identify. One of his favorite recollections was a time when he arrived
at a new spot and tried preaching during the roundup and branding. At
first, the cowboys were mostly dismissive of the unknown Anderson.
Suspicious of the unlikely possibility that a preacher could also be a cowboy, the men made wagers among themselves about what kind of fraud he
would turn out to be. But within a day Anderson proved himself by working alongside them, demonstrating he was not merely a passable cowhand
but a superior one. The men were duly impressed by his unusual combination of talents, and word spread to nearby ranches. People came out to
"hear the new man preach who could throw the lasso and catch the wild
cow." Anderson was able to attract sizable groups to his preaching services
all during the roundup and afterwards, and considered it one of his more
successful life moments. His story contributes to the conclusion that a
man who was truly skilled as both a preacher and a cowboy was a rarity.[23]

The aforementioned Will S. James (b. 1856), a Texan who gave his
life to Christ at age twenty-seven, is another Christian cowboy who left a
record of his religious work. James did not feel called to formally pastor,
but instead "went out among cattlemen and worked as a missionary" in
a lay capacity. Proving that debates about cowboy authenticity are nothing new, his memoir shows that James was particularly concerned with
the differences between genuine cowboys and imposters, the latter being
men who had accepted a popularized image of the cowboy and attempted
to remake themselves in that image. Most especially, James had a distaste
for men who called themselves cowboy preachers yet had no background
in cowboy culture. As he wrote, "It is certainly quite amusing to see a little
six-bit fellow start out to slinging slang from the pulpit, posing as the cowboy preacher. He usually procures a ten-ounce hat with a leather band, a

pair of high-heeled boots, and then he is sailing." Commenting on one man of this type that he met, James wrote, "[T]o my astonishment and disgust, he had never been on a regular cow ranch in his life. His experiences consisted, I am convinced, in sitting on the fence and seeing the herd go by, or watching his mother milk an east Texas dogy cow. He didn't know the first letter in the cowman's alphabet."[24]

Among those like Anderson and James who left records discussing cowboy preachers, the issue of authenticity was key. It seems to have been a given that some people might be fraudulent in their presentation of religion, and so there was already a general skepticism regarding itinerant preachers. But on the specific issue of *cowboy* preachers, or at least men who presented themselves as such, their cowboy credentials were put to even greater scrutiny. According to James, most did not hold up. Cowboys would tolerate the presence of a "counterfeit" cowboy preacher for a day or so, but he served as mere amusement; he could not earn the men's respect without demonstrable grounding in the western culture by virtue of ranching and horsemanship skills.[25]

Though there were (and continue to be) numerous markers of authenticity in the cowboy context, a key aspect during this period had to do with language and communication style. A man's ability to imbue religious talks with illustrations and references drawn from cowboy life made his message more relatable. In the title of James's memoir, he refers to himself as a former "mavrick [sic]," or unbranded calf, which is cowboy idiom for an unsaved person. He advised cowboys against running wild on the range without being branded, warning that on judgment day "the great herdsman claims nothing that is not in His own legitimate earmark . . . . In the last great round-up . . . you and I will take the place of the range herd and there we are to be rounded up and the herd cut." In other words, the saved and unsaved ("branded and mavericks") would be judged by God, with sinners sent to hell ("sorted and cut"). On multiple levels, then, James conveyed his Christian journey in cowmen's lingo. Furthermore, the ability to show biblical support for one's message gave the cowboy preacher ministerial validity. As James noted, plainspoken truth about Christianity was more likely to appeal to cowboys "than all the clap-trap plans adopted by so many workers . . . . When dealing with him be certain your argument is backed with God's word or, as [cowboys] would put it, 'with bible.'"[26]

Anderson, too, mastered the analogic approach of preaching. For example, he referred to daily activities that cowboys would be familiar with, such as the task of lassoing a frightened horse when it was running wild in order to prevent the animal from hurting itself. This was just what Anderson himself was trying to do, he taught the cowboys he met along the way, by "throw[ing] the gospel net" on them. They were unsaved souls who were running wild on the range like the horse, only hurting themselves. He added biblical support by using language specific to Matt. 13:47–48, which refers to fishermen netting good and bad fish, with the good ones going to the kingdom of heaven. In this way, Anderson demonstrated a deeper credibility for those who might want to test not only his cowboy skills but also his religious knowledge.[27]

Beyond encounters with various types of cowboy preachers, the other noteworthy religious outlet on the frontier during the golden era was the multidenominational camp meeting. Much like Methodist endeavors elsewhere in the nation, western frontier camp meetings lasted for a week to ten days and sought to make more, and better, Christians. Some were specifically called *cowboy* camp meetings, and this was likely an effort to suggest that all were welcome regardless of religious background or commitment, as well as that the environment would be rugged, just as it was on the trail. Families traveled long distances to attend, often bringing their entire ranch staff and a team of horses; they camped out in wagons or slept under the stars, and they made communal meals. Religious fellowship, Bible study, and prayerful contemplation were all significant parts of the agenda, but the basic social aspect of these gatherings was likely just as important for many of the people who lived in remote areas.[28]

The most famous Cowboy Camp Meeting was held every August in the Davis Mountains of west Texas. William B. Bloys (1847–1917) moved to Texas in 1879 as a newly ordained Presbyterian pastor. West Texas at that time was characterized as "sinful frontier country," rife with crime, but "the cowman and his family was [Bloys's] mission," recalled a surprised local. Bloys visited saloons, gambling dens, and ranches, preaching to anyone who would listen. The lore says that Exa Means, of the Means Ranch, suggested "that there should be some place for the cowboys and the ranch people to meet together and worship the Lord." Bloys agreed but knew a church would not suffice, because people would not travel long distances merely to attend a weekly service. In October 1890, he held his first experimental camp meeting. It was small and had logistical challenges, but he committed to the endeavor, especially because "only a small per cent of these beginners were Christians." Garnering support from several other denominations, Bloys was able to grow the event each year.[29]

Before long, the annual Cowboy Camp Meeting offered four services a day led by preachers from different Protestant denominations. Ironically, Bloys himself was not considered a particularly good speaker, but he kept a list of all the "unsaved cowboys and ranch men in the country" and spent years trying to reach each one personally. During the evenings at camp, they held gender-segregated prayer sessions. The men met under the "prayer tree," a large tree at the camp that Brother Bloys had dedicated for that purpose. Sitting in the grass under the tree, a few might share testimony, or read a Bible passage, while others just listened. As historian Evans described it, "The prayer tree is the spiritual power house for the camp meeting. Scores of old hard sinful cowboys have found the Lord under the Prayer Tree . . . . The cowboys have named this tree their spiritual Hitchin' Post." The significance of the prayer tree being called a "hitching post" should not be lost: a hitching post is something dependable in its immovability, able to hold any wild horse that might be tied to it. So too was this meeting spot a spiritually significant place for the men, many of whom spent the rest of the year without any connection to organized religion but knew they could revitalize that part of themselves each August.[30]

The meeting continued to grow, with increasing numbers of attendees and permanent physical structures added to the campsite as they were able to finance them. The success of Bloys led to satellite Cowboy Camp Meetings being established over the course of the next several decades. Twelve camp meetings were founded in eight states all over the West, and, like the original, each one had a dedicated prayer tree. Though most of these meetings eventually died out, the Bloys Camp Meeting has continued on to the present day, meeting every August in the same location in the Davis Mountains.[31]

The Cowboy's Changing Reality

By 1900, the work of the cowboy had been altered by a variety of social and technological changes. Homesteaders, who were populating the West in increasing numbers, began to privatize their parcels of land, making it unavailable for public grazing. In tandem with this, the newly introduced barbed wire fence was an affront to the concept of open range cattle ranching. The fences created both confusion and conflict between those who felt the land should be open to all and those who wanted to protect their property from the intrusion of people and animals. There were also environmental problems with the open range cattle industry. At times, cows died in large numbers due to issues like drought, overgrazing, blizzards, and disease. Meanwhile, other advances made it possible to raise cattle on a single ranch. Windmill-pumped water tanks and wells began to dot the land, and new railheads reached further and further into the West. All of these factors made long trail drives impractical and increasingly unnecessary.[32]

These changes piled one atop the other such that by the late 1890s the job of the cowboy had become drastically different. Most ranchers diversified their livestock, and many added crops. Ranch tasks were becoming mechanized, requiring fewer workers—a trend that has never abated. Round-ups and branding continued, but they were done on a smaller scale and now represented only a portion of the work cowboys might do. Only the largest ranches still needed drivers and line riders, and in general the work became more permanent than seasonal. Maintaining a ranch required differing skill sets in climates as diverse as Texas, Kansas, and Wyoming, and as cowboys became more geographically constrained, the regional differences in their work became more pronounced. In most places, regular breaking and training of horses became part of the job, whereas previously it had been a specialized task performed by independent contractors who went from ranch to ranch. In his memoir, J. B. Cranfill remembered that in the 1870s a bronc buster could earn five dollars for taming a wild horse, which was about four times the daily pay of a regular ranch hand.[33] The job included teaching the horse to wear a saddle, respond to a rider, and ignore random noises and distractions. But like many other changes that became permanent, bronc busting was a job now relegated to the ranch hands, with specialists only being called upon for the most unruly animals.

In fact, horses came to have much greater significance in the cowboy's work life as he moved into the twentieth century. During the era of trail drives, the cowboy had used the horse as both a means of transportation and to assist with control and management of the herd. Most working cowboys did not own their horses; rather, they used whatever horses were in the remuda provided by the cattle owner. From the perspective of the cowboy, the horse was a tool that served a purpose, just as cattle were property being managed for specific purposes—growth, breeding, slaughter, and sale. Despite what is often portrayed in popular culture, there was not, typically, a *special* relationship between the cowboy and the horse in the 1800s; as Slatta has written, they were "not pampered pets and companions."[34] While the cowboy of the golden era had little personal concern for the horses, what he did need was a firm understanding of cow behavior. Erickson calls this "cow psychology" and explains that the best cowboys would study the eyes, ears, tails, and other subtle movements in an effort to anticipate what the animals would do.[35] But beyond the intimacy of cow psychology, cowboys have never been particularly tender toward livestock, and in fact many commentators today would classify some aspects of the animals' treatment as cruel.

The romanticized cowboy with his loyal horse, which came to be a part of the stock image of the American cowboy, is at least partly a genuine reflection of his changed work experience. The working cowboy of the twentieth century no longer needed multiple horses each day because he was not traveling great distances. It would be a natural development that a person using a single animal for daily work would begin to have a relationship with that animal. Hence, the portrait of a cowboy as a horseman does make sense, but the cowboy-and-horse combo is anachronistic if imagined to be part of the life of the original trail drive cowboy. The notion that a cowboy has an intuitive connection with his horse seems to have developed much later, most especially through depictions in film and television. By the second half of the century, horses on ranches were largely replaced by trucks and four-wheelers, though in certain conditions or for certain tasks, horses remained important. Nonetheless, the idea of a cowboy as a man who has a special connection with horses has persisted to the present.

The Cowboy's Changing Image

By the turn of the century, there were few opportunities for thrill-seeking young men who wanted to spend several months traveling the West working as a cowboy. One might expect that as the reality of the cowboy job changed, losing its aura of drama, travel, and adventure, the American fascination with him would have waned. But the inverse is true. Public interest in the cowboy became even more prominent after the turn of the twentieth century, though it was primarily nostalgia for a version of the cowboy that was by then obsolete, if it had ever existed at all. Americans' initial love for the cowboy came from presentations of his imagined life in different types of popular culture, including novels, magazines, art, and "Wild West" shows that toured the country. Many weeklies carried serial fiction that centered on the frontier, and whimsical travel narratives and western-themed human interest stories were published in magazines like *Lippincott's* and *Harper's Weekly*. Illustrations by artists such as Charles M. Russell and Frederic Remington often accompanied magazine stories. Russell's cowboy was usually engaged in standard herding work, if not also trying to ride a bucking bronco, while Remington's cowboy was doing the same activities but on a scale suggesting heightened intensity and danger. Both artists, ultimately renowned for sculpture and painting, provided visual explanations of life on the frontier to those who lived far from it, reinforcing ideas that it was a place of constant adventure and excitement. Some modern critics have pointed out that the works of these artists also glorified white settlement and the domination of Native Americans in the fulfillment of manifest destiny. As Sweeney has written, for example, "The cowboy hero—a macho figure of the imagination who has been enshrined in the consciousness of the world as an archetypal protagonist of American history—is the mythic persona fostered in this historical vision of the past as a national morality play." Critics such as Sweeney would urge contemporary viewers to recognize the editorial elements of fantasy and violence conveyed in many of the early images of the West, rather than viewing them as strictly historical renderings. Viewers at the time, however, may have accepted them more at face value.[36]

Live theater versions of cowboys were first presented in *Buffalo Bill's Wild West*, created by William F. Cody in the early 1880s. It was a western-themed variety show that grew to have many imitators, and as these shows increased in popularity, they also affected public perception of life in the West. *Wild West*'s acts, many of them rodeo prototypes, included races, shooting demonstrations, and men performing tricks on horseback in a section of the show called "Cowboy's Fun." In 1884, Cody added a new figure to his lineup: Buck Taylor, the "King of the Cowboys." The character Buck was billed as an orphan from the frontier who became a cowboy at a young age. Program books described the tall, handsome man as "genial" and "amiable" yet also someone with many "sturdy qualities" that had carried him through hardship. He primarily performed riding tricks in the show. Buck Taylor was the first specific personification of the cowboy image that came to dominate the American imagination, and he made impressions on audiences nationwide as the show toured the country. Taylor's character was also promoted in dime novels about his life and adventures, published beginning in 1887 with author Prentiss Ingraham's book *Buck Taylor, King of the Cowboys; or, The Raiders and the Rangers: A Story of the Wild and Thrilling Life of William L. Taylor*.[37]

Novels featuring cowboys and/or trail drive settings had been prolific since the 1870s, and they came in both high- and low-brow form. Some were written for adult audiences, others for juveniles, and their wide range meant they did not particularly put forth a single image of cowboy character traits. That changed definitively in 1902 with the publication of Owen Wister's *The Virginian*. The unnamed cowboy star of this novel takes the strength, masculinity, likeability, and horsemanship of Buck Taylor and adds several traits. The new standard for the cowboy added depth and complexity to him, such that he had all of Buck's charm and was also a loner, quiet, trustworthy, and a stalwart upholder of "good" over "bad." Ironically, as many have noted, both Buck and the *Virginian* were cow-less cowboys, which meant the image of the man had already been severed from its original labor context. For the public, this seemed to matter very little. *The Virginian* was immensely popular and a quick bestseller. The year after its publication, it was turned into a stage play; the first of many film versions appeared in 1914, and the book itself was republished numerous times. The basic plot of cowboy stories was also fixed by the example of *The Virginian*. Cowboy stories were, henceforth, morality tales about good versus evil, law versus chaos, and civilization versus savagery. American audiences loved this cowboy so much that they did not need him to change with the times, and so for the next five decades or more he was always on the winning side. As Don Russell has written, "*The Virginian* halted the evolution [of the cowboy image]. For half a century or more the cowboy isolated himself on the ranch of 1902, and those who wrote about him ignored such improvements as the automobile, tractor, telephone, advances in animal husbandry, and other appurtenances of the twentieth century."[38]

One question is what lay behind the popular attraction to this particular type of hero and his predictable story. Some commentators have attributed the surge of interest in the cowboy around the turn of the twentieth century to a kind of insecurity in the American psyche that the strong cowboy image assuaged. Fussell, for example, has written that "as the cowboy left the land, his legend lit up the imagined stage of the West . . . . I wonder if our cowboy myth didn't first take root in the all-too-human fear of being nothing and nobody in an alien land . . . . The fact that farmers began to migrate to cities to become wage earners fired the fantasy of an independent loner in the wild." Taylor more specifically pinpoints it to the vast number of social challenges that Americans grappled with as they encountered record numbers of immigrants, increased racial violence, and wide-scale industrialization and urbanization, among other things. The Anglo cowboy on the open range became a fantasy image of what American manhood was all about, and it was an image white Americans could cling to in the face of a rapidly diversifying society. The cowboy thus became almost a messiah figure, serving as a representation of hope as well as a nostalgic reflection on "a disappearing breed of men," like they felt themselves to be.[39]

One consequence of the advent of the cowboy as all-American hero was that the image could be abused. The newfound public admiration for and trust in the cowboy meant that people could establish a degree of legitimacy—or at least try to—by portraying themselves as cowboys. Perhaps this is the reason that a bevy of charlatan cowboy preachers in urban settings seemed to bubble up in the years around the turn of the twentieth century, as newspapers from across the country attest. Jack Mulcahy, for example, promoted himself in Los Angeles and beyond as a "cowboy preacher," yet the only records of his deeds are unflattering ones. After marrying a young woman whose parents disapproved of their union, he was twice charged with abandoning her in various stops along his national preaching trail. Another man who seized the opportunity was Samuel Bettes, originally known as a temperance speaker, who refashioned himself as a "cowboy preacher" in the mid-1890s. Bettes spent years raising money to finance the construction of a sailing vessel for world evangelism, though he never made such a journey. In the midst of his "cowboy" preaching career, he also became embroiled in a scandal when his much younger mistress discovered he was married, which certainly went against the upstanding cowboy image. And perhaps the most notorious, or at least the most newsworthy, "cowboy evangelist" was Justin Rice. Rice and his wife, Emma, traveled the country preaching on the streets. Rice was repeatedly arrested for disturbing the peace, spending weeks at a time in jail, and during his incarcerations Emma took up the burden and preached on her own. Everywhere they went, the couple attracted vehement opponents who considered them to be deceptive swindlers, but they also attracted supporters, too. On one occasion in Chicago, Justin's prosecution inspired a protest group to form a "Free Speech League"; police pointed out, however, that Rice's freedom to speak on the streets was not at issue, but rather the problem was the crowds and other disturbances that increasingly accompanied his speaking events. The Rices also managed to find themselves in trouble in other places. In Atlantic City, for instance, they got into an argument with their landlord, and Mrs. Rice scandalously threw a Bible at him. Mr. Rice was arrested for public intoxication in Los Angeles and again in Sacramento. The preaching couple made themselves known in places including Pennsylvania, New York, and Arizona over a period of eight years before finally disappearing from the headlines.[40]

More than once, reporters took the time to describe preacher Rice's appearance, with one paper even including a sketch of him alongside an article entitled "Fakes and Fanatics." Rice had long hair and a beard, he wore a hat similar to a sombrero and a jacket with fringe, and he was otherwise adorned in a popular interpretation of cowboy-style clothing. In this and other stories, his visual description was invariably juxtaposed against statements meant to indicate he was putting on an act, from mild comments like "the real cowboys of the plains never wear their hair long," to more explicit descriptions of Rice as "the long-haired genius who exults in the sobriquet of the cowboy preacher." In other words, it was not enough that Rice may have been a swindler posing as a preacher; rather, writers wanted to emphasize that he committed the double sin of passing himself off as a *cowboy* preacher, making a mockery of the American hero. For the most part, the motives of cowboy preachers like Mulcahy, Bettes, Rice, and others like them cannot be known, so while they appear to have operated out of self-interest, it is possible this is an unfortunate distortion of sincere evangelistic intentions. However, stories about them do stand in stark contrast to the many other humdrum news reports about speaking engagements of various cowboy preachers, which suggests that there was something distinctive about a few of them that induced widespread skepticism.

Cowboy History through Song

Golden era cowboy nostalgia also made itself evident in early twentieth-century attempts to reconstruct cowboy trail life via songs and poetry. Songs, as folklorists generally agree, can be keys to understanding the daily life and concerns of cultural groups. Cowboys did sing—though when and where is debated—so theoretically their songs might yield a wealth of information about their lives, and if we were to look for signs of religiosity in these lyrical texts, it could certainly be found. A song such as "The Cowboy at Church," for example, is told from the perspective of a cowboy who wanders into a service one Sunday morning on a whim. Though the people there look at him askance, he reflects on his boyhood salvation and knows that he is rightly a part of them. Observing their outward differences, the narrator's voice says, "Though the congregation doubtless thought / That the cowboys as a race / Were a kind of moral outlaw / With no good claim to grace. / Is it very strange that cowboys are / A rough and reckless crew / When their garb forbids their doing right / As Christian people do?" The lyrics of many songs, such as "The Grand Round-Up," "A Cowboy Alone with his Conscience," and "The Cowboy's Sweet By-and-By," portray a concerned cowboy wondering about his eternal future, fearing hell and hoping he will go to heaven. Based on the content of these and many other poetic and musical texts, one might conclude that the average late nineteenth century cowboy was familiar with the Christian church and sentimental toward it, that he believed in God, and that he often pondered the afterlife while out on the range. All of these assessments have indeed been made by people reading history from—or into—cowboy verse.[41] Unfortunately, most of these conclusions about the cowboy's religion are based on flimsy evidence, because few of the songs ever came from range cowboys themselves.

In order to accurately interpret history from cowboy songs, we must first delineate different strains of cowboy music and evaluate their provenance. Songs and poems written *about* cowboys were published for their artistic value in newspapers and magazines of the times, and later in small books and various reprint volumes. Few of these pieces were written by actual cowboys or former cowboys, but rather by talented writers. They have limited historical use for understanding the thoughts and concerns of the trail cowboy because they indicate little more than individual authors' notions of cowboy life during that era. An early example of a collection of this type is N. Howard Thorp's 1908 book, *Songs of the Cowboys*. Thorp, who lived in Nebraska and New Mexico during the waning years of cattle drives, was himself a writer of poetry and fiction. The verses in his first volume are predominantly Thorp's sentimentalized musings on a cowboy life that he did not experience; other songs included in it, culled from old periodicals, were written by people whose connection with cowboy life cannot be known. Other well-known authors whose work falls into this category include poets Charles Badger Clark and William Lawrence Chittenden; while many of their poems are beautiful from an artistic point of view, historically speaking they only serve to perpetuate a cowboy mythology that was already in vogue.[42]

The well-known Lomax collection of cowboy songs and poetry, which became quite influential and authoritative, is particularly vexing. John

A. Lomax was a native Texan and English professor who spent years gathering cowboy verse; the first of his many volumes was published in 1910. He posited that cowboy work songs, which are identifiable by their commentary on aspects of the job, were usually composed communally by cowboys on the range. The dissemination of his work via publication led to many people providing evidence to the contrary and highlighting significant flaws in his research. Most of the alleged cowboy work ballads were traced to specific poet-authors, and often they had been written after the demise of the trail drives. Some scholars have also pointed out problems with Lomax's logic: Logsdon, for example, has argued that ideas of cowboys singing during their workday, especially as they rode along the trail, are not plausible given the nature of the job. While they might have used yells or musicalized calls to drive cattle, overall "the work was hard, dusty, non-rhythmic activity, and to think that a cowboy, face covered with a kerchief, eating dust, trailing cattle, could sing, is ludicrous."[43] Likewise, cowboys would not have played instruments on horseback, though a few may have pulled out a violin or banjo at the evening campfire.

As numerous scholars have pointed out, in this early project, Lomax let his personal love for the cowboy taint his objectivity, which is evident not only from his method of collection but also in his commentary on the songs.[44] In the introduction to a 1919 collection, for example, Lomax waxed poetic, regretting that "[t]he trails are becoming dust covered or grass grown or lost underneath the farmers' furrow; but in the selections of this volume . . . men of today and those who are to follow, may sense, at least in some small measure, the service, the glamour, the romance of that knight-errant of the plains—the American cowboy."[45] It was this version of the cowboy and the West that Lomax sought to preserve via songs. Lomax edited many of the songs prior to publication, in some cases to cleanse them of off-color references and in other cases to streamline several different versions of a song into one. Taylor provided numerous samples of Lomax's redactions. For instance, the lines, "My foot in the stirrup, my ass in the saddle / I'll bid goodbye to these God damn cattle," became, in Lomax's collection, "Feet in the stirrups and seat in the saddle / I hung and rattled with them long-horn cattle." Other lyrics that Lomax found too racy were not published at all, because he found them unsuitable for polite reading, such as, "I'm going down south just whooping and yelling / If I don't get a woman I'll take a heifer yearling."[46] Lomax's editing cleaned up the cowboy to fit the image of the upstanding man Americans believed

him to be, but it did a disservice to those interested in his more complicated, and often murky, cultural history.

Though cowboy work songs must be disregarded for reasons of authen-
tication, what is more clearly agreed upon is that cowboys sang for entertainment around evening campfires, and there is mixed opinion on the
degree to which men sang alone during nighttime watches. Evidence suggests that many cowboy campfire songs were popular melodies of the day
with words spontaneously changed by the group of men singing them,
and various collections indicate that entertainment songs were often
humorously raunchy. Folklorist Logsdon, for example, has commented
that many songs dealt with "phallic size and virility, venereal disease, and
sodomy," and to his mild description I would add that they also refer to
rape, prostitution, incest, and bestiality. As for night herding songs, they
have been described as low-toned serenades or lullabies, intended to keep
the animals calm. Some people recollected that most often these were
church songs with lyrical modifications; yet, as McCoy noted in the mid-
1870s, "the spirit of true piety does not abound in the sentiment."[47] If this
description of night-herding songs is accurate, the historical information
it provides is that some cowboys were familiar enough with formal religion that they knew hymn melodies, even if they felt no compulsion to
sing the original words.

Entertainment Cowboys

After World War I, the cowboy figure became even more beloved in entertainment realms. Traveling shows of the Wild West genre were declining
in popularity, but they were being replaced by more athletically oriented
shows that were increasingly referred to as "rodeo." As rodeo worked
through a long process of becoming a uniformly regulated competition,
in the interim it was a sport-entertainment hybrid that contained fanci-
ful elements of cowboy performance, like tricks on horseback. Audiences
flocked to see film versions of cowboys just as they did to see live cowboys
perform. The cowboy milieu had become a fertile setting for many movies, such that they numbered in the hundreds by the early 1930s and an
entire film subgenre, the B-Western, had begun. Many B-Westerns told
ongoing stories about a set of characters, and the major cast pool of these
films remained fairly stable. Perhaps most importantly, B-Westerns served
as an influential source of cowboy imagery to the public at large for several
decades.[48]

The cowboy also found a place in radio starting the 1920s via the creation of the singing cowboy, who was a new variation on the stock image. This lighthearted, good-natured cowboy was quite far from ranch work as he strummed his guitar and sang simple songs from the heart. Though some of these men performed original material, many of the early singing cowboys performed what they called "cowboy traditionals," which were primarily songs taken from the Lomax collection. Among the early singing cowboys were Stuart Hamblen, who at first used the stage name "Cowboy Joe"; Carl T. Sprague, "The Original Singing Cowboy"; and John White, the "Lonesome Cowboy." These men made names for themselves through regular radio station gigs and product endorsement deals. It was not long before singing cowboys gained starring film roles, too. Some, like Ken Maynard, were known performers whose singing was passable, while others, like Gene Autry, were singers whose acting was passable; the cowboy credentials of many of them are another matter entirely. Regardless of the paths they took to gain fame, singing cowboys became immensely popular and made a significant imprint on the standard cowboy image, which came to include the characteristic of musical talent. As Lonn Taylor has opined, "the thirties were the great years of the cowboy singer, whose costume, demeanor, and action on screen generally indicated that he was an entertainer first and a cowboy second."[49]

Cowboy shows of dramatic, melodramatic, and lighthearted tenor also unfolded on the radio waves, and some of these shows remained quite popular until being outmoded by television in the 1950s. Programs such as *Death Valley Days* (1930–1945) and *The Lone Ranger* (1933–1955) gained such loyal audiences that they spawned variations in other forms of media; the latter program continues to be discussed as a show that "attached religious significance with American progress, piety, and expansion."[50] A radio program that more overtly promoted ideas about cowboy religion was Stuart Hamblen's *Cowboy Church of the Air*, which originally ran from 1949–1952, then was restarted a few years later and ran for fifteen years in syndication. It is also the first known use of the term "cowboy church."

Hamblen, the son of a Methodist preacher in Texas, had worked on ranches as a teen before pursuing a career in music. His early work in radio taught him that he preferred to be in charge of programming rather than subject to it, and he expressed annoyance with entertainment professionals who thought the cowboy aspect of his persona was a gimmick. He sought work opportunities that allowed him to express his cowboy side and did not infringe on his creative control, and in addition to film and radio work, he wrote a catalog of his own songs. Hamblen described the earliest iteration of *Cowboy Church of the Air* as an unscripted gospel singing program. Members of the live audience, who could sing along, were often drunk. Though he had not yet become a devout Christian, Hamblen felt it was a moral conflict to mix religion and alcohol. As he recalled in 1986, "Everybody was walking around there half-stoned, which to me was sacrilegious, you know, because of my dad. And I had some guys that'll sing those hymns, and they were standing up there stoned-out, you know, and that used to worry me, because I believe, I thought, 'Well, it's a wonder God doesn't strike us dead, putting on that kind of stuff,' you know." Not long after his 1952 conversion at a Billy Graham event, Hamblen refused to allow a beer company to sponsor his show, and as a result he was fired from the station. When Hamblen was encouraged to restart the show a few years later, it had a more subdued live audience, and the content mixed music with religiously themed stories. He claimed that his goal was to "lift the hearts of men from the moral down-drafts that plague our times." The music included some of Hamblen's originals, such as "My Religion's Not Old Fashioned," "It Is No Secret," and "Open Up Your Heart (and Let the Sun Shine In)." Though the show's content as well as its title, *Cowboy Church of the Air*, promoted the idea that a cowboy's form of religion was in some way distinct from the norm, after listening to Hamblen's shows, audiences might have also characterized cowboy religion as casual, down-home, and fun.[51]

Meanwhile, the most popular singing cowboy of film, Gene Autry, had a weekly radio show called *Melody Ranch* (1940–1956) that also came to promote religious ideas. *Melody Ranch* included music, cowboy stories (sometimes with a moral lesson), and discussions with guests, and its varied content meant it held appeal for both adults and children. Occasionally, Autry promoted a list of good behaviors that was originally called the "cowboy code" and later renamed the "Ten Cowboy Commandments," which was invented by his managers in the late 1930s. This list included points about being truthful, clean, patriotic, and harboring no religious prejudice. Particularly after World War II, Autry's management team closely aligned the Cowboy Commandments with his public image, making sure that frequent mention of them was made on radio, in magazine articles, and in press for his films. As Autry biographer Holly George-Warren has commented, the more Autry's private life veered toward debauchery in the late 1940s and early 1950s, the more heavily his managers promoted his public image as a moral leader and representative of what young American men should strive to be.[52]

Autry, along with Roy Rogers, was among the few cowboy stars who navigated successful careers across radio, film, and television. Part of the long-lasting appeal of Autry and Rogers was that they managed to straddle different cowboy images, morphing from simply singing cowboys into wise father figure cowboys, a new variant on the image that emerged in the late 1940s and early 1950s. Television shows marketed to children facilitated the promotion of this new surrogate parent cowboy image. Like Autry before him, Rogers too promoted a list he called the "Ten Commandments of the Cowboy," which members of his "Roy Rogers Riders Club" agreed to follow. The list was similar to Autry's but more simplistic in its wording, and it included the very explicit religious instruction to "love God and go to Sunday School regularly." By veering somewhat from the biblical Ten Commandments, the implication of these lists for impressionable children might have been that cowboys live by a different set of rules than other people, a point that was by then certainly a part of the basic cowboy mythology.[53]

Entertainment Cowboy Preachers

During this same period, the entertainment cowboy had a parallel in the religious realm: the entertainment cowboy preacher. Just as the cowboy lit up the airwaves of radio and television and sang on the stage and the screen, so too did preaching cowboys find places in the pulpits of American churches large and small, rural and urban. Completely removed from the ranch context, this new crop of cowboy preachers marketed themselves as formal guest speakers. Their religious and cowboy credentials were mixed and varied, just as had been the case when trail cowboys of the golden era had found some itinerants to be likeable and authentic while others were rapidly dismissed as posers. The list of "cowboy preachers" and "cowboy evangelists" speaking at churches from the 1920s through the 1950s is a long one. Some of these men seem to have had short-lived careers, passing through a given city only once or twice, while other more popular speakers had frequent engagements in a wide variety of places.

One "Preachin' Cowboy" who came to be fairly well known was Leonard Eilers (1898–1996). Eilers grew up in South Dakota and as a child became fascinated with the roping tricks he saw performed at a Wild West show. After working at the Diamond Ranch in Wyoming, he moved to Hollywood in 1922 with hopes of becoming a cowboy actor. The movie world, however, was disillusioning for him, because he encountered many behaviors that were a challenge to his deep Christian beliefs; furthermore, he realized that there were hundreds if not thousands of men just like himself trying to break into film. Eilers grounded himself in his faith and attended a two-year Bible education program. He abandoned what he called the "goal of my dreams . . . a job for which thousands were longing and striving," in order to "get into the saddle for God." During the Depression years, he survived by melding all of his skills into one package and traveling the country as an itinerant guest speaker/cowboy preacher, and although he eventually returned to work at the studios as a cameraman, Eilers continued his cowboy preaching endeavors on the side. His religious talks emphasized a western context, with titles such as "God and the Rancher," "Trouble on the Range," and "Brand Inspection." He used rope tricks to both catch the attention of attendees and to illustrate religious principles, and his programs, which also involved slide shows and live music, appealed to youth and adults from all different denominations of Protestantism.[54]

Furthermore, Eilers and his wife, Frances, opened their eleven-acre ranch to teens who were troubled or in need of better living situations, and they estimated they had provided temporary homes to more than five hundred young people over the course of four decades. When interviewed by a reporter for the *Los Angeles Times*, the couple said that although their work was based on their religious beliefs, they did not pressure the teens to accept Christianity. Eilers also worked on more direct evangelism and organization. In 1946, for example, he started a worship group in his home that eventually became the First Presbyterian Church of Granada Hills. In 1948, he attended an international conference focused on ministry to youth, about which he later wrote a book. In the early 1950s, he was involved with the "Hollywood Group," a meeting of Christians working in the film industry who sought to use their work to spread the gospel. By 1950, Eilers had published half a dozen works on Christian faith, with one specifically focusing on being a Christian while working in the movie business. And Eilers continued performing his "lariat-lasso tricks" at religious gatherings, even into his eighties.

Eilers is an example of a cowboy preacher who helped sustain the idea that a distinct cowboy Christianity existed. As a person, Eilers had genuine roots in western culture, but he stepped away from that context and spent most of his life in show business. Though at times he had speaking engagements in Texas and parts of the Great Plains, it seems that Eilers's primary audience was in Los Angeles. He was presenting ideas and imagery about cowboys that were contextualized within religious teachings, and he imparted these ideas to people who had little or no contact with real working ranchmen. Like Hamblen, Autry, and Rogers, Leonard Eilers—and the many other men who fit his mold—was an entertainment cowboy who promoted ideas about "cowboy values." The story of his work serves as an example of one type of cowboy preacher that existed during this part of the twentieth century, through whom the American public absorbed ideas about "cowboy religion."

Very few entertainment cowboy preachers maintained a long-standing ministry, as Eilers did. For instance, "cowboy evangelist" Jay C. Kellogg (1893–1961) was a man who burst into prominence and then seemed to vanish. Kellogg hailed from the West and spent his teen years working with cattle. In December of 1931, Kellogg was promoted in Chicago newspaper church pages as an "expert cowboy" who gives "soul-stirring, thrilling, and enlightening" talks. The following year he began offering a handful of his sermons for sale in booklet form, advertising in places like the Pentecostal magazine *The Latter Rain Evangel*. One advertisement described his books as "rip-snorting, right from the Western Plains and written in true American cow-boy style." It was not long before Kellogg was invited into the pulpit of the famous Angelus Temple in Los Angeles during the vacation of its founding pastor, Aimee Semple McPherson. She and her followers greeted the "chaps-clad and gun-toting evangelist" at his train with "the crack of a six-gun" and a "parade . . . of Indians and cowboys" to lead him to his hotel. Although Kellogg continued publishing and having large speaking engagements through 1936, the cowboy preacher abruptly disappears from the record of public history after that year. Could it have been caused by something he said? He was no stranger to controversy, having indicated support for the KKK in 1932 and having made disparaging comments about women even as shared the pulpit with McPherson on several occasions. This is possible, but it is just as likely that people tired of him and found him somewhat incongruous. Kellogg liked to portray himself as a simple man without formal education, which was not entirely true. His religious messages, which bordered on extreme, conflicted with his advertised easygoing cowboy persona. A "cowboy" who preached with great specificity about the League of Nations, capitalism, prophecy, and demons may have felt like an oddity; Kellogg would have stood in contrast with the more popular idea of a cowboy as a straightforward man who conveys a basic message in easy terms. Perhaps his attempt to capitalize on the cowboy image led to his decline; many others like him similarly seemed to come and go rather quickly.[55]

In contrast with the work of entertainment cowboy preachers, there were also people who still tried to reach out to the ranch men who were the new incarnation of the working cowboy. Ralph J. Hall (1891–1973), a cowboy preacher and Sunday school missionary, exemplified this dwindling group of itinerants. Hall was born and raised in the cattle country of west Texas. As a young man full of Christian zeal, he secured a job as a missionary with the Presbyterian Church. Starting in approximately 1910, Hall worked as an itinerant preacher in areas of New Mexico and west Texas, at first traveling on horseback. He had almost no formal education, but based on his success as a missionary and an intensive course of study with two ministers, he was ordained in 1916. Year in and year out, Hall made home visits, he spoke with men in gathering spots like ranches and mines, he preached sermons whenever he could gather a group, and he initiated Sunday school programs in small towns by enlisting an instructor and providing the curriculum. But he became known as "the cowboy preacher" because of his special gift in this area. When dealing with cowboys, he preferred to first work alongside them, and only after gaining their friendship would he disclose that he was a preacher. He recalled a time when, for example, he spent several days assisting as a hand during roundup at the FLY Bar Ranch. The men there "accepted me as just another cowboy riding chuck line." When he finally told the boss he was a minister, the incredulous man replied, "The hell you are!" Hall got the chance to preach to the men that evening and for several more afterwards, trying to impress upon them that being a Christian was a personal commitment, rather than something that was about big churches and lots of other people. At the end of his time on the ranch, he baptized several of the men with water poured from a tin cup. This story was typical of many of the ranch evangelism experiences he recalled.[56]

Furthermore, Hall's memoirs attest to a great number of western people who, even well into the twentieth century, still had no access to an organized religious community because of their geographic isolation. During his years on horseback, he could sometimes ride an entire day and encounter no one, and perhaps for that reason he considered himself "a trailblazer, a pioneer in the things of the Kingdom." In a 1928 report, Hall estimated that he had traveled twenty-four thousand miles that year, en route preaching more than three hundred times and making more than one thousand home visits. In 1940, he was promoted to a regional supervisory position, which meant significantly less travel. Photographs and films from after that time show Hall as a man who was more typically wearing a suit and working on projects involving the institutionalization of religion. But at least during the prime of his missionary years, he was deeply engaged with trying to bring religion to western people, sometimes one by one, who felt they had no access to it. As he expressed to fellow missionaries during an event in Denver, "We are sent to the neglected people of America . . . . It is our [task] to become the pastor of the pastorless, to visit the isolated homes, to establish family religion."[57] Ralph Hall's words could easily be spoken by many of the cowboy pastors of the present day, and they would be just as accurate in describing the common goal. Though "cowboy churches" did not exist during Hall's lifetime, this common thread of the cowboy ministry runs consistently through the lives and work of men like John Anderson, Will S. James, Ralph Hall, and hundreds of cowboy preachers today.

From the postbellum era to the 1950s, the image of the cowboy changed numerous times. The entertainment cowboy was perhaps the most drastic departure from the original; though old range cowboys probably showed off horse or lasso tricks when they could, they were unlikely to croon sweetly to young ladies or play guitar while riding horseback, and most would have been ill-suited for advising children about morals. Certainly, through the first half of the twentieth century, men still worked on ranches with cattle, but the chasm between their reality and the popular image Americans absorbed through television and film grew more vast every decade. After World War II, ranch cowboys began to marry in greater numbers than ever before, which further changed their cultural reality by making them more "settled."[58] Surprisingly, greater religious involvement does not seem to have accompanied this domestication process. The itinerant preacher was gradually disappearing because there was no moving population (cowboy or otherwise) for him to follow, and so outreach to working cowboys and their families declined. The men who called themselves cowboys still had a degree of geographic isolation, and they still had muddy boots and jeans on every Sunday when they came in to breakfast after a long morning of work. These facts of their lives meant that Protestant churches, with their emphasis on respectability and appropriateness, were not environments in which cowboys felt particularly comfortable. And so they mostly stayed away.

As the entertainment cowboy finally began petering out, his popularity was replaced with a very different kind of man. The 1950s and '60s saw the emergence of the rodeo cowboy who was as worldly, tarnished, and dangerous as the outlaw cowboys of days long gone. Increasingly, the popular cowboy image on film and television was a lone rodeo man haunted by demons, and we rooted for him to conquer his demons just as we cheered him on when he occasionally became a vigilante. Concurrently, in the real world of horse people on ranches and at racetracks and in rodeo, a cadre of people worked to counter the reality on which the dark cowboy image was based. As the next chapter will show, the increasing dominance of this rough image is part of what spurred some people to attempt to "save" the cowboy from himself, and through their work, the first serious efforts at establishing a distinctive church for cowboys was born.

3

Ministry to Rodeo Cowboys

A TEXAS BREEZE blew through the olive green shotgun-style building that served as the headquarters of Cowboys for Christ (CFC), an outreach ministry and publisher of the newspaper *The Christian Ranchman*.[1] President Dave Harvey and I sat across from each other at his broad desk, talking and laughing, while his wife, Margie, quietly knitted on the sofa behind us. The afternoon was prematurely hot for mid-March, and Harvey had opened both the front and rear doors of the building to get some air moving; at times, the wind suddenly kicked up a plume of papers.

"I got involved in Cowboys for Christ in the early eighties, and I've been with it ever since. It's just a neat ministry because you don't have walls." Harvey spoke at a rapid clip, moving seamlessly from one story to the next, and occasionally he jumped from his seat to find a document or picture to show me. He was pure adrenaline and enthusiasm for the CFC enterprise. In the two hours that followed, Harvey regaled me with stories about CFC ministry and history, recalling noteworthy incidents from horse shows and rodeos, and drawing my attention to particular testimonies that had been printed in the newspaper over the years. One of these was the story of Jack Favor, a former rodeo champion wrongly convicted of homicide. While in prison, he ran Bible study groups as well as working to produce the then-new Angola prison rodeo. Not long after his exoneration in 1974, Favor became actively involved with CFC, joining its board and often doing speaking events with founder Ted Pressley to promote the burgeoning rodeo ministry.

Harvey, who became CFC president after Pressley's 2011 death, spoke to me about the importance of a ministry being accessible to its target audience on a variety of levels. He recalled a time when Pressley entered a hotel in Europe. "He walked in with his cowboy hat on, and he said people were almost wanting to bow to him! 'Oh, this is an American cowboy!' And when they found out he was an American cowboy *preacher*, that really did stir 'em up, I guess!" Harvey used this anecdote to make a point about strategy in ministry. As he put it, "That really is what we use as the door opener for the Lord: the cowboy image. You would think that it would have lost its impact, but it has grown. Because look at your PBR—Professional Bull Riding, the whole horse industry, and any given weekend—almost any given day in this area—there's a livestock activity of some type. And usually in Texas there's probably fifty or a hundred every weekend. So, that's why we really got the urge to go and take the gospel there, because all these cowboys and cowgirls were there."

From its start as a form of religious outreach at rodeos, CFC has grown and expanded, now including approximately fifty chapters and an extensive prison ministry. Reflecting on CFC's overall work, Harvey cheerfully says, "My philosophy is, there's a little cowboy in everybody. So you can reach just about one hundred percent of anybody with that cowboy image." Then he adds, "And let me tell you, rodeo's a fun ministry. There is no atheist behind the bull chutes."

Rodeo and Its Cowboys

Rodeo moved in to absorb the market for western-themed live entertainment as its Wild West show predecessors began fading from popularity around the time of World War I.[2] There was no system of national organization; therefore rodeos could be arranged and produced by anyone with the means to do so, and this begat various problems. One consequence was that rodeo came in many different types, from small to large, with a range of possible events, and a portion of them were not actual contests at all despite appearing to be so. A fake rodeo would have a cast of contracted competitors who typically rotated the jobs of winning and losing among themselves, and attendees were none the wiser. Another rodeo problem was the "bloomer," or exploitative producer. After organizing a legitimate-looking rodeo and attracting genuine contestants, bloomers disappeared with the entry fees and ticket profits, leaving winners cheated of their prize money. These and other issues led to the first step in organizing rodeo as a sport on a national level through the creation of the Rodeo Association of America (RAA) in 1929, an organization comprised of people working in rodeo management. The RAA, though limited by the monolithic perspective of its members, began creating policies about competition and prize money. A second step came with the creation of the Cowboy Turtles Association (CTA), a group formed by rodeo contestants in 1936, and which advocated for additional forms of fairness and standardization.[3] As the years passed, more layers were added to the sport: for example, geographic regions distinguished rodeo circuits and helped in the tracking of points toward annual championships, and strict rules about contestant attire and behavior helped keep a family-friendly atmosphere in the arena. Although the influence of these two organizations evolved over time, in their first decades they were crucial to the development of consistent rules for competition, judging, awards, and safety, among other aspects of rodeo.

Rodeo was also becoming more male dominated during this time. Women had built careers in rodeo since the days of its nineteenth century prototypes, competing in events including bronc riding, bull riding, steer wrestling, and roping. By the 1940s, however, they were increasingly being shut out of the competitions and relegated to performance roles as parade leaders and rodeo queens. Mary Lou LeCompte, a historian of women in professional rodeo, has attributed this change to several things that happened at management levels, none of which was an overt attempt to shut women out of competition but which did have that cumulative effect. One factor was the death of bronc rider Bonnie McCarroll at the 1929 Pendleton Roundup. After being horrendously trampled during her last planned appearance prior to retirement, McCarroll lingered in critical condition for eleven days. Her tragic death caused many rodeos to become hesitant about hosting women's competitions, despite the fact that the events posed an equal danger to men. A second factor was that women were not allowed real participation in the CTA; they were nonvoting members, and no one was advocating for protection of their events within the developing organizational structure. And a third important factor was the format change in the early 1940s instituted by Flying A Rodeos, a production company owned by Gene Autry. Flying A deliberately outbid its competitors to win as many contracts as possible, essentially creating a monopoly in the business of large rodeo productions. Autry's reformatted rodeo included fewer competitive events—partially achieved by eliminating those for women—and adding spectacle, such as music and dance performances, which capitalized on the popularity of singing cowboys. Though rodeo women subsequently organized and worked to get some of their events back in the competitive lineup, by then the damage was nearly irreparable. From the 1940s on, rodeo was perceived and promoted as a male sporting environment that was somehow unsuitable for women, who were considered too delicate for competition, both physically and psychologically.[4]

Despite the gradual elimination of women's events, rodeo was growing in popularity across the nation. During the years of the second World War, deliberate efforts to imbue rodeo with Americana pushed audiences to perceive it as a sport deeply connected with national identity. The use of patriotic music, an emphasis on the flag, and the presence of speeches or recordings that referenced moments of American history became part of Autry's rodeos in the 1940s and left an imprint that can still be observed today. In the shadow of war's uncertainty, more widespread nostalgia grew for the cowboy hero, and rodeo was a way for the masses to see him live and in action and feel like they were part of his story. The narrative of the cowboy as a symbol of national pride also aligned well with the emergent paternal cowboy image, discussed previously, on whom parents could depend for children's moral guidance.

Rodeo cowboys themselves were also transforming. In the 1920s and into the '30s, rodeo men were popularly regarded as rough and unsavory, partly because they tended to engage in pursuits like drinking and card playing during their off time, and partly because people were wary of their transience. According to historian Kristine Fredriksson, even ranchers regarded them as "undependable, [and] too lazy to hold down a job," and therefore avoided hiring men known to compete in rodeo.[5] As rodeo professionalized and more contestants made it their central career rather than a side job, the men involved put greater attention on training and physical fitness. This also coincided with the increased patriotism in rodeo, such that the public image of the rodeo cowboy in the 1940s was becoming much more respectable. By the 1950s, individual men whose skills dominated the competitions developed personal followings and thus began to draw audiences merely because of their participation. National media outlets also put attention on the sport, with full-color articles about it in places like *Time, Newsweek,* and *Sports Illustrated.* Attendance reached new heights, and the calendar for serious competitors essentially ran year-round.

Rodeo changed once again with the invention of the National Finals Rodeo (NFR), which ushered in the style of rodeo most people are familiar with today. The NFR, first held in 1959, is an annual competition that crowns a "world champion" in each event, with all participants drawn from among the year's biggest winners on the circuit. It is a heavily publicized and sometimes televised multiday extravaganza with large monetary prizes. Like football's Superbowl or baseball's World Series, the NFR put a culmination point on the rodeo calendar, which gave spectators more of a reason to track particular events and/or competitors they found interesting. Furthermore, it was conceived and designed by a diverse group of men that included both contestants and rodeo planners. By putting the focus on the competitions, there was little time left at the NFR for the inclusion of pageantry and performance, and that did not seem to affect anyone's appreciation of it. In essence, the success of the NFR showed that a format based strictly on athletic competition would continue to attract big audiences. Gradually, the influence of Autry's rodeo template waned, and the professional circuit readjusted its programs. Professional rodeo has been, ever since, a gritty environment of serious athletic competition.

Although rodeo cowboys of the 1940s and '50s were generally notable for their upstanding public image, in fact a career in rodeo has always created serious lifestyle challenges. Foremost, it required a heavy travel schedule and thus a somewhat nomadic life; stops at home, if the rodeo cowboy bothered to maintain one, were typically only for a few weekdays at a time. The schedule made it difficult to build marriages and families, though some alleviated the conflict by marrying rodeo cowgirls. Most of the time, the cowboy slept in motels, trailers, or cars en route to the next competition, and each rodeo had its own new set of social circumstances based on who happened to be competing. Furthermore, because entry fees and travel expenses came out of contestants' pockets, the net income—even for winners—was not typically very high. It was an erratic lifestyle that created its own forms of stress, and this stress became more evident in the rodeo world in the 1960s and beyond.

Another crucial aspect of the life of the rodeo cowboy—as true today as it was in the past—is the constant danger. Physical injury is common. Broken and dislocated bones are typical, and there is always the risk of being pinned, crushed, or trampled by an animal. The chutes and arena dirt can be rife with animal microbes and other bacteria that may cause serious illness. But from a young age, rodeo participants are encouraged to minimize injuries and continue competing regardless of what pains them. Many observers have attested to a culture of injury denial in rodeo that is linked with a badge of pride. It is not unusual to hear contestants boast about having competed despite serious injury, and some oft-retold stories about particular contestants have become akin to legend. James Thor, a doctor who has worked with rodeo cowboys, has written that the men are often reluctant to accept any medical assistance and can be "unforthcoming on health issues" when asked, such as not disclosing previous injuries that may affect medical care or recommendations.[6] Thus, it is not unusual for a rodeo cowboy to be actively competing in spite of pain.

All of these factors combined—the unstable nature of the contestant life, the high risk of injury, and the heightened attention on the sport—contributed to the change in the demeanor of many rodeo cowboys starting as early as the 1960s, and certainly evident by the 1970s. The public image of the upstanding, respectable rodeo cowboy morphed into a tougher, harsher one; he was no longer a clear role model for young children, but rather someone who should be approached with caution, if at all. Retrospectively, we can see this reflected in movies that featured rodeo cowboy characters, including *The Misfits* (1961), *JW Coop* (1971), and *The Honkers* (1972). In these and other films, desperation and self-destructive behavior represented the mood of the rodeo circuit, and while that would not have represented the experience of all rodeo cowboys, it surely represented the experience of a portion of them.[7] The solution was clear to one letter-writer to the *Christian Ranchman*, who lamented, "The American people think of cowboys as ungodly. In fact, the young person who wishes to be a cowboy thinks he must become a sinner, spitting and chewing tobacco in order to be a true cowboy. Wouldn't it be wonderful if we could change this image so people could think of Jesus when they thought of the American cowboy?"[8]

There is some data, though not extensive, that helps us to understand this transition of both image and reality. Researchers studying personality traits and stress levels of professional rodeo cowboys determined that they have higher levels of stress than average Americans in relation to home, health, money, time, and interpersonal issues. The cowboys studied also tended to have more trouble than average with experiencing and expressing their own emotions.[9] It would not be surprising, then, that high levels of stress in combination with an inability to express it to others might lead rodeo cowboys to engage in risky stress-relieving behaviors. Supporting this, many of my interviewees who were involved with rodeo in the 1960s, '70s, and '80s anecdotally portrayed it as an environment of relative depravity. Pastor Tuck Whitaker, for example, referred to rodeo during that period as "a cesspool for drinking and drugs."[10] As a former contestant, Glenn Smith has written, "In the years I was competing, it was understood that if you didn't drink, cuss, chase women, and fight, you were not accepted. I figured this was still the attitude, in general; and in 1973, I was right."[11] The image of the hard-partying cowboy is also reinforced by the work of

Bob St. John, a journalist who chronicled rodeo in the early and mid-1970s. His accounts about various rodeo cowboys with whom he traveled reveal heavy drinking, drug use, fights, arrests, and casual sexual encounters. At great length, for example, he told the story of a bronc rider who drank all afternoon with other contestants by the motel pool, then tailgated with them again in the early evening, right up until the time they were all due in the arena for competition. The moderately successful ride was capped with more drinking. Another cowboy recounted to St. John a time when he drank so much on the way to the next rodeo that he decided he should take over the driving because, he reasoned, "It'll sober me up." Instead, he wound up in a high-speed chase with police that became an accident, and the injuries prevented him from competing for two months. Other cowboys St. John encountered during his research casually indicated that they took unprescribed pills for purposes including staying awake and masking pain, and more recent studies show this pattern has continued.[12] Doctor James Thor has observed, "Drugs that contestants are typically associated with are animal narcotics not intended for human beings. Riders use these narcotics to control pain and achieve a state of euphoria."[13]

It is difficult to know how much anecdotes like these do, or do not, represent more than the moments and individuals they describe. Little statistical or sociological data was collected in professional rodeo during those decades, so the collective culture cannot be described in absolute terms. However, the aggregate picture suggests that for a significant portion of rodeo cowboys of the 1960s through the '80s, debauchery ran amok behind the scenes. And certainly, some men veered in the opposite direction, as will be the case in any group. Tuck Whitaker recalls that the cowboys who preferred to live a cleaner lifestyle tended to gravitate toward one another, which he found helpful.[14] And in the midst of this rough environment, it was precisely these men—specifically, clean-living, Christian men of the rodeo—who decided to try to change things. In various places around the country, they looked around at their fellow competitors, brothers in their subculture, and they did not like what they saw. And they vowed to make a change.

Ministry at the Racetrack

"It all goes back to ol' Salty Roberts," Sam Ed Spence says.[15] On a dusty July afternoon, I meet Spence in his office at the Lone Star Racetrack in Grand Prairie, Texas. I am there to talk with him about the historic parallels and connections between rodeo church and racetrack ministry. We are on the "backside" of the track: the environment of the trainers, groomers, jockeys, and other people who work with the horses. It is not an area that is normally visited by members of the public. Spence has told me Salty's story once before, on the phone a few weeks prior. Now, he tells it to me again in person, perhaps to emphasize its importance to the history of cowboy Christianity. Mid-story, he chokes up with genuine emotion, as many cowboy preachers do when recounting instances of the power of God changing peoples' lives.

Horace W. "Salty" Roberts (b. 1931) had aspired to become a jockey from adolescence. He worked seasonally at tracks in Florida and New Jersey, sometimes as an exercise rider and other times as a parking attendant. But, similar to the kinds of troubles some rodeo cowboys faced, Salty had lost his family and his career goals as a result of alcoholism and drug use. Despondent, in 1969, he decided to commit suicide. Roberts was sitting in his apartment with a gun in his hand when he made a final plea to God. As Spence tells it, Roberts said, " 'Lord, if you're really real, help me!' " Spence's voice quiets as he recounts what happened next. "The Holy Spirit just came into that room, and filled him. And he laid that gun down, and went and resigned, and went back home to Florida." Not long afterwards God spoke to Roberts again, telling him to return to the racetrack. He protested: " 'That's where I got into all the trouble!' But God said, 'Now, I want you to go back and tell them what I did for you.' " Roberts was reluctant. Although his personal faith had been renewed, he was not a confident speaker. So he "pulled a Moses," as Spence says, and enlisted Baptist preacher Al Dawson to evangelize on the backside of the Gulfstream track, with Salty by his side acting as a social gatekeeper. Laughing at the thought of this, Spence says, "If you ever met Salty today, Salty would preach to that telephone post out there if God told him to! And I mean, *convert* it!" But at the time, Roberts felt he should be more of a facilitator than an evangelist.[16]

Their work began slowly. Both track officials and denominational officials were reluctant to do anything more than allow it, as no one was certain about what it was Roberts and Dawson were actually doing. One Baptist missions director, for example, called it "a most unusual chaplain ministry" but felt there was no need to interfere, since it was being done on a voluntary basis and thus cost no money.[17] Other administrators were more clearly hesitant about appearing to condone, or even support, institutions of gambling, and so they cautioned against creating any official relationship between Baptists and racetrack ministry. Even some trackers were suspicious: as chaplain Norman Evans recounted, when he showed up to the first day of work, the trackers thought he might be an undercover investigator of some kind, since they had never heard of a racetrack chaplain. Despite the hesitation of others, Dawson and Roberts persevered. Describing his work, Dawson simply said he would "walk the shedrows in the afternoon," inviting people to a weekly Bible study he conducted in the paint shop, and making a regular presence of himself. When the racing season ended a few months later, Salty Roberts returned to New Jersey, where, after some difficulty, he set up a ministry at the Atlantic City Racetrack. "Praise God!" Salty is recorded as saying. "We had claimed another track for Jesus." While this was, perhaps, an overdramatization of what he had actually accomplished, Roberts's confidence and fervor were both growing, and he had the momentum he needed to establish chaplaincies at other tracks. Two years later, an official body to support the ministry network was incorporated as the Race Track Chaplaincy of America (RTCA), a nonprofit organization. Although the majority of its founding board of directors was Baptist, the RTCA had no official denominational ties.[18]

From track to track there were variations in how much a chaplaincy was welcomed, and that continues to be the case today despite more widespread acceptance. In some places, for example, track managers were willing to pay a portion of a chaplain's salary and to designate a meeting space. Others provided neither, but permitted a minister to be present on the grounds; typically this meant the chaplaincy was an extra duty for a local pastor. Regardless of the circumstances, it seems that the day-to-day work of racetrack ministry has been relatively consistent since its beginnings. Track chaplains provide an additional form of support for those who work on the backside, primarily through informal religious counseling but also through formal worship services and sometimes via benevolence programs. In simple terms, its goal is "[t]o bring people to God and to bring God to the people."[19] It is further described by officials as a "ministry of presence," a common phrase among chaplains of all sorts.[20] In the racetrack context, this essentially means having a chaplain who walks the grounds, entering the different offices, barns, and buildings of the backside, always willing to stop and talk with anyone who works at the track. For those chaplains who are lucky enough to have a dedicated office space, they might also hold drop-in office hours. But whether the track chaplain provides religious counsel that is applicable to people of differing faiths, or limited to Christianity, may vary; those who work through the RTCA follow a mission statement that specifies their lens is Christian.

Sam Ed Spence has worked in racetrack chaplaincy since 1981, and he concurs that the job itself has not changed very much. He attributes that to its initial design. "I think Salty had a real leading of the Lord in the way he went about it. The way he set up his Tuesday night Bible studies, and had the chaplain just be available, not go around beating everybody over the head, not condemning in any way. Just be available and share the love of God." In addition to walking the barns, on race days Spence leads a devotional service in the jocks' room before racing begins, and he stops into the maintenance barn and prays with the start gate crew. This loose structure has never been "enough" for some religious people, who continued to criticize the racetrack ministry even once it was fully established. For example, in 1982 a letter of protest was sent to the RTCA from members of a church in California, listing biblical verses that supported their position against racetrack ministry. Among other things, they objected that the chaplaincy did not seek to "encourage people out of the race track and into some fundamental local church," and that it was a form of "cooperation with doctrinally opposed individuals."[21] Various RTCA chaplains responded in kind, using biblical verses to show they understood the Christian goal as evangelism to all, and that following in the footsteps of Jesus could not preclude ministry at a racetrack. Chaplain Norman Evans preferred to refocus the conversation on the writers, saying, "I sure hate to get into a proof-text debate with someone whose mind is already made up . . . . These deacons strained to get their Scripture texts to apply, but they sure didn't strain their mercy."[22] Mercy, forgiveness, and the embrace of all people were (and are) key to the racetrack chaplaincy approach.

Back in his office, Spence concurs that he still occasionally encounters similar judgmental attitudes, but it is far less often than in the past. He also acknowledges that there are always trackers who do not want to be involved with religion and generally avoid the chaplain, which is true with any type of corporate or industrial ministry. Nonetheless, the RTCA has remained a steady organization, developing a structure typical of other national nonprofits. It has a board of directors, regional circuits, and a small executive staff; it offers continuing education programs for chaplains and benevolence funds, as well as national networking opportunities. In some places, racetrack chaplains have financial support from a local church, and while the organization has strong ties with Baptists as well as Assembly of God churches, it remains nondenominational.

Perhaps most importantly, RTCA has periodically re-examined its mission and consciously assessed its own relevance. In Spence's estimation, the organization today is in better shape than it was in years past, with better order and "less strife"; this is particularly weighty considering that Spence served as its executive director for five years in the 1980s.

For two basic reasons, the RTCA is important for understanding developments in cowboy Christianity. First, there has been continual overlap in the personnel of these ministry cultures. Many of the men involved with starting racetrack ministries were also involved in starting rodeo ministries; and some men who began as racetrack chaplains or rodeo preachers later became cowboy church pastors. All three ministries operate within the same milieu, which in its most simple terms relates to people who work with horses, and therefore it is shortsighted to discuss any one of them as a completely isolated enterprise. And, second, because of its early beginnings, racetrack chaplaincy served as an important example of an unconventional ministry geared toward horse people. While the culture of trackers is distinct from the cowboy culture (in some places more strongly distinct than in others), there is crossover in the communities because of the centrality of working with horses; this crossover is both ideological and literal. There are also commonalities in lifestyle, most especially between jockeys and rodeo cowboys. For these reasons, ministry to both of these groups—trackers and cowboys—is rooted in similar principles.

Cowboys for Christ

Curled up on my sofa and staring at the television, I was getting to know Ted Pressley (1938–2011), the founder of the first rodeo-specific ministry, Cowboys for Christ (CFC). In addition to speaking with people who knew him personally, I was able to watch several hours' worth of video that Pressley filmed in the 1980s. The videos took some finagling to see, as the mysterious contraptions I was loaned turned out to be U-Matic tapes, a form of industrial video that had become outmoded long before someone filmed Pressley on it. Figuring out what the tapes were and how to get them converted took months, but it was worth the wait. The man before me on the television screen was lively, and passionate, and clearly a charming person. He made me laugh out loud, sometimes because of his asides and other times because of the unpredictable behavior of his horse. Most of the video is raw and unedited: it includes footage and interviews from a 1985 stock show, and there are close to forty spots filmed as potential public service announcements about Christianity. My favorite part turned out to be twenty-three minutes of continuous film in which Pressley attempts to nail down two short promotional ads for a Christian-focused western culture show he was putting together called *Country Roads.*[23]

The first spot was intended to woo potential advertisers. In it, Pressley assures his audience that he would "produce a show that will lift up Jesus and sell your products," implying it should be doubly enticing for business owners who were Christian. The second spot was a more general advertisement for the program, which Pressley described as a show filmed on location with cowboys, ranchers, and others working in the livestock industry. "If you've ever been down a country road," he said in several of the takes, "then you need to watch *Country Roads* with me, Ted Pressley." Pressley did not use a script or cue cards, perhaps because of his dyslexia. Thus, he spoke off the cuff, a tactic that at times seemed to frustrate the director as well as Pressley himself; in fact, they finally gave up on getting a decent single take of the second spot and hoped they could edit some bits together. In between takes, Pressley was self-critical, and the director offered advice about things such as how quickly or slowly to speak, and how to position his gaze at the end of the take. At one point, he advised Pressley not to mention Jesus, because that might deter the general public from watching the program.

Through it all, Pressley comes off as an affable man with a high level of energy; he seems to have been the kind of vehement but light-hearted cowboy preacher who makes researching the cowboy church fun. Sam Ed Spence, who worked with Pressley, struggled to describe him. "I never met anyone quite like him, I'm telling you! Ted just . . . he kinda *captured* me when I heard him preach." Both Spence and another early CFC member, Steve Womack, used the same phrase to describe Pressley: "a preaching machine." Similarly, his successor at the Cowboys for Christ organization, Dave Harvey, said, "Ted was a dynamic preacher! . . . He just didn't really feel called to pastor a church."[24] Instead, Pressley was instrumental in institutionalizing rodeo ministry, one of the building blocks in today's cowboy church movement. By the time he filmed the television spots at hand, he was a well-respected cowboy preacher, the founder of an international organization, and a man who traveled all over the world speaking about his Christian faith. He had come a long way from the first days of his rodeo ministry in 1970, which just happened to coincide with the first days of the racetrack ministry.

Ted Pressley had grown up on a farm and learned to rodeo from a young age. Prior to his conversion at age twenty-one, his time was mostly spent hell-raising and trouble-making. "I was rank," he said frankly in a 1999 interview, "and had been thrown out of most schools because the way I lived my life."[25] Pressley's career led him down many paths: he worked in ranch management; he ran hotels; and he trained horses for rodeo, racing, and show. But he said that for a long time, God kept telling him that he was meant to preach. He returned to school, earning a college degree and graduating from Southwestern Baptist Theological Seminary in Fort Worth. Through a friend he made in seminary, Pressley also came to embrace charismatic gifts of the Holy Spirit. In the late 1960s, Pressley became a settled pastor, working at churches in Texas and then Colorado, but he kept feeling a drive toward something different. "Bloom where you're planted," God continued to instruct him, and he finally realized what it meant. A single bloom can produce seeds that blow in all directions, creating more plants and blooms, and this was an analogy for a new kind of ministry. But where was Pressley planted? In his heart, he felt planted among horse people, and so he knew he was to be a "flower planted in the middle of the livestock industry—that's rodeo, ranching, cattle ranching, farming, horseshows, sheep farming . . . . And we began to bloom there."

He started as a single-man operation in 1970, in the exact same year that Salty Roberts and Al Dawson began to walk the shedrows at the racetrack, Bibles in hand. Pressley packed up his station wagon and traveled to rodeos and horse shows, sleeping in his car and washing up in gas station bathrooms. He would sneak into the shows to avoid paying, and then chew the ear of the announcer until someone agreed to give him a few minutes on the microphone, usually at the end of the program. "And I'd end up preaching," he said, implying he may have been overstaying his welcome. The very first time, in Colorado, people left in droves when he began speaking; he claimed that the arena was completely empty by the time he finished. He learned that tailoring his message made people more receptive, so he increasingly framed his biblical teachings with ranch and rodeo lingo and analogies. He recognized that many people have "awe" or "nostalgia" for the cowboy, and because he was a man who both dressed like a cowboy and truly understood that realm, western culture people seemed more likely to pause and listen to his message when he overtly drew on his background.

However, Pressley admitted that at first "it was tough." Religion and rodeo made awkward bedfellows, and he faced repeated rejection. "He never talked about it much," said Sam Ed Spence, "but just the comments that he made here or there, [indicated] he was not well received at the rodeos." Steve Womack, who began preaching at rodeos in 1975, concurred: in addition to general animosity toward their work was the fact that services were often so poorly attended. "If I got five people there, I felt like Billy Graham!" Womack recalled.[26] But Pressley described himself as being "like a Missouri mule," which meant he refused to quit. He was focused on bringing the gospel to people who, he believed, were unlikely to seek it on their own. He overlooked it when rodeoers called him "stupid, and crazy Ted," because he finally felt he was preaching in the way God intended. Early on, Pressley's successes were in preaching to the audiences at rodeos and similar events. It is not clear exactly when he began to make inroads with contestants and other workers, but it does seem to have happened within the first two or three years. By then, he was no longer begging for a few minutes on the sound system; he was running a worship service in tandem with the rodeo, which he eventually began referring to as "cowboy church." Whether or not Pressley was the first to try having a worship service at rodeos is unknown; however, he was certainly the first person who tried to institutionalize it as a regular part of rodeo. Always insistent that it was not to become a church or replace church, Pressley's rodeo ministry was simply an effort to bring a Christian message to people who he believed were not being exposed to it elsewhere.

By 1972, Pressley had incorporated his "interdenominational" nonprofit organization as "Cowboys for Christ," and he was enlisting others to help. As more people joined, he expanded the ministry, and CFC's four official areas of focus became rodeo, the cattle industry, the racehorse industry, and the show horse industry (the latter group called, simply, "horsemen"). All of these ministries were in place by 1975, the year Pressley began sending out the early versions of what eventually became the *Christian Ranchman* newspaper. In it he wrote about their evangelistic successes, and he listed types of support that would help, ranging from prayer to donations to more volunteers. The newsletters contained reports on rodeo services held in places like Texas, Nebraska, and Colorado; discussions of new ventures such as prison ministry in Louisiana, and racetrack ministry in New Mexico and Washington; announcements about upcoming events like a cowboy camp meeting or a radio interview with Pressley; and photographs from events at which CFC was represented.[27] In the late 1970s and early 1980s, by which time the *Christian Ranchman* was a monthly eight-page newspaper, the CFC listed more than twenty-five chapters all over the

West, and offered services to Christian cowboys including employment referral, teaching tapes, and Bible curricula.[28] Never letting up, Pressley's organization continued pursuing its goals in an effort to normalize the existence of small devotionals and even large worship services in the rodeo environment.

Fellowship of Christian Cowboys

Shortly on the heels of Cowboys for Christ, a second organization formed to support ministry to rodeo cowboys: the Fellowship of Christian Cowboys, a spinoff of the Fellowship of Christian Athletes (FCA). The FCA was founded in Oklahoma in 1954 as an organization geared toward nurturing Christianity among young male athletes in a wide variety of sports. Through school programs, conferences, summer programs, athletic camps, and other ventures, the FCA brought youth in contact with professional athletes and coaches, with the latter groups serving as Christian role models whose guidance might not be ignored as readily as that from parents and pastors. The FCA later expanded to include programs for adults as well as including female athletes.[29]

The Fellowship of Christian Cowboys (FCC) originally started as a chapter within the FCA. In 1974, rodeoers Mark Schricker and Wilbur Plaugher got the idea to launch a ministry for their fellow competitors. For some time, they were each "undercover Christians," as Schricker's wife Lynne characterized them; the two men casually shared their faith with others in the rodeo environment, trying to gauge what interest there was and to find like-minded people. It appears that they had not yet heard of Cowboys for Christ, because as Schricker later told a reporter for *Western Horseman*, when he thought about trying to organize, he "didn't have any idea where to start." Through suggestions from acquaintances, Schricker and Plaugher connected with a regional director for the FCA, who offered assistance. The men also wanted rodeo organizers on board in support of Christian fellowship, which they obtained by pointing out that it could help improve upon the hard-partying image of rodeo cowboys. After an initial meeting in Phoenix with a handful of interested people, in July 1974 the men launched an FCA Cowboy Chapter for the rodeo and held their first service at the Cheyenne Frontier Days. "We used the name Cowboy Chapter instead of Rodeo Chapter because we want[ed] all cowboys to feel free to join our group—students, stock show people, ranchers, contestants . . . all cowboys," Mark Schricker said.[30]

The FCA Cowboy Chapter's activities and goals were similar to those of Cowboys for Christ, in that they held cowboy church services at rodeos open to both contestants and the public, but they were not trying to replace or compete with institutional churches. They hoped people would become involved with a local church after being inspired by their experiences at the rodeo. As the Cowboy Chapter grew, it added components such as rodeo Bible camps for youth, and local competitions at which someone would share the gospel. According to Schricker's widow, the FCC eventually became so large that it no longer made sense for it to be a part of another organization. Furthermore, aspects of the FCA structure, particularly its geographic divisions, did not work as well for rodeo because many of its constituents were constantly traveling. As a result, the FCC separated and became an independent group in 1991.[31]

It appears that Fellowship of Christian Cowboys and Cowboys for Christ mostly worked harmoniously rather than competitively, despite their identical purposes. Sometimes the two groups even worked cooperatively at a single event: for instance, at the 1976 PRCA rodeo in Burwell, Nebraska, a Sunday worship service was conducted by the FCC at which the primary speaker was supplied by CFC. Ted Pressley explained in a 1999 interview that he was never disturbed by other rodeo and livestock ministries coming onto the scene. "God's got many other men," he said. "If these men are preaching Jesus Christ, why should I worry?" And, he added, there was far more ministerial work than a single organization could handle. On the other hand, Pressley was clearly proud that, in his opinion, he had made the inroads for the others, repeatedly mentioning to the interviewer that he had been "the first preacher ever" at a long list of well-known rodeos and stock shows.[32] As with other ministries in the cowboy Christian milieu, even in the organizations' formative years some men were involved with both CFC and the FCC as preachers, planners, officers, or other kinds of volunteers, and that fact further blurs the historical lines of influence and development.

Methodists in Colorado Springs

It is possible that Ted Pressley and/or Mark Schricker picked up the name "cowboy church" from elsewhere, building on a basic idea to create a much larger entity. A strong possibility is that they each heard the name in Colorado Springs, as both men lived in that area at the time they founded their organizations. From 1968–1984, the First United Methodist

Church of Colorado Springs sponsored what it called "Cowboy Church" for three months every summer, which a brochure advertised as "the most unusual worship service in the West." The "informal" early morning worship service was held at a drive-in theater, with preaching taking place at the concession stand. Based on handouts from various years, it appears the cowboy church services were fairly straightforward and followed a format that included prayers, a sermon, a short scripture lesson, and live religious music in western style. Preaching and other duties rotated, so the services were not always run by the same people. Men and women on horseback directed traffic as well as riding from car to car collecting the offering. Although the church was formally organized by the United Methodists, it was billed as "interdenominational," and records show that speaking guests indeed came from a variety of denominations.[33]

According to church documents, in its first year, 1967, the venture was called Drive-In Church, and it had low attendance. After they whimsically added ushers on horseback for a service in August, the numbers increased. That success prompted organizers to rename the services Cowboy Church for the following season, keeping the riders and adding western style music. In an undated newspaper article, an associate pastor described cowboy church as appealing to many different kinds of people: "to some of our tourists as a novelty; to some of our members who are not physically able to sit in the sanctuary; to young parents with babies that are too young to stay in the nursery and to others who just enjoy the unconventional setting of worship out-of-doors under the western sky." Notably, the services were not geared to a population that was, or even wanted to be, immersed in western culture. In other words, this cowboy church was not for cowboys. Early polls taken showed that many of the attendees did not normally attend church, but went to cowboy church because they appreciated the unusual worship style being offered. Therefore, while the Colorado Springs cowboy church may have only a slight genealogical connection to cowboy churches of today via Pressley and Schricker, its deeper similarity is church leaders' willingness to be innovative in order reach people who would not otherwise seek out a church. Attendance at the Colorado Springs cowboy church dropped from several hundred per week in the 1970s to only about sixty people in 1984, and so the annual cowboy church folded at the end of that season.[34] Since that original foray, Methodists have not become involved in the cowboy church movement, which is relatively surprising given their roots in the camp meeting tradition. But it was not long after their Colorado summertime church ended that a new type of cowboy church opened in Texas, this one a nondenominational fellowship under the leadership of Jeff Copenhaver.

Sundays at Billy Bob's

It was the first week of June, 2014, and after nearly a five-hour drive it was a tremendous disappointment to knock on the cabin door of Jeff and Sherry Copenhaver and have no one answer. No one was home. When I called his cell phone, it went right to voicemail. Fearing that Copenhaver had forgotten our appointment, I brushed some leaves from a chair on the side porch and sat down, dejected. I didn't know what to do. The surroundings, at least, were peaceful: tall, aromatic pine trees, a dry Texas heat, and the distant sound of traffic that a city person like myself finds comforting. I waited.

Copenhaver, who maintains a public ministry and busy travel schedule, arrived about a half hour later, full of excitement and exuberance. He took me across the road to an unusually beautiful cowboy church built of giant timbers brought from Washington state. We sat and talked all afternoon, his wife Sherry joining us for part of the time. In anticipation of my visit, Copenhaver had pulled together articles, brochures, flyers, photographs, and other personal memorabilia from his earliest days of cowboy church, which he had thrown haphazardly into a giant plastic bin. Struggling from the weight, he dragged the bin into the sanctuary and proceeded with a kind of show-and-tell. Story after story tumbled out of him in a random order, each sparked by something he pulled from the pile. Sherry, mindful of the time, tried to keep him focused, but his passion for the subject could not be easily contained. What was particularly refreshing about Jeff was his ability to navigate from serious to lighthearted and back again, and his willingness to laugh at himself. Months earlier another cowboy pastor had described Copenhaver as "the first happy Christian" he'd ever met, and that turned out to be an apt description.[35]

Copenhaver grew up in Idaho and, like his bronc-riding father, built a career in professional rodeo.[36] His most prestigious rodeo win came in 1975, when he earned the PRCA World Champion title in calf roping. He describes himself in those days as having "a cowboy mentality. I'm not saying that's good, bad, or ugly; I'm just saying I thought like a rodeo cowboy." He was familiar with the Baptist faith, having attended church as a child, but semijokingly referred to his younger self as a "heathen." Copenhaver rededicated himself to Christianity in 1978, and within a short time, evangelism became central to all that he did. He gradually stopped competing because after conversion, "my heart wasn't in it at all." With Sherry, he spent time traveling, studying the Bible, and teaching rodeo skills in the United States and Canada. Most importantly, Copenhaver became involved with ministry to other rodeo cowboys. He and Sherry found that by being open about their faith, people came to them as they traveled the rodeo circuit. "We were in the ministry full time and didn't know it . . . . People would be coming to our camper, and we'd be discipling people without putting a tag on it. Just loving people and sharing the Lord with them." Copenhaver also got involved with some of the formal organizations working the circuit, eventually serving as the president of the Cowboy Chapter of the FCA for two years. In December 1985, Copenhaver had the privilege of attending the National Finals Rodeo in his role as chapter president, and he was scheduled to preach in the arena on Sunday morning. As it happens, 1985 was the first year that the NFR was held in Las Vegas, an important geographic change that led to higher prize money for competitors and greater exposure for rodeo overall.

Among Copenhaver's acquaintances in Las Vegas was Benny Binion, a man described by one biographer as "a barbaric outlaw of terrifying means," and by another as "one of the most feared and successful racketeers of his day."[37] Since 1951, the Binion family had owned the Horseshoe Club in downtown Las Vegas, though by 1985 the casino's heyday was behind it as "the strip" increasingly pulled gamblers to a different part of town. Binion, originally a Texan, also owned a ranch in Montana, and it was through common interests in rodeo and horses that the Copenhaver family had come to know Binion many years earlier. Jeff's sister, artist Deborah Copenhaver-Fellows, had been commissioned to sculpt several pieces for Binion, and during the NFR weekend she invited Jeff to join her on a visit to his estate.[38] This trip to the elderly gangster's home led to a series of encounters that, ironically, launched a new incarnation of cowboy church.

Copenhaver's face lights up at the memory. "I didn't know Benny, really. But we go out in this limo, which is the only way you get to see Benny," he explained. "Well, obviously, you get permission, but then you gotta get in one of his limos. You go out, through their guard gates, and the dogs and everything. And we get there, well, Benny's in this bathrobe!" Jeff laughs, commenting that it unfolded like a clichéd movie scene. Binion signaled for his people to leave the room, then sat down at his desk in his robe and slippers with Jeff across from him. Jeff recalls that God directed him to thank Binion for several things, including his role in helping the NFR to move to Las Vegas. Knowing Jeff, I also assume he took the opportunity to evangelize in whatever way he could; this likely would have fallen on receptive ears, considering that just months earlier Binion believed he had encountered Jesus during a medical emergency.[39] After their talk, Binion arranged for Jeff to ride back into town with visitors Billy Bob Barnett and Tex Whitson, both of Fort Worth.

Barnett was the owner of Billy Bob's bar, a famous honky-tonk that opened in the Stockyards section of Fort Worth in 1981. His massive country-western themed nightclub had approximately one hundred thousand square feet of space that included dance floors, bars, gaming areas, private party rooms, a gift shop, and an arena featuring weekly bull riding. Some sources imply that Binion was an investor; Whitson, who formerly worked in the music industry and later worked for Binion, was at that time the manager of Billy Bob's. In the car heading back into Las Vegas, Jeff mentioned that he was interested in finding a place in the Stockyards area to hold Christian youth meetings. He also invited the men to his arena service early the next morning. To his surprise, Whitson showed up at the service, although it appeared he had been partying for most of the night and "you could tell he'd probably slept about fourteen minutes!" Afterwards, Whitson said that Jeff should come see him at the bar to talk. Back in Fort Worth a week later, Whitson proposed that Copenhaver hold church services in the arena at Billy Bob's during the rodeo weekends in January and February 1986. Jeff must have paused before answering, because then Whitson said, "You *do* want to start a church, don't you?" Jeff surprised himself by answering in the affirmative.

And so it was that a few weeks later Jeff Copenhaver had pulled together several Christian friends from the rodeo to help him convene what he called Cowboy Church.[40] Approximately 350 people, mostly visitors in town for the rodeo, attended church in Billy Bob's Bull Arena on the morning of January 26, 1986. On the bill as speakers alongside Copenhaver were professional rodeoers Bobby DelVecchio and Paul Luchsinger, and Luchsinger's then-wife, Susie McEntire, provided music. Copenhaver recalled that there was a lot of "hooptola" and publicity, including a local television station that sent a crew to the service. The following week, speaking and musical guests shifted; attendance was about the same. Chairs were set up right in the arena dirt for service, and when it was over, they quickly transformed the space back to a working arena. The attire was come-as-you-are, and the services offered what they called "a 'no bull' gospel," in that the goal was to be as straightforward as possible about faith and the Bible. Copenhaver kept the services going even after the rodeo crowds left town in February, though in our interview he was unable to pinpoint the moment when he fully committed to making it a regular thing, paradoxically saying that it "instantly evolved." Posters plastered all over the Stockyards advertised that everyone was welcome for "Sunday's [sic] at Billy Bob's." Cowboy Church averaged about a hundred people in Sunday morning services with a core group of approximately thirty; by the following year, attendance had doubled. They added a second service on Sunday evenings and a third on Wednesdays, a schedule that Copenhaver found taxing, especially because his home was nearly an hour away.

It was not long before Cowboy Church grew to include various activities and ministries. They started outreach to the poor involving donated goods, and they started a "riding ministry," in which riders on horseback carried flags to advertise the church at parades and other events. Next door to Billy Bob's was the Cowtown Coliseum, where the church held a number of events like rodeo schools and competitions that generated publicity and interest. "One of our events was called the bull slinging," Jeff remembers. "It was a match bull riding, with the bull riders giving their testimony with a cordless mic right after they got off of their bull . . . . It was awesome. The audience loved it." The church also added what was called "Eagles Training," a program of intensive study for those who wanted to become better Christians in their daily lives. Because Sunday mornings typically had about twenty-five children in attendance, they added a children's church called the Buckaroo Club. Sherry Copenhaver recalled, "The back of the bar was very grungy and dingy and dark, and we would have the children's church in the back part of the bar in the green room, which was where all the stars would come when they'd perform at Billy Bob's . . . . It was out of our comfort zone. We didn't know any better at that time, either, because we weren't really churched . . . . I just took 'em, and we'd learn about Jesus in the back room!" By the following year, the uniqueness of Copenhaver's church was creating such a buzz that it was profiled in the front section of the *New York Times*, where it was described as "a blend of rodeo ambiance and evangelical Christianity."[41]

Copenhaver fondly says that Cowboy Church in the Stockyards was never predictable, and anything could happen in a service. "It was not tame. It was not religiously orchestrated," he remembers. Early on, the church was sometimes called nondenominational and other times interdenominational; the key for Copenhaver was that he did not want to be limited. He felt strongly that Cowboy Church, not only at Billy Bob's but also in the present day, could and should transcend denominational barriers. Rather than trying to model the church on, or against, a denomination he was familiar with, he describes their approach as "we just began to *do* out of who we *were*." He and other members took what they knew from rodeo and applied it to their faith: make a plan, get a coach, work as hard as you can in practice, and always strive for excellence. Like almost all cowboy preachers I have met, Copenhaver resists accolades for having started something significant; instead, he attributes the idea and its fruition to God. Secondarily, he gives credit to people who provided personal guidance, such as Sam Ed Spence of the RTCA and Chuck DeHaan of Cowboys for Christ, both of whom were on the first board of directors when Cowboy Church incorporated in 1986, and whose influence further demonstrates the kind of cross-pollination that took place among the early horse-related ministries.

In fact, Copenhaver insists he never thought cowboy church was particularly new. "It's not like we invented anything original," he demurs, and refers to Eccles. 1:9.[42] What he felt was truly different was the passion for outreach ministry that enveloped the church. "We had the mentality of, we want to *go after* God. We want to see what he has for us." Everyone at Billy Bob's was so excited about their faith that they were eager to share it, and they even had a group called Western World Ministries visit to provide training in street witnessing. In our interview, Sherry Copenhaver concurred that the exuberance of the church was distinctive. She recalled that when they were new Christians in the late 1970s, she and Jeff were naïve in their faith. "What did *I* know about God?" she asked rhetorically. "I'd never had a relationship or been acquainted to Him, introduced to Him, anything. So when you all of a sudden have this experience, it's like, what do you do with yourself?" The excitement of it propelled the Copenhavers forward and gave them a hunger for religious knowledge. Though they were just a few steps ahead of many church members on their religious path, they tried to be the best leaders they could in the new-convert environment. Their situation was, perhaps, less unusual than the Copenhavers realized, as many newly-formed religious groups experience something similar in their earliest years. As sociologist of new religious movements (NRMs) Eileen Barker has written, "Converts . . . tend to exhibit far more enthusiasm (even fanaticism) and commitment than those who have been brought up in their faith," and the impact of this reality is exponentially greater when the majority of the organization is comprised of new converts.[43] Considering the Stockyards Cowboy Church as a type of NRM helps contextualize its rapid growth as well as its premature end. Sociologists have found that intensive excitement about newfound faith is not usually sustained indefinitely; overall commitment levels in religion typically change over time, and this is not a commentary on the value of the religion, the strength of the leadership, or the belief of the members themselves, but rather a basic fact of social development.

When I asked Copenhaver to discuss some of the early pitfalls, he laughed: the first thing that came to his mind was when he realized that the bulk of his Sunday night service crowd was made up of single people who were looking for a date more than they were looking for Jesus. But more broadly, he said he could have used better skills with organization, delegation, and team leadership, all of which he acquired through trial and error as the years passed. He also implied that the distance from his home to the church made things difficult. When Billy Bob's closed down for a period starting in 1988, Cowboy Church moved to the nearby Fort Worth auction barn. Copenhaver described that building as quite old and rough: "It wasn't very civilized. The restrooms looked like . . . ugh!" "Not good," Sherry added. After another year, the church moved to the Stockyards Hotel, and then in 1990 it permanently relocated to Granbury, where the Copenhavers lived. Although a few members made the trek out to attend the Granbury church, now called New Frontier, most dispersed in different directions: a few went on to begin their own types of ministry, but Copenhaver surmised that others probably stopped going to church altogether. In time, the traveling ministry became Jeff and Sherry's primary focus. New Frontier church still offers Bible study on weeknights and gets rented out for weddings, but it is no longer the home of a regular congregation.

Despite its demise, the work in Fort Worth inspired other people to start ventures that were also called cowboy churches. Copenhaver's recollection is that the earliest spinoff occurred in Canada after a visit to Fort Worth by his friend Phil Doan, a former rodeoer. Doan returned home and started a church in Calgary at the Ranchman's Bar, a space very similar to Billy Bob's.[44] That also led to another cowboy church after a visit to Calgary by Joanne Cash Yates, the sister of Johnny Cash, and her husband Harry. They launched a cowboy church in the lounge of the Nashville Holiday Inn in 1990 that is still going strong today, with live radio broadcasts and an emphasis on music.[45] In a written piece about his memories of Cowboy Church, Copenhaver states that sometimes "people came to one of our services and went to their hometowns and started a cowboy church in a bar, an auction barn, hotel, feed store, barns, or any other number of creative places to have church." In fact, he said that he was not always aware of these other cowboy churches, sometimes hearing about them only much later. When I inquired whether people sought advice or guidance from him, Copenhaver said no, but felt that was not surprising. "That's kind-of the western mentality, you know?" he said, meaning that cowboys pride themselves on independence and self-sufficiency. In other words, if they visited his church once, many would have felt secure in returning home and starting their own version of it. Cowboy Church at Billy Bob's therefore seems to have served more as an inspiration for people than as a specific model, a fact that could explain the diversity among styles and approaches of cowboy churches that began in the 1980s and '90s.

Cowboy Churches of the 1990s

A variety of cowboy churches came into being in the 1990s, particularly in Texas and Oklahoma. There is no clear benefit to enumerating every cowboy church start, particularly because having been among the earliest does not necessarily convey anything significant about originality, authenticity, or influence. However, a passing look at a few of the early churches demonstrates the diversity in what occurred. What we find is that in the 1990s there was little coherence among cowboy churches, primarily because each one started independently even when founders were aware of other examples. Some of these churches grew into their identities over time and now, in hindsight, are better equipped to articulate who they are as institutions and what they seek to do. For others, the identity has changed in a significant way.

The Cowboy Church of Henrietta, Texas is perhaps best known for being the creator and owner of the iconic image that has come to represent not only cowboy churches but cowboy Christianity more broadly: a cowboy kneeling at the cross with bowed head, his horse by his side. The original version is a larger-than-life sculpture positioned on a hill above Highway 287, just a stone's throw from the single-story church building. The sculpture's cross is built of "bridge timber" set in rock, while the horse and cowboy are two-dimensional pieces cut from steel. Randy Wood designed the image using his father as the model for the cowboy, and the second model was a horse named Miss Kitty who belonged to church member Donna Gee. Lights illuminate the piece so that it can be seen from a distance at night. The sculpture dates to 1997–1998, and the church subsequently registered its ownership rights simply to prevent someone else from staking claim to the image; they make it known that the image can be used freely by others, and they like to see it proliferate.[46]

The Henrietta church is an early pioneer of the cowboy church realm and one of the oldest continuous bodies. It grew out of the collective efforts of people who were, in 1992, attending a cowboy church that met twice a month in Iowa Park, Texas. It was Donna Gee who first suggested that someone should start one in Henrietta, which was more centrally located for many people traveling long distances to the Iowa Park arena.[47] Beginning in March 1993, a group of about thirty people met every other week in Henrietta, fellowshipping in an unheated sale barn or outside under the trees, depending on the weather. Though they started with several men rotating the speaking duties, former rodeoer Larry Miller eventually became the sole pastor due to attrition. As part of making it official, Miller was ordained by Jeff Copenhaver in January of 1995. This continued the lineage among cowboy ministries, since Copenhaver himself had been ordained by racetrack chaplain Sam Ed Spence in 1982, and Spence had been licensed for ministry by Cowboys for Christ.[48] Miller insisted that he was never a gifted speaker, and in our time together he repeatedly joked that he has never understood why people would want to hear him preach "unless they want see how bad I can mess up!"

Regardless of Miller's estimation of his own abilities, the small and relatively steady group of worshippers muddled along, celebrating baptisms, creating youth programming, and increasing the frequency of services. In their fourth year, they were organized enough to incorporate and buy an acre of land; their first building was a forty-by-forty-foot barn-like structure completed in 1998. Miller disagreed with some of the church elders about the initial building: he insisted it be kept small, consistent with the size of the congregation. But Miller underestimated what would happen with better facilities. He shakes his head at his own folly, saying, "The first building, in a year's time, it was standing room only. And so we added on . . . . And the next year, *both* of them were full, so we added a third one. And then *it* filled up, and we added on a fourth." These additions are evident when one visits the church in Henrietta: the somewhat awkward, oblong layout of the main sanctuary makes sense only once this architectural history is revealed. Finding a place to sit where one can see all the focal points—the band, the pastor, and the announcement screen—is quite difficult. But people there do not seem to mind, and in fact the unusual seating configuration allows many people to see each other during the service, giving it a comfortably casual feeling. Both before and after the service, members wander around to meet and greet each other; in my visit there I found it to be a particularly hospitable church where people treated the stranger in their midst quite well.

Over the years the church in Henrietta has been invited by other denominations to join their ranks, but Miller prefers that it stays nondenominational. "If you ask me," he admits, "I'm a Bapti-costal." That is to say, he is aware that he draws on both Baptist and Pentecostal traditions, but he also finds strong reasons to not affiliate with either one. The church membership has always been varied in terms of people coming in with different sorts of Christian backgrounds. Perhaps for that reason, Miller says, "I don't get into denomination bashing. None of 'ems perfect, and all of 'em have some good golly people in 'em." After more than two decades in existence, Miller notes that one of his greatest challenges is that the Henrietta cowboy church has become "established." "We are comfortable in what we're doing," he says, and while there may be some peace in that, there is also a danger. In a subsequent conversation, Miller added that "it's hard to get Christians today fired up, to take a stand against things in the world." Instead of changing the world, they allow the world to change them, which he implies can quickly lead to compromises in the faith. He sees that as an ongoing challenge in his ministry as well as something that should be a widespread concern for all Christians.[49] Whereas the first church in the Stockyards seemed to run its developmental course rather quickly, what Miller describes suggests his church is following a more common path of social development. Essentially, he speaks to the fact that social differences between his church members and the wider society have softened, which is a normative part of religious institutionalization. Additionally, the first generation of members has aged, and it has been supplemented with succeeding generations of members who may encounter the faith differently.[50] Sociologically speaking, the very traits that concern Miller about his church are also indicative that it has achieved a certain level of stability that may sustain it for the long term.

A different path for a cowboy church is demonstrated by Shepherd's Valley, a bustling church that today offers two Sunday morning services and a variety of specific ministries for different ages and interest groups.[51] The church is a fine-tuned operation with more than a dozen people on staff. Various workers wear headsets on Sunday mornings to facilitate instant communication, and they refer to their facilities as a "campus."

Though the main section of the sanctuary has arena dirt underneath the chairs, every week the dirt is carefully raked, and mats are rolled out to create tidy aisles for people to walk on. The pastor, Russ Weaver, is the cohost of a cable television program called *Cowboy Church* that began in 2007, so the presence of video is quite normal at Shepherd's Valley; in fact, services begin when the lights dim and all attention is focused on a glitzy video montage of church event advertising.[52]

Weaver's journey to this level of ministry was a long one that he pursued since his youth. Through an appointment with the Assemblies of God "Home Missions" division he worked in rodeo ministry in the 1980s, and later he was involved with racetrack chaplaincy. However, Weaver found himself frustrated with the limits on his ability to build Christian disciples in those temporary environments. For example, although some rodeo attendees were deeply touched by his church services, even experiencing salvation, without a permanent church home they often lost touch with their initial commitment. Weaver remembers his exasperation: "The next year we'd come back to the same rodeo and the same people would come back and say, well, we don't have a church like *this*." He admired what Jeff Copenhaver had done in Fort Worth, and he was also familiar with the cowboy church in Calgary. Weaver prayed for guidance because he felt strongly that he was supposed to start a cowboy church of his own.

Serendipitously, in 1997 Weaver was contacted by some friends from a Baptist organization. They had purchased an arena in Benbrook, Texas and thought it might be a good place for a cowboy church. Because of the denominational difference, Weaver arranged to rent the space and hold his services there, but the church was not an instant success. For its first three years, it had fits and starts, growing in membership and then dropping back several times. Similar to the experience of Larry Miller in Henrietta, it was only once they bought a piece of property and had a better meeting space that the church experienced swift growth. By 2002, they averaged five hundred people per week at their new facility in Egan, Texas, and today the church is even larger. Shepherd's Valley is particularly unique among cowboy churches because it is part of a charismatic denomination. Weaver says that he neither hides nor advertises the fact that the church is part of the Assemblies of God, but aspects of the service like anointing with oil for healing very quickly reveal that identity to visitors, or at least signal to them that it may be different from other cowboy churches, which rarely include charismatic aspects. As part of building and sustaining his particular cowboy community over the years, Weaver deliberately cultivated a sermon style that evokes serenity and comfort. His hope is that the western culture people he is trying to reach will feel like he is personally visiting with each one of them when he speaks. As he told interviewer Jake McAdams, "When I set the atmosphere right, they don't mind me addressing things in their life" that are difficult, personal, or challenging. He also came to see that his church needs to be active in the local community, offering events and programs that appeal to people who are not necessarily church members. Weaver is no longer surprised by the growth rate of cowboy churches but admits that the movement has certainly become bigger than he ever imagined. His future plans assume continued growth both within his own church and among new church plants that he hopes to be involved with.

Pastor Paul Lutz sums up the present-day cowboy church situation by advising me, "You're not going to find any two of these churches the same."[53] Former rancher Lutz and his wife, Donna, had originally heard of cowboy church in Texas, and after completing seminary in 1999, Lutz accepted an offer to use an arena for services in southwest Oklahoma. "When we first came here, traditional southern Oklahoma thought it [cowboy church] was almost blasphemy," Donna said. Local reception was chilly, and the congregation was slow to grow. For Lutz, calling it "cowboy church" was a symbol of antitraditionalism; as he explained, he could just as well have put up a sign reading "This is not a church," because that would have forthrightly articulated his concept. What was important for him was breaking away from the "paradigms and traditions" found in static denominational practices in order to simply focus on the story of Christ and its meaning for humans. In time, his cowboy church split; the pastor's discussion of the reasons was circumspect. Lutz and a portion of his congregation moved into a brand-new barn structure that offered a more comfortable environment, including heat and air conditioning. Another portion remained behind in the more rustic arena. By 2012, when I visited each of these churches, the distance between them felt vast. Lutz is an educated and serious man, and his approach to sermonizing reflects that. His fellowship has a relatively mainstream feel to it, from the arrangement of the music to the atmosphere of the building; my field notes include words like "shiny," "clean," "arranged," and "churchy." His rejection of hollow tradition became clear on an intellectual level when having a deeper discussion with him, but it is unlikely that that would be evident to the average person walking through the door for the first time. In contrast, the original cowboy church that remains in the arena feels quite spontaneous, and rather unlike any mainstream Protestant church. Contemporary pop music played on the loudspeakers prior to the service; the pastor's sermon was peopled with extras and involved elaborate props; and my field notes contain words like "vehement," "energetic," "dynamic," and "loud." Lutz's earlier point about cowboy churches being so different from each other has truth to it, as these two bodies prove; that fact is one of the things that complicates any answer to the question, "What *is* cowboy church?" As Lutz said to me, if he were starting all over again, he would not call it a cowboy church, because he feels that in the ensuing years that name has begun to carry its own baggage and cultural expectations. Perhaps that is because at the same time that Lutz was starting his first cowboy church, another man decided not only to start cowboy churches but also to organize and unify them. In short, that man determined to define cowboy church once and for all.

The Architect of the Twenty-First-Century Cowboy Church

I took it as a high compliment when cowboy pastor Ron Nolen called me "persistent" and "a woman who just won't take 'no' for an answer." Nolen himself, the White Whale of the cowboy church researcher's world, had previously been described to me by others as "passive-aggressive," "hard to get along with," "a strong personality," "an unusual personality," "manipu-lative," and "demanding."[54] After more than a year of trying to get an inter-view with him, I felt great joy the day I finally tracked him down—not that he was lost. He was simply minding his own business, pastoring a lively little church in Waxahachie, Texas, and utterly disinterested in having his voice become part of the historical record. Nearly every conversation with a cowboy church pastor sooner or later comes around to the subject of Ron Nolen, whether or not he is identified by name. The modern day cowboy church movement cannot be discussed without referring to him unless one is making a deliberate attempt to obliterate his role in it; some people would like to do exactly that.

In the 1990s, Nolen was "a suit and tie" man, working as a church planter for the Baptist General Convention of Texas (BGCT, also referred to as the Convention).[55] The main focus of his job entailed starting new churches and serving as the initial minister. Once the congregation was solidly established and a permanent pastor could be found, Nolen moved along and "planted" elsewhere. In October of 1999, Nolen stopped in to the cowboy church in Henrietta and visited Larry Miller. He found Miller's church intriguing, and the two men talked and prayed about whether Nolen might start a similar venture under the Baptist aegis. Nolen returned for a second visit with his wife, Jane, after which they began to seriously consider whether a cowboy church might succeed in Waxahachie. As pastor Gary Morgan explained it, Nolen "believed that he could put together a church that would appeal to the team ropers, and would appeal to cowboy people. He also saw an opportunity to do church a little bit differently than Baptists had done the church before. It was an opportunity to start with something that was really new and a different kind of approach."[56] Exactly what caused Nolen to launch fully into organizing remains unclear, because the story gets framed in several different ways by different interviewees.[57] Encouragement from his rodeo contestant son seems to have been one factor; the sponsorship of a local Baptist church also seems to have been relevant; and there is also talk of a moment when Nolen was sitting in the stands in Glen Rose, watching team roping, when he began to wonder if he could offer the ropers a kind of church they would actually want to attend. He told his superiors at the BGCT that he wanted to start a cowboy church, and they asked, "What is that?" "I don't know," he said, "but we'll figure it out."

By December of 1999, the Nolens were in serious church-plant mode, holding "core group" meetings in their home for all interested parties. In the first meeting, they thought about their mission and target audience and possible locations, they brainstormed ways to insure the services would have a low-key atmosphere, and they looked at photographs Nolen had taken in Henrietta. By their second meeting, they were engaged in discussion of budgeting, small group ministries, and branding. The group continued to meet weekly and hammer out specifics as they geared up for their first planned cowboy church service, to be held in the Ellis County Expo Center on the morning of February 27, 2000. It was a soft-launch "preview" service that was not advertised, but even with just friends attending, sixty-four people were there. After a few minor adjustments, one week later they held their first publicly advertised cowboy church service. Nolen's sermon was entitled "The Cowboy's Secret to a Great Life," and in addition he brought in professional team roper Kory Koontz as a guest speaker, and a full country and western style band provided music. Three hundred and eleven people were counted in attendance that morning.[58] In all, their work was an extremely organized venture that stands quite apart from the more spontaneous beginnings of churches like those in the Stockyards or Henrietta. Though no one knew it yet, the road to an entire movement of cowboy churches was being paved.

Growth at their church, named the Cowboy Church of Ellis County, was explosive. Nolen continued building the internal structure, experimenting with things like the number of elders and different methods for reaching and keeping new members. In May, he proposed that they purchase 8.8 acres on which they could build; by November they had broken ground.[59] By the following year, the church had more than five hundred members, and a permanent pastor had been found: Gary Morgan, a seminary-trained Baptist who grew up on a ranch in rural Texas. The wheels were turning in Nolen's mind, and he was beginning to see that there was great potential for more cowboy-style churches. He was eager to get to it, so once Morgan was up and running, Nolen moved on to start cowboy churches in other Texas towns. "Ron was the engine and the driver of this thing, without any shadow of a doubt," Morgan says.[60] Already, other people were starting to take notice and launch their own cowboy churches, just as some had done after visiting Jeff Copenhaver's church in Fort Worth. Ellis County became a kind of mother church: a role model for everyone else, many of whom called upon Morgan and Nolen for advice. The two men had trouble keeping up with the demands for their expertise, and they began regularly holding "Ranchhouse School," an educational seminar to support cowboy church pastors and other leaders.

Meanwhile, Nolen appealed to the BGCT for increasing amounts of support. He recalls it being a mixed experience. On the one hand, he compliments the Baptists for "their willingness to think outside the box" and for the significant amount of money they put into church starts and educational resources. But on the other hand, he calls it "narrow-mindedness" that the BGCT slowed the funding after a couple of years rather than continuing to expand it. He attributes some of the problem to aspects of cowboy church that went against standard Baptist practice, such as the emphasis on team leadership and the aversion to having deacons. "To go against what your own constituency . . . there was a lot of anger, or behind-the-scenes criticism over what was being done," he admits. Others, such as Morgan, indicate that a large part of it had to do with Nolen's approach, in which he hotly demanded resources from the BGCT. Morgan put it this way: "You know, quantum theory says if you walk into a wall long enough, enough trillions of times, eventually you might get to that lucky place where all the atoms align and you just can walk right through it. If anybody ever walks through the wall, it'll be Ron Nolen. He is *that* focused."[61] But in this case, the atoms did not align, and his persistence at the Convention created hostility and resistance. Among the ranks of Baptist leadership there was increasing ill will toward cowboy churches. Nolen seemed to be the source of everything that was right and wrong with the cowboy church, or at least, his visibility made him an easy person to blame. As Nolen himself put it, there were people at the Convention who "didn't appreciate Ron Nolen at that time."[62]

What happened next appeared, at first, to alleviate the tension. In 2004, Nolen enlisted a number of cowboy pastors and collectively started a new organization separate from the BGCT: the Texas Fellowship of Cowboy Churches (TFCC).[63] The TFCC became a network, allowing pastors to share educational resources, create an atmosphere of mentorship, and have stronger lines of communication. According to an internal document about its history, "The BGCT gave its blessing to this organization and directly funded it for the first few years of its existence"; likewise, Nolen insisted that TFCC member churches donate money to the BGCT every year. According to Gary Morgan, "the intent was for the TFCC to be the cowboy church arm of the BGCT."[64] Though they hoped this would better define boundaries and generally create a more harmonious relationship between the cowboy churches and the Convention, ultimately it seemed to change nothing. Instead of vilifying Nolen, some people at the Convention began to vilify the entire TFCC. In 2006 Nolen resigned as a church planter in order to work full time as director of the TFCC, and the Convention hired Charles Higgs to fill the newly created position of cowboy church liaison. Movement historians write, "While Higgs and Nolen tried to work together to promote unity between the organizations, the relationship was cool at best . . . . Cooperation at the grassroots level was low and the relationship continued to deteriorate."[65] With things going relatively well on his end, the following year Nolen formed a suborganization within the TFCC to support cowboy church plants outside of Texas, called the American Fellowship of Cowboy Churches (AFCC).

Ron Nolen's management style, it seems, continued to be perceived as forceful and abrasive, and everyone's tolerance of him expired in 2010. Amid much controversy and many bad feelings, the board of the TFCC/AFCC voted to fire him from his own organization, though technically Nolen had already resigned, one day prior to the vote.[66] Seizing what appeared to be an opportunity of chaos and transition, the BGCT tried to persuade the TFCC to dissolve and have all the churches come under the formal wing of the Baptists. The TFCC member churches saw the benefit of accepting this offer and thereby separating themselves from any notoriety associated with Nolen, but their firm distrust of denominational hierarchy won out. They decided to collectively regroup under the AFCC banner and hire a new executive director, allowing the TFCC name and structure to fizzle out.[67] As the AFCC, the group was now stronger than before, because it unified the Texas churches with what had become a national network of cowboy churches.

As the AFCC's independence grew, the Convention continued to pursue its own program of support for cowboy churches through an entity named Western Heritage Ministries, directed by Higgs. However, it appeared to some that the BGCT was actually trying to compete with and marginalize the AFCC, possibly even trying to render it unnecessary by replicating its services. For example, whereas previously the BGCT had recommended that pastors attend educational seminars taught by the AFCC, now the Convention created its own educational program for those interested in cowboy ministry. There was also a perception that the BGCT was planting new cowboy churches but cutting the AFCC completely out of the process, as though it did not exist.[68] Tension was building, even if only on an institutional level. Cowboy church leaders with whom I spoke had a wide variety of opinions on this somewhat awkward situation: some saw no problem with having two cowboy church networks and were actively involved with both, whereas others thought a clearer separation would be better for everyone. One cowboy church pastor I met said he was unwilling to join the AFCC as long as it had Baptist ties, which for him included faith statements in the by-laws that implicitly suggested Baptist identity.[69] Others were more overtly angry, such as the pastor who said, "The guy in the Baptist building has continued to try to usurp, pretty much, what we [the AFCC] have spent a lot of time building up, and take ownership of it. It's not setting well."[70] And yet others seemed relatively unconcerned, in some cases because they did not feel these conflicts affected their daily life, and in other cases because they were mostly unaware of the politics. In 2014, the AFCC board voted to formally sever all ties with the BGCT, though its bylaws continued to include statements that most would consider Baptist in nature.[71] In the short term, there may be little observable impact of the latter decree. The AFCC did not make a big public announcement about the change, and it did not require individual member churches to separate themselves from the Baptists if they already had a relationship. In the long run, the change should help to clarify the independence of the cowboy church movement from Baptist identity and control, even though many of its churches do remain squarely in the Baptist tradition. Pastor Mike Morrow said that although his church is technically interdenominational, the Baptist influence cannot and should not be denied. "People need to know your DNA: they need to know who you are, when you peel back all the layers of how you do church, who you are here. We want them to know that we're a cowboy church and that we have Baptist in our DNA."[72] For some, that Baptist DNA is exactly what makes them want to keep their distance from the AFCC. Nonetheless, the organization started by Ron Nolen is clearly the largest entity linking cowboy churches and providing them with stability, and that is unlikely to change in the near future regardless of how many internal feuds and scandals bubble up.

The Prophecy

Today, some cowboy Christian leaders refer to a prophecy that anticipated their ministry. This prophecy, allegedly delivered by the internationally renowned charismatic preacher Smith Wigglesworth in the 1930s, provides them with a heightened sense of significance about the work, and assuages them in times of great difficulty. As Ted Pressley explained it in a 1999 interview, Wigglesworth "prophesied that the last and great revival would be ushered in by the American cowboy. I just feel so blessed and honored that God would allow me to be a part of that group of His chosen."[73] Though numerous pastors have mentioned the prophecy to me, few have ever articulated anything more specific about its content. In most cases, it seemed they had learned about the prophecy via word of mouth. The most detailed explanation was provided by Jeff Copenhaver, who explained not only his knowledge of the prophecy itself but also where he heard it, which was important to his belief in its veracity. As Copenhaver said,

> A lot of people wonder how this is documented; well, I can tell them. It comes from Smith Wigglesworth, prophesied to David du Plessis . . . . Du Plessis prophesied to Murray McLeish, who was a pastor in Eugene, Oregon. In 1978 Murray McLeish came to the Cheyenne rodeo and told us that prophetic word. Wigglesworth, du Plessis, and McLeish. And here's what he said: he said in the very end times, he named three groups but obviously the one we're excited about was—he said one of the three groups that God's going to use in a mighty way is going to be cowboys. God's going to use cowboys in a mighty way.

The other two groups included in the prophecy were "blacks and youth," according to Copenhaver. The essence of the prophecy, as Copenhaver explained it, was that a future religious revival would sweep the earth and it would begin among these unexpected audiences.[74] From discussion, it was clear to me that Copenhaver is the kind of man who wants to be certain about his sources. Prior to telling me the prophecy, he was careful to explain why anyone should believe a man such as Wigglesworth. Essentially, it was "documented" that Wigglesworth had raised twenty-six people from the dead during his lifetime, in addition to a few additional failed attempts.[75] For Copenhaver, the repeated miracle coupled with Wigglesworth's own admission of failures rendered his power more believable, so a prophecy uttered from the lips of such a man should also not be taken lightly.

Another cowboy pastor who referred specifically to Wigglesworth was Ron Nolen. He recalled having read the prophecy in a small paperback book years earlier. When I asked what it was about Wigglesworth that made his prophecy so important, Nolen dispelled the notion that the importance was related to the person who uttered it. Rather, it was the complete randomness of such a prophecy in combination with the fact that it had occurred many decades before anyone was even thinking about a cowboy church. It was incredulous that a British man delivering a prophecy in 1936 would anticipate a religious revival that would begin among cowboys, of all things. That kind of insight, Nolen explained, could only be inspired by God.[76]

One other noteworthy reference to Wigglesworth is found in the autobiography of Glenn Smith, a book spoken highly of by many cowboy pastors. Smith, a former rodeoer who converted to Christianity in 1972, had a vision that God wanted him to save rodeo cowboys from hell. Smith closed his business, started a ministry, and he and his wife traveled the circuit in a camper, making progress in the rodeo environment only little by little. Over the next two decades he persevered in creating a presence with his organization, Rodeo Cowboy Ministries, which later became Western World Outreach Center. Like Copenhaver, Smith was also present in Cheyenne in 1978, which may be where he heard about the prophecy. However, Smith's rendering of the content is significantly different. He writes, "It is interesting to note the Rev. Smith Wigglesworth is reported to have prophesied that when the Lord begins to move mightily in Australia, look out! The second return of Jesus is just around the corner."[77] Thus, as Smith remembered it when writing in the early 1990s, the prophecy contained no reference to American cowboys.

Copenhaver, Nolen, and other cowboy pastors I have met sincerely believe in the significance of a revival beginning among cowboys, though they do not all place equal emphasis on the prophecy. Despite their trust, it has a dubious provenance. As Wigglesworth biographer Desmond Cartwright has written, "Some of the stories about Smith Wigglesworth are, in my opinion, exaggerated, and a small number strain credulity beyond legitimate limits."[78] Cartwright would count "the prophecy" among them. Pentecostal evangelist David du Plessis was the only witness to Wigglesworth's prophetic word, and although he both wrote and spoke about it many times in the ensuing decades, the first time du Plessis made any public mention of said prophecy was in 1948, more than a year after the evangelist's death. Over time, du Plessis made subtle and significant changes to the prophecy's content, as can be seen in variations published in the 1950s, '60s, and '70s. Most scholars who have carefully evaluated it imply that du Plessis singlehandedly invented the "prophecy" in 1948, attributing it to Wigglesworth because it imbued the message with greater status, and embellishing it with more details over time. And yet, perhaps in deference to his legacy as a religious leader, those same scholars politely excuse du Plessis for what appears to be an elaborate and long-running fabrication.[79]

For cowboy Christians, even more important than the question of transmission from Wigglesworth to du Plessis is the total absence of cowboys from the message. Among the many published variations of the prophecy, some by du Plessis and others by those who heard him speak about it, there is never any mention of three groups being singled out to jumpstart the revival, and in turn, no mention of cowboys. In addition to reading many variations of the prophecy, I consulted several scholars who are well versed in the work of du Plessis. None were familiar with anything du Plessis had said that might relate to cowboys, and they all confirmed that he was prone to exaggeration and "storytelling," as one put it. If du Plessis was guilty of lying about hearing Wigglesworth utter the prophecy, and also guilty of altering the message to suit different circumstances, it is conceivable that he could have added a new detail about cowboys when speaking in a particular context.[80] However, the cowboy detail is not included in his 1977 autobiography, which came out only a year before Murray McLeish spoke about the prophecy at the Cheyenne rodeo. So while it is possible that du Plessis added cowboys to the prophecy, an equally likely scenario is that McLeish added the detail about cowboys himself, either deliberately or as the innocent result of miscommunication.[81] What we can be certain of is that the prediction of a religious revival among cowboys does not date to the 1930s, and it did not come from the mouth of Smith Wigglesworth.

Thus, when large numbers of cowboy culture people began stepping into churches in the year 2000 and beyond, it was not the fulfillment of a prophecy. It was nonetheless the spark of a subcultural movement within American evangelicalism that is succeeding in bringing new people into the fold of conservative Christianity. With most of its experimental church starts behind it, the cowboy church movement in the twenty-first century has begun to both grow and develop its own institutional norms. As I have learned through my visits to churches and my participation in cowboy church leadership seminars, stable ideological concepts underlie the cowboy church approach, even as tangible implementation of those concepts can vary greatly. What the cowboy church looks like today, what it understands itself to be, and how it is perpetuating a singular identity are the subjects of the next chapter.

4

The 21st-Century Cowboy
Church Movement

"THEY DO THINGS a bit *different* over there," said the woman who told me about a cowboy church in Joshua, Texas. "I'm sure you'll have an . . . interesting experience." Her "Midwestern nice" way of describing it came through loud and clear, such that I knew she held the church in low regard. That made me want to go there even more.

Since its website was defunct and its phone just rang and rang, that was all the information I had before arriving one morning in April 2013. An elderly man in overalls at the door told me that pre-service Bible study groups met in two rooms. "Just pick a room. Doesn't matter which," he said. Though I entered with some trepidation, I ultimately felt perfectly comfortable as a visitor to the Bible study, neither excluded from the conversation nor pressured to speak. I was dressed differently from the other women; in jeans, a t-shirt, and my "church shoes"—a pair of rugged men's shoes suitable for walking in arenas or mud—I stood out from the ladies in their dresses and hose. But in the Bible study and later at worship, no one even glanced at my attire, appearing to greet me the same way they did everyone else.

On my way into the worship service, I spoke with a man who had been attending for several years after moving to Texas from Oregon. He had gone to many different churches in his life, he said, and most of them were "cold." This one, though, was defined by its warmth, friendliness, and openness to all kinds of people. "That's what makes it cowboy church," he said, expressing a new twist on what "cowboy" might mean.

This same idea was reiterated when I spoke with the pastor's wife, Bunny Reid. She explained that their church philosophy is "like that of the cowboys. We accept anyone who comes through the door." Elaborating that the heart of the idea is "love and acceptance," she said that their church considers sanctification gradual and therefore does not turn anyone away "just because they're divorced, or they wear jeans, or they smoke, or for any reason."[1]

Reid encouraged me to meet other members during fellowship lunch, where I found more people eager to give their spin on the essence of cowboy church. "Cowboys were once the future of America," an elderly man explained to me, and likewise he believes their church is the future of what religion will be. Said another, "It's a place where everyone is welcome." Another suggested, "People will give you a helping hand if you need something, just as cowboys would." And no fewer than three people said this exact same thing to me, indicating it must be a kind of catchphrase in their church: "I'm no more a cowboy than I am a rocket scientist, but that's not what cowboy church is about."

I had to agree with the woman who advised me this cowboy church was different; indeed, it was unlike any other I ever went to, with a peculiar mix of formality and informality. Its distinction was partly caused by its lack of affiliation with other cowboy churches, and partly due to it being a Seventh-day Adventist church, which is unusual in the cowboy church milieu. And yet, even in its total independence from other cowboy churches, this congregation's ideological essence is aligned with those in the large networks. Its differences are not a bad thing; it is just proof that in a world of cowboy churches that are striving to become increasingly consistent and streamlined, some strong and persistent contours remain.

Teaching People How to "Do" Cowboy Church

From random church starts in the 1990s to the deliberate structure codified by the Texas Fellowship of Cowboy Churches (TFCC), cowboy churches in the twenty-first century have begun to align around certain core principles and approaches. Because cowboy churches exist across denominational lines and usually outside of seminary preparation, a key method of perpetuating core ideas is through grassroots education. This takes the form of pastors educating pastors, as well as educating anyone who serves in a lay leadership capacity or aspires to do so. By 2004, the TFCC began holding what it called Ranchhouse School, a one-day seminar on all things cowboy church, meant to support those in leadership. Similarly, several years later, the Nazarene Church began to sponsor Cowboy Church University (CCU), a weekend seminar for anyone interested in starting or developing a cowboy church. These programs are held in all kinds of places—a large Ranchhouse School I attended, for example, was conducted at a multi-building church complex in Tyler, Texas, and a small CCU was held in a barn with a sawdust floor in rural Colorado, with a port-a-potty and a bottle of hand sanitizer out back. Other more formal educational programs have been developed through Dallas Baptist University and Truett Seminary at Baylor University to support interested cowboy pastors. All of these have contributed to the relatively quick development of a model for cowboy churches that provides a surprising degree of uniformity in approach.

Ranchhouse School was named for one of its early venues: the Ranchhouse Cowboy Church of Maypearl, Texas. As Ron Nolen explained it, the school was desperately needed to support the many new pastors—easily several dozen of them—who had jumped into cowboy church ministry based on a strong religious feeling but without much serious preparation. Like what had occurred with Jeff Copenhaver's church in Fort Worth, people learned of the church in Ellis County and decided to start one of their own. Some of their churches grew very quickly, and the newly minted pastors were ill-prepared for the kinds of challenges that came with that. "These guys would get a church and it grows to over two hundred in one year," Nolen says. "Most pastors live and die and never pastor a church running more than two hundred. Well, they're in a church that's up here exploding . . . and everything in [members' lives] is brought with 'em . . . . They lack[ed] a frame of reference to work with as a pastor." The messy result was a situation with "inexperienced pastors [and] a deluge of hurting people."[2] Jon Coe, a pastor who worked with Nolen on some of his early cowboy church starts, gave an example of the challenge: in a traditional mainstream church, parishioners may call the pastor and complain about the appropriateness of the shirt he wore last Sunday, or gripe that the piano has been moved from one side of the room to the other. In cowboy church, no one cares about that sort of thing, but you will regularly get phone calls in the middle of the night because a member has been kicked out of the house by his wife or has landed in jail on an intoxicated driving charge. "Your parishioners in a traditional church woulda never called you, 'cause they wouldn't want you to know about it!" Coe says. "So, we don't have *church* problems," but cowboy pastors nonetheless have a long list of serious issues they need to learn how to handle.[3] Especially in the early days of the movement, many cowboy pastors worked regular full-time jobs in addition to serving their church, and this contributed to the challenge of ministering to a congregation. For several years, Nolen felt inundated with the crisis-management needs of pastors. His goal was to "try to help the pastor survive his own mistakes" and become an effective leader without turning into a "potentate."[4]

The Ranchhouse schools were a way that the more experienced men tried to help the situation. Drawing on their knowledge from both Baptist church plants and cowboy churches, Nolen and his wife put together a workbook that outlined ten topics of instruction and discussion, combining theory, ideology, method, and practical matters. An outline is really all the workbooks contained; attendees were supposed to take their own notes and fill the blanks with relevant information.[5] The first two schools were held in the Nolens' barn in Maypearl, and the next were held at the new Ranchhouse Cowboy Church, with the goal of having them there quarterly. However, they soon realized that it would be more helpful to people if the school could travel around to different regions. Funding for some of the schools, as well as production of the workbook, was provided by the BGCT.[6] The interest in cowboy church was exploding, but only a small number of people were able to teach what it was all about. Gary Morgan recalls that "by 2004 or '05 our model that we were putting out was pretty firmed up, and things began to get pretty clear-cut so far as how we taught people, what we taught. The schools began to get massively big. We would have five to seven hundred people at some of these schools, from all over the United States, that would come to these clinics to learn how to do cowboy church."[7] Little by little, cowboy churches were founded in states all across the country that had communities of horse people, combining what had been learned in the schools with characteristics appropriate for the local culture.

The popularity of the schools was sustained even during the years of organizational flux among the TFCC, AFCC, and BGCT. In 2015, the AFCC changed the name of Ranchhouse School to Cowboy Church Clinic, reflecting a desire to make the event feel more accessible. "Ranchhouse School" was not a descriptive name, and the AFCC leadership felt that the inclusion of the word "school" might scare some people away from attending.[8] In contrast, a "clinic" in the western heritage context is a kind of instructional and coaching affair that focuses on a narrow equine topic, and it is an event that horse people would be comfortable attending. The change of name was not mirrored with any content changes, though by 2015 the program had certainly expanded from its original 2004 format.

It remains a single-day, free event, and preregistration is recommended but not required. Attendees include men and women who come from all levels of experience with cowboy church, and they may arrive late or leave early as they wish, which contributes to the informal atmosphere. Many people attend clinics year after year, which is made easier by the fact that they are offered about every six weeks. The idea is that attending the clinic multiple times allows a person to learn about different aspects of cowboy church as needed rather than trying to take it all in at once. The AFCC leaders who attend offer themselves as coaches in the cowboy church experience, insisting that they do not and cannot have all of the answers all of the time.

I attended AFCC clinics three times from 2013–2015, twice in Texas and once in Oklahoma. Consistently, each clinic started with at least an hour of worship, and each topical session began and ended with a prayer in which God's guidance was sought for the discussion. Every session included multiple reminders to keep things "Christ centered." Thus, the clinic is framed as an inherently religious event, not merely an educational one, which is a notable approach. Perhaps related to this, it always struck me that few people arrived prepared for seminar-style learning; they did not bring notebooks, for instance, and they frequently commented on my copious note taking on my laptop as being unusual. Mostly, people just sat and listened. Leaders of some workshops passed out fill-in-the-blank sheets that carefully mimicked the lesson to follow, and some attendees did engage in filling them out once they were able to locate a pen. These sheets bore some relationship to the original Ranchhouse School workbook but tended to be far more simplistic in content, even as the individual lessons had become more extensive.[9] For example, headings in the original workbook included things like "Elder Role" and "Staff Issues," with blanks left for note taking on specifics. In newer versions, the handouts were more like busy work, where people were asked to fill in the obvious rather than filling in ideas that might be more complex to remember. Examples from newer handouts include sentences such as: "Existing church culture is not reaching the _____ heritage culture" (western), and "Conflict resolution needs to be _____ based" (biblically).

The largest clinic I went to had close to one thousand people attending. The day's program was divided into six thematic sections—Cowboy Church 101, Church Development, Ministry to Children and Youth, Leadership Development, Arena Outreach, and Administration—and within those there were shorter topical units. In the Arena theme, for example, there were forty-minute sessions on arena devotions, ranch rodeos, rough stock, bookkeeping and legal requirements, and liabilities. People were encouraged to select one theme and stick with it all day, but many of us ignored the instruction and attempted to bounce from session to session based on our personal interests. In contrast, the smallest clinic I attended in Lenapah, Oklahoma, had about one hundred attendees including the program facilitators. The entire group stayed together for most of the day in the session called Cowboy Church 101, and we only moved into breakout sessions for the very last hour. At the end of a typical clinic, the average person has received about four hours of instruction, some of which may have been workshop-style conversation about particular problems that can arise in cowboy church.

The AFCC events are somewhat impersonal, mostly because of the size, though leaders I knew were very welcoming to me just as they probably were with other familiar faces. The clinics fail to take opportunities to foster connections among people from different churches, regions, and interest groups, which would require some restructuring of the basic program. The event does not facilitate mingling, and all but the most gregarious people tend to stay with their friends. Leaders, rather than spreading themselves throughout the crowd, congregate among themselves. At every clinic I attended, I honed in on other lone individuals like myself, who were diligently attending sessions but rarely seemed to speak to anyone. During breaks, we would wind up lingering in the same places—places that allowed us to stand around alone without looking lonely. As a woman attending without a husband or church group, there was an added layer of difficulty for me in trying to speak with male attendees, particularly those who were alone and within my age bracket; they usually skirted away if I approached.[10] When I attended sessions that were meant for men such as "advanced training for lay pastors" or "cowboy preaching," it was clear that my presence caused some people discomfort. In two such sessions, a speaker censored his language because "there's a lady present," though in the second case I went ahead and called out the censored word for him. I did not fit the mold of the average clinic attendee, and that sometimes made things awkward for everyone. Though my experience of the clinics was obviously not the usual one, it seemed clear that the structure would be most beneficial for team building of groups that attend from a single church.

The parallel program run by the Church of the Nazarene is called Cowboy Church University (CCU). The content of this intensive weekend-long program is quite similar to that found at the AFCC clinics; however, the event has a distinctly different feel to it. One difference is that CCU has more diversity, because attendees come from a wider variety of horse-oriented subcultures and thus bring more perspectives to the table. For instance, when I attended CCU in Colorado in 2012, people had come from places including Arkansas, Missouri, and New Mexico; when I attended in Texas in 2014, the group included a man from Virginia. Attending CCU requires a high level of commitment because it is held only once or twice a year; most people will need to travel and find accommodations in addition to paying a registration fee.[11] The CCU program begins Friday afternoon and goes into the evening, lasts for about twelve hours on Saturday, and may include additional workshops on Sunday morning. No sessions run concurrently; therefore each attendee is able to learn about every topic on the agenda. It is a serious event, and the small group of participants—fifteen to twenty people—tends to be quite invested in everything that is offered, including opportunities for individual mentorship. During breaks and over meals, there was rarely any light banter; people networked and discussed church questions, and even when standing around the arena in the evening, conversations tended toward the practical. At the conclusion of a CCU weekend, attendees were likely to feel confidently equipped with the knowledge needed to both launch and develop a cowboy church, and they were sent home with a notebook dense with information in addition to whatever notes they had taken.

Perhaps because of the small size of the Nazarene training sessions, I felt more like a full participant. CCU leaders appeared to have been informed about who I was and why I was there, and most of them made a point to approach me and offer input as well as giving kind words of support. "We're really glad you're here," they told me, repeatedly. I doubt that was entirely true; nonetheless, I appreciated that they chose to be consistently helpful and positive. At CCU they sat with me at meals, they introduced me to people, they made suggestions about my project, and they invited me to visit their churches. During arena activities one pastor even helped me ride a horse for the very first time, which was surely my most vulnerable moment in the entire course of research. This more personal experience at CCU did not seem to be mine alone; it was clear that leaders made efforts to connect individually with every attendee. Something that Nazarene pastor Jon Coe said about attracting new members to his own church may be apt here: he believes the first, most important thing is to welcome people into the community and make them feel like they belong to it; all the rest, belief and behavior, can come later. Likewise, CCU itself models the very atmosphere they are teaching people to create.

These two training grounds for people interested in cowboy church leadership should not necessarily be measured against each other, as I have implicitly done here. In many ways, the different styles of education are catering to two different approaches extant in the cowboy church. The AFCC continues to play catch-up, trying to unify a vast number of independent people and groups. Because many churches existed on their own before affiliating with the AFCC, they may come in with unique approaches or ideas about what cowboy church is that run counter to the standards the AFCC wants to promulgate. Additionally, some churches have a denominational affiliation that creates another layer of structure, while others are totally independent. The AFCC is trying to assist all of these kinds of churches yet also maintain a set of methodological standards. The frequency of AFCC clinics means that people can constantly be brought into the cowboy church leadership fold, which keeps momentum going; the consequence is that sometimes those churches crash and burn due to inexperienced leadership. For Nazarenes, cowboy church planting is a more deliberate endeavor that is denominationally supported; therefore, all new churches are founded within certain established boundaries. The intensive weekend training of CCU reflects and underscores the seriousness with which any church plant is made. Although in the past some independent cowboy churches did come under the Nazarene wing, it would be unusual for that to happen again because now such starts are managed within the denomination from the outset.

The Low Barrier Method

As Jeff Bishop semijokingly said in an AFCC clinic, it takes tons of work to make cowboy church seem chaotic and unstructured. Despite how it may appear, the majority of the churches follow a careful model. At its core is the "low barrier method," a term that was used by Ron Nolen to explain his new approach to church, and which became a buzzword among leaders.[12] The low barrier method has been explained to me by countless pastors and again at CCU and AFCC clinics. As Mike Meeks boiled it down, "[It] simply means denominations create their own barriers, their own sets of rules. Cowboy church: no barriers. Just come as you are. Dress how you are. Be who you are."[13] The perception is that mainstream Christian churches have, over time, erected virtual barriers to people of the cowboy culture; although these are primarily psychological barriers, the consequence is that they prevent people from attending because they feel unwelcome. This pattern of ostracization from churches is not unique to cowboys: it can be observed among a variety of minority groups that could be delineated by race, socioeconomics, cultural identity, or other factors. In fact, though not precisely parallel, it is akin to what occurred among African Americans who were part of the Great Migration in the early part of the twentieth century; many found that cultural differences prevented them from being accepted in northern mainline black churches, and so there was a burst of new storefront churches in which alternative modes of worship and participation were validated.[14] In this particular case, the minority group is a cultural one: the cowboy, and by extension, others who work in ranching, farming, racing, rodeo, and related industries.

Nolen says he first read about the low barrier idea in a newsletter from a church in Kentucky in the 1980s, and that he was further influenced by the book *Church for the Unchurched* by George Hunter III (1996).[15] Hunter's book is actually just one in a long line of texts dealing with concepts of modernizing the traditional church to make it appeal to younger generations, some of which date back as far as the 1950s. Influential thinkers on this subject have included Robert Schuller, Lyle Schaller, Elmer Towns, Bill Hybels, Leith Anderson, and various professors affiliated with Fuller Theological Seminary in California, where new strategies for church growth were being taught as early as the 1970s. The ideas that came from these myriad men built upon each other. In the books they authored, we can see both prototypes for and alignment with aspects of today's cowboy church method and overall ethos, albeit without any specific use of the term "low barrier method."[16] By the mid-1990s when Hunter wrote about the low barrier method, he was really pulling together ideas that were by then tried and true. In one example of an earlier version, the book *Inside the Mind of Unchurched Harry & Mary* (1993) is a popular text mixed with memoir, meant to help Christians evangelize nonreligious people. Author Lee Strobel discusses focusing on a target audience and strategizing to make every aspect of church appeal to that group. He writes, "It should drive what kind of building is rented or constructed, what sort of music is used, what kind of drama or multi-media are employed, the titles and illustrations in messages, the design and contents of the bulletin, the manner in which ushers greet visitors, the way the parking lot is handled, the way the grounds are kept, the times of the services, the way participants are dressed, and on and on."[17] Many of the same ideas were elaborated on in Rick Warren's *The Purpose Driven Church*, where one does find specific language about "eliminating barriers," and even more so by Hunter, who devotes nearly an entire chapter to the concept of "culture barriers." The work of Hunter and related thinkers does not seem to be on the radar of cowboy church leadership; in conversation with me, only three pastors ever referred to any of these authors, and in two cases the references were garbled. Like the Smith Wigglesworth prophecy, this is another instance in which there is murkiness within cowboy church circles about the foundations of particular ideas, and nearly a complete disconnect from the originating sources.

Regardless of whether cowboy church leaders read or understand primary sources on the low barrier ideology, they are articulate about what it means and how to implement it. It should be seen as a strategy of eliminating things about church that make western heritage culture people uncomfortable, as well as adding or highlighting things that will increase the comfort level for them, and it applies to attire, physical space, music, sermons and biblical discussion, general terminology, leadership, treatment of people, church activities, and other aspects of worship. Ultimately, the goal is to bring people into, or back into, the fold of Christianity by eliminating the barriers that appear to keep them away from it. As Nolen put it, "The body of Christ is an organism, not just an organization. Don't keep throwing every barrier you can at it and think it won't be affected . . . . Figure out what the barriers are to its growth and health, and remove them. Leaders in the cowboy church, I hope, view that their role is to help lower barriers, and empower others to do what it is they've been created and called to do. That gets exciting if they're practicing that."[18] Thus, ideally, in cowboy church, attire is of no concern. The physical space is devoid of typical church ornamentation like stained glass windows, chandeliers, and carpeting. The music is up-to-date. The sermons, biblical discussions, and general terminology incorporate familiar western language. The leadership structure has parallels with ranch and rodeo examples. People are welcomed to participate regardless of their sins. Church activities and other aspects of worship are similarly made culturally relevant and comfortable for the target group of people. Barriers are lowered, and so people come in the doors, and these material changes are the primary means that cowboy churches use to distinguish themselves from mainstream evangelical Protestant congregations.

According to many leaders—regardless of whether they are associated with Baptists, Nazarenes, or another Christian path—sticking closely to the model is absolutely key to success. Leaders warn that churches that have deviated significantly have gone astray; whether that is actually true is a different question, and perhaps also a subjective one, because "astray" does not necessarily mean "defunct." Additionally, the specific points that today define cowboy church did not all emerge at once; many aspects developed through trial and error, and because it is still a young movement, additional changes to the model should be expected. For instance, the TFCC added points of "functional church structure" to the model based on experience gained by pastors in the earliest years of cowboy church. This term is taken from Christian Schwarz, who argues that structures of leadership and organization in a church must be based on what actually works for sustaining an engaged membership, rather than based on familiar traditions or patterns.[19] Churches on today's AFCC model de-emphasize hierarchy so that as many people as possible can take active roles in church functioning via teams and consensus decision-making, but responsibilities are clearly designated for those who are elders, lay pastors, and team leaders.[20] The Nazarenes have a similar structure, in their case making use of a western idiom and calling certain leadership positions Segundos and Point Riders. They have also developed step-by-step instructions for long-range planning, they strategize about different types of cowboy church plants, and they offer very specific financial guidance. Ultimately, though the model is the goal, it cannot be achieved instantaneously. In the several years it may take a cowboy church to get from its start to ideal functioning, it will go through all kinds of makeshift formats and stages.

While the package may look different, in its core beliefs the cowboy church is not significantly different from mainstream evangelical Christianity.[21] Some cowboy pastors are forthright about that. As one said, "I don't think we're any different, really. When they invited me to come out here and start preaching, I said, 'Naw, that cowboy church deal's kinda hoaky.' . . . I just believe that church is church. The message is no different."[22] As another said, "People ask me what cowboy church is and I tell 'em, it's just church."[23] One other made the point more directly: "The cowboy *believes* himself to be unique . . . . They have this concept that they're somewhat *different* from other people groups, particularly when it comes to organized religion or Christianity or what they identify as church . . . . I've been starting churches for a long time, and the truth is, every group thinks that they're unique, but they're not."[24] However, in order to reach those people, he explained, you have to act as though your church is different and is "unique" in the same way the people imagine themselves to be. In contrast, other cowboy pastors—and based on my interviews, a smaller group—appear to believe that their churches are both different from and inherently better than mainstream churches. In some cases, this relates to the Wigglesworth prophecy: they believe they are part of a great and final revival that begins with the cowboy. In others, they express that cowboy churches are one of the few places where core "American" values are being upheld, and therefore they are building a kind of remnant community that may serve to save American society from an impending cultural downfall. One pastor even explained that the value of cowboy churches is that they deal with real heartaches and real trauma, as opposed to "daycare" churches where no one is ever challenged to grow spiritually. And yet other pastors simply take pride in their ability to bring Christianity to the western culture community via a different approach to doing church, while traditional congregations appear to idly ignore attrition. But even among those who feel their organizations are an improvement on church, this still relates primarily to matters of structure and approach. Theologically, nothing truly separates the cowboy church from the vast majority of evangelicals; rather, the strategies for lowering barriers for western heritage people are what sets it apart.

The Physical Space

Low barriers find their first expression in the physical space of cowboy church, where the guiding idea is that everything should be functional and not fussy. This begins outside the building, where there needs to be enough room to accommodate a lot full of pickup trucks.[25] Inside, the space should be completely comfortable for people who may be grubby from work, rather than causing them any self-consciousness. Randy Reasoner epitomized the attitude of most pastors I met when he reminisced about an important moment in his first cowboy church: "One service, we're done, and we're walking out, and I look back in the back row and there's great big chunks of red mud all over the concrete in front of these two or three chairs. And I saw that, and I got excited! Whoever this was felt comfortable enough to come in here muddy and dirty from whatever they were doing that morning to come and worship the Lord. We set up an atmosphere to make that possible."[26] Sometimes that atmosphere is natural, but other times it is created rather studiously. I was reminded of Reasoner's story about a year later when, sitting in a Texas church after the service ended, I happened to overhear the pastor say to a broom-carrying member, "Don't sweep up! I don't want it too clean around here."

Cowboy churches that build from the ground up typically use a modern barn design, which is a rectangular wood-frame structure with metal siding. The interior of the worship space will have a high ceiling, and the walls may be finished in corrugated metal or particle board. The floors are polished concrete, though in some places they have stayed with a dirt/sawdust floor; the latter are also spaces without HVAC or plumbing in the building. The decor of cowboy churches is as spartan as possible, almost intentionally looking as though no thought has been given to the issue, though I rarely find that to be the case. One may see a few props hung on walls or piled near the main door, especially things that are evocative of cowboy identity or farm culture, like horse shoes, old milk pails, cattle skulls, lariats, well-worn boots, antique hand tools, bales of hay, piles of logs, and cowboy-themed art. Western nostalgia is typically the rule with decor, though quite often a church will be nearly devoid of all of these things because careful attention has been paid to minimizing accoutrements.

The ethos of not focusing on creature comfort is commonly reflected in the seating. Rather than a set of pews, cowboy churches have folding chairs, benches, and other sorts of mismatched seating that can be moved around, thereby maximizing the potential usage of the space; a clear exception is any church being held in an arena or sale barn where the facility's built-in seats are used. In one creatively arranged church in Texas, the worship space was furnished with assorted kitchen tables. Attendees sat around the tables during the service and therefore had as much ability to look at each other as at the pastor. This fostered a particularly social environment, especially because all of the tables were small enough that people could really talk to each other. It was surprising how a simple seating alteration could change one's expectations and have a ripple effect on other elements of the experience.

Contrary to what popular news stories portray, few cowboy pastors preach from horseback; in most cases this would be impractical. Instead, they typically stand on a low dais with a rustic-looking, movable lectern. Sometimes the chancel has a special design to visually set it apart, such as cedar paneling at the back, or a small covered area that makes it look like a porch. A common though not universal theme is to have two saddles on either side: one old and beaten up, the other shiny and new, representing one's life in relationship to Christian conversion. A head mic allows the preacher to move around the room, and these are used in all but the small-est churches. In a few cases of churches meeting in arenas, I have seen pastors preach from horseback; ironically, because they want to keep the horse calm, this causes them to be more stationary as they speak.

Many cowboy churches start out in a makeshift space loaned to them, such as a bar, an arena, or an arena outbuilding. A few others meet in a traditional space that was formerly home to a mainstream church; in my opinion, in all churches where this was the case, something signifi-cant felt lacking.[27] The physical space of the church is deeply influential on the mood, as well as who will be comfortable there, and I found that no amount of cowboy music, cowboy decor, or cowboy preaching could entirely eliminate a churchy atmosphere in spaces that had been designed as traditional churches. Perhaps more than any other point of the cowboy church model, I most strongly agreed with the importance of having a physical space that is comfortable and nonthreatening in order to "lower barriers" or otherwise influence who will want to walk through the doors. Of course, secularizing the space is not the invention of cowboy churches; American megachurches are well known for their nondescript sanctuar-ies, unadorned with religious symbols, intended to make everyone com-fortable and remove the expectations brought by visual cues. By making the environment of church relatively indistinguishable from the spaces that suburban middle-class people pass through during the rest of the week, such as an office or mall, megachurches press the point that "reli-gion is not a thing apart from daily life," as Paul Goldberger has phrased it.[28] The similarly dressed-down spaces of the cowboy church also intend to create a comfortable environment, quite like buildings that ranching and farming people would pass through during their work week. But, more than just supporting the idea that religious life is not separate from everyday life, cowboy churches also seek to convey a deeper message: that the crux of being a Christian takes place within a person. No part of reli-gious identity is inherently tied to, or limited by, a designated sacred space. Thus, by downplaying physical space, they convey a theological message about introspection and focusing on a personal relationship with Jesus. Anything else, such as what the worship space looks like or what you are wearing there, is irrelevant.

The casual space is certainly part of what makes it feel acceptable for everyone to wear boots and jeans. Those who wear cowboy hats momen-tarily take them off during prayer, but aside from that event, no one is expected to remove their hat inside. In some cowboy churches, peoples' attire seems somewhat contrived: for example, men wearing pressed jeans with shiny boots that look like they were in the closet since the previous Sunday, and women with matchy-matchy western outfits. In other words, there are those who deliberately dress in their "cowboy best" for church, which feels beside the point. But this variation also reflects different kinds of church populations. In some places, the majority of members feel themselves to be deeply rooted in the western heritage culture, but in actuality they live in a suburban condominium and spend their week driving to an office, so they relish the chance to wear their western gear on Sunday, and the intent is genuine.[29] Other churches serve different kinds of western heritage communities. Shane Winters, a pastor in central Texas, describes his cowboy population: "We're pretty rural. Mexia is pretty good cowboy country. Quite a few ranches, small and big. A little bit of farming."[30] In a church like his, the attire feels less deliberate, so you'll see people in pressed plaid shirts as well as in t-shirts, wearing cowboy boots or workboots or sneakers, with cowboy hats or baseball caps or no hats at all. In the end, most pastors would agree that the point of having casual attire is to get people in the door. As Scott McAfee of Owasso, Oklahoma, put it, "Come filthy. Come neat. Just come in and relax. We're not looking for a dress code, or how much money you got."[31]

Cowboy Church Music

Another barrier-lowering point occurs through music. A typical cowboy church service begins with about thirty minutes of music and ends with a lively and/or standard song (for example, in some places "Happy Trails" is always the ending). From the perspective of leaders, music plays a significant role in attracting the target group, and getting it "right" is often articulated as one of the top priorities. In fact, leaders consider music more of a hook than an engaging pastor, and they caution that the lack of a band can, by itself, cause a cowboy church to fail. As articulated in training seminars, ideally the church music should sound similar to what people listen to on the radio because that will make them feel comfortable. Contemporary country-western is assumed to be the most popular genre among the target audience, so that should be what one hears; the occasional inclusion of older country songs, or bluegrass, is also acceptable.

In practical terms, this means that the average cowboy church strives to have an amplified band with drums and several string instruments. Five members is good, and fifteen is even better. When they start rocking out, the whole cowboy church should be filled with sound. This is not a place for hymns, choirs, praise music, or sentimental contemporary Christian numbers; if someone wants to hear or sing those, they have a wide range of other places to attend. Pastor Gary Morgan explains that "the music is typically more spectator-driven, as opposed to being participatory . . . . It was the feeling that that would be a higher comfort level for unchurched people who are used to going to rodeos and country-western shows and it would just feel more at home for them, and less churchy."[32] In other words, the assumption is that today's cowboys do not want to sing along, and so it should always be comfortable to just sit and listen, or even mill about if they prefer. Pastor Paul Lutz said that he is perfectly fine with the fact that some of his members stand at the back of the room or even outside during the music portion, socializing over coffee or cigarettes until it is time to come in for the sermon.[33]

The subject of bands is elaborated on at AFCC clinics and CCU. They emphasize that the band is not an activity; it is a ministry. The band should support the most important part of the church service, which is the pastor's sermon. One way it does this is by energizing people in preparation for it. Slow songs should always be buried in the middle of the music, with lively songs played just prior to the pastor stepping up to the lectern. In a perfect situation, the band makes its song choices so that the musical messages are aligned with the pastor's message, though this requires both good communication and an experienced band. In terms of musical content, traditional hymns and old gospel songs are acceptable as long as they have been arranged in a contemporary country-western style. There is also a subgenre of western-themed Christian music, old as well as new, that can be drawn from. But just as often, bands take popular songs and change a few lyrics to make the song appear to have a religious focus, such as altering a romantic love song to make it about love for Jesus. Other examples of changes that I heard included Gary Stewart's "An Empty Glass" sung with a final religious verse added, Bob Seger's "Turn the Page" made into a song about prayer and conversion, and Kenny Rogers's "Lucille" with the chorus lyric changed to "You picked a fine time to get born again." Sonny Spurger, a church member in Waxahachie, summed up the music situation of cowboy churches this way: "I laughingly say, if it's on the radio, and it's got 'God' in it, it passes. It'll work. And so, you know, some of it's really good."[34] But there are other people who are wary of allowing any secular music in church; as an AFCC leader advised, they should always pray about it first and then make individual decisions.

A strong and developed music program can also have negative consequences. In training seminars, pastors and other leaders are warned against
allowing the band to become too much of a focal point. The music is not
worship, they reiterate; it just draws people in so that they can be reached
with the gospel. Band participation can become a prestigious or even cov-
eted form of lay ministry in places where many members have musical
talents, fomenting envy. In one situation, though it was probably atypical,
I met a woman in Texas who attends two different cowboy churches on
alternate weeks. The reason was that she very much wanted to play in the
church band, but at her original church the band was "full." Thus, she
found a cowboy church forty-five miles away that did have a place for her
in the band, and so she was dividing her time. How long will it be before
she transfers her membership full time to the church that supports her talents? This kind of exclusion, or perhaps just lack of participant rotation, is
precisely the sort of thing that leaders caution against with church bands.

In some cowboy churches, the music is truly memorable. I will not
forget the stellar six-piece band I heard in a tiny church inside a former
gas station in Grapevine, Texas, or the elderly lady in Yukon, Oklahoma
who knocked out the crowd with her harmonica solo, or how the band's
sound literally made the walls vibrate in the temporary trailer space of a
church in Waxahachie, Texas. Great bands are worth coming back to hear,
even if one is only modestly interested in the message, and cowboy church
leaders count on that. And yet, in my visits to cowboy churches, I have
witnessed *all* of the forbidden kinds of music. I have felt obliged to stand
and mumble along in unison from a standard hymnal. I have seen lyrics
of praise songs projected onscreen, overlaying pastel landscapes. I have
listened to wobbly solos sung to prerecorded music by well-intentioned
church members or even visiting guest artists. I was nearly put to sleep
with a slate of slow, sentimental songs that led right up to the pastor's sermon at the "flagship" cowboy church in Waxahachie. In cowboy churches,
I have even heard an organ, and I have seen a choir. Despite the strong
articulation of what cowboy church music *should* be, the musical realm
was one of the most common places where I found frequent discrepancies
between the ideal and the lived.

Part of the problem is that the model may be unrealistic when it comes
to music. A unified and polished band is not easy to put together, and compromises are often needed in smaller and/or newer churches. It may be
that musical talent is simply not present among the congregation, which
forces the church into makeshift solutions. Yet paying guest musicians is

frowned upon; the fact that they are playing for money "doesn't help the spiritual level of your service," as an AFCC leader moralized.[35] Talented pastors are discouraged from being band members primarily because the opportunity should be given to others, though I have seen exceptions to this in several places. Lowering the barriers via music thus becomes a complex undertaking, because at the end of the day it is much easier to have everyone stand up and sing some familiar hymns.

Some start-up churches actually borrow a band from a larger, more established cowboy church, and at other times bands are recruited from local bars. Over time, I observed division about permitting people to be in the band if they are not church members, especially if they also play in a bar; ultimately this issue is decided at the level of the individual church. At an AFCC clinic, one speaker advised that it is probably acceptable for nonmembers to be in the band as long as they are not the leader. He suggested that such people should be considered lost souls who have the potential to be reached with the Word through their participation; it is a state of "prediscipleship," as it was called at CCU. Pastor Jason Taylor recalled a relevant story about a man who formerly played in the band of Taylor's east Texas church. "He was a drunk, a full-blown alcoholic, drunk every night. But he would come to church Sunday morning, he'd be red-faced, and he would play, and he'd look at the wall." At some point, the man admitted his problem and asked Taylor what he should do. Taylor told him, "You're supposed to ask Jesus to be your lord; I can't fix you. I love you. I don't care that you was drunk last night . . . . [Jesus] loves you when you're slobbering drunk last night, and he loves you when you stand up and play a guitar in the morning." Slowly, the man began to grow in his Christian faith and in his newfound goal to overcome alcoholism. Several years later he had moved on to another church, where he continued playing music and also led a men's Bible study group. In this situation and others, Taylor's approach tends toward the more radical end of the cowboy church spectrum in terms of embracing everyone who comes through the door. Here he lowered the barriers not only through music itself but also through the musical participants, and many other such stories of conversion and transformation come from his congregation.[36]

Worship

The ideal cowboy church worship service is defined by an atmosphere of unpredictability. Although this is partly established through the casual nature of the space and attire, it is also made clear through the light-hearted attitude of the pastor and other speakers. At the start of the service someone may tell a funny anecdote from their week, or a joke involving a rancher, or a story about the stock bumpkin character known interchangeably as "Cowboy Joe" or "Cowboy Bob." The sermon may also be laced with humorous asides. I have even heard profanity used on the pulpit, uttered not as random expletives but as contextual adjectives in a story. Or consider this example that got the crowd warmed up in a Texas cowboy church:

> Cowboy Joe is riding fences one day when he comes upon a rattle-snake. The snake tries to slip over to the other side, but Cowboy Joe catches him. The snake pleads, "Cowboy Joe, if you allow me to go free, I'll grant you three wishes." Cowboy Joe says, "Okay, that's a deal. See how beautiful my horse is? I want hair just as thick and golden as his." "Done!" says the snake. "And see how great my horse's teeth are? They're big and pearly. I want teeth just like 'em." "Done!" says the snake. "And last, you see how big my horse's equipment is down there? I want to be built just like that!" "Done!" says the snake. Cowboy Joe lets the snake go on his way, and he rides off to finish his work. That night he gets home and turns on his bathroom light. Looking in the mirror, he takes off his hat to see that he has a head full of beautiful golden hair. He smiles, and sees he has a full set of excellent teeth. Then he unzips and pulls down his pants. "Oh shoot!" Cowboy Joe says. "I was ridin' a mare!"[37]

The point of a joke like this is obviously not religious. Rather, it is to get peoples' attention, and to put them at ease. Anything can happen in a church where a joke with a punch line about genitalia is one of the first things you hear from the pulpit. It signals that this place is unpredictable, and that atmosphere is a distinctive marker of cowboy church.

At other times, a service may be more dramatic than jokey, but the effect on peoples' engagement is the same. Unusual approaches and/or sermon props can be used to set the atmosphere and hold attention. In McLoud, Oklahoma, Randy Reasoner sometimes brings his horse into the worship space to use as his assistant in sermons. In McAlester, Oklahoma, pastor Mitch Arteberry can make an entire sermon interactive, inviting questions and comments and using each person's response to explore the topic more deeply. In Tatum, Texas, Jason Taylor once lit a fire in a barrel on the dais of his large wooden church, squirting it with streams of lighter fluid for extra effect in relation to his message. And Sonny Spurger recalled a cowboy preacher in Alpine, Texas who frequently turned church into participatory theater. One time, "he came in and had big chains all over him. He was towing about a fifty-pound anvil, and I mean, it was tough. He worked his way to the front. His sermon was [about] setting aside the slavery of sin, and what it is to be free." In another instance, the same man drove his pickup truck into the middle of the church, locked it up, and then said he needed the congregation to figure out how to move it, all of which led to a message about working in unity.[38] Cowboy preachers like these are intentionally changing the paradigm of what worship has to look and feel like, and showing their target audience that church can be interactive and engaging. By extension, we are to understand, religion can also be a source of excitement in their lives.

Although dramatics of this type are viewed favorably, there is a conscious effort to stay away from religious emotionalism in cowboy church. At CCU, Jon Coe advised leaders to "avoid religious extremes" in services, which includes charismata. Mike Meeks, formerly of the Nazarene Cowboy Church Network, elaborated that "'charismatic' doesn't work well, because it puts a lot of fear into a culture that's not with that."[39] As Ron Nolen put it more plainly, speaking in tongues, spiritual dancing, and other forms of charismata just "tends to spook the cowboy people."[40] There are exceptions to this, most obviously in cowboy churches affiliated with the Assemblies of God, but also in some independent churches. For example, at an unaffiliated cowboy church in Jones, Oklahoma, the preacher spoke in tongues on the day I visited, and the musical guest insisted that everyone come to the front corner of the room and crowd together for an intensive prayer activity. Later in the same service, healings commenced. Although I am no stranger to charismatic worship, all of this made me want to slink out of the building mid-service, so I would not have been surprised if this approach alienated others, too. Just as with charismata, many cowboy pastors say that altar calls should be avoided because of the heightened visibility. Gary Morgan explained that "there's the feeling that a lot of individuals don't want to do their business with God in front of five hundred people," and being expected to do so creates yet another barrier.[41] However, though not technically altar calls in which people come forward to make commitments to Christ, I have seen many cowboy services in which people were invited forward for special prayer requests, and this is no less public. At one large church in east Texas, a segment of special prayer at the altar was immediately preceded by a band member ironically announcing, in total seriousness, "We don't do altar calls in cowboy church." In sum, the reality of religion on the ground is much more varied than the ideal, and there are many times when individual emotions are put on public display.

When it comes to sermons, the cowboy church model dictates that they should be short, practical, and focus on a specific biblical message. Hellfire and brimstone preaching are to be avoided, as are abstract ideas, theological terms, and doctrine. Straightforward messages are better than complex ones, and sermon illustrations should draw on cowboy culture by making use of parallels that come from ranching, rodeo, the racetrack, or even just generalized aspects of rural living. In my experience, preachers do stick to the guidelines, with the exception of the length: sermons most often run thirty to thirty-five minutes rather than the prescribed twenty. But the aspect of drawing on the western culture is usually strongly present. In doing so, today's pastors tap into a longstanding tradition of using cowboy vernacular for preaching, as exemplified by Will James, John Anderson, and other cowboy preachers of the late 1800s. Today they may refer to rodeo competition, or trail riding, or the way a particular animal—a cow, or a horse—relates to humans, and compare that with how humans can relate to God. Some references might simply be to ranch chores. Perhaps the best example was given by pastor Jake Shue, who summed it by saying, "You know you're in a cowboy church when you hear 'rectal palpation' used as a sermon example."[42] There is, of course, a range: some pastors seem to deliberately pepper their references and stories with the cowboy idiom, while others are far more understated. In an interview, one pastor who grew up ranching actually groaned when I asked him about his use of such language. "Horse metaphors," he said, disgustedly, shaking his head. "The analogies are just *annoying* . . . . We're trying to do something real. We don't try to cowboy it up."[43] Though it is impossible to say in absolute terms, in my observations there seemed to be an inverse relationship between cowboy-style references and the rootedness of a given pastor in western culture; in other words, those who lack confidence in their cowboy credentials sometimes overcompensate with their language. In contrast, men who had grown up working on ranches and felt deeply embedded in the culture did not appear to try quite as hard. In seminars, a few have even warned against overuse of cowboy lingo, advising that credibility and respect have to be earned rather than put on like a costume. As one AFCC leader put it: "Don't be a poser." Just be yourself, he said, and surround yourself with leaders who are more genuinely immersed in the culture if you feel you aren't cowboy "enough."

In terms of sermon content, many pastors indicate that the new Christians in their congregation are not ready for a complicated religious message. Pastor Terry Hill says that for that reason, he avoids "heavy, deep theology."[44] Some deliberately keep the Sunday message light and only get into more serious discussion with those who attend a mid-week service. One AFCC affiliated pastor is rumored to have preached from a child's Bible for an entire year, because he felt that was the depth his parishioners were ready for. Another said that he makes sure to always be very explicit with his meaning, but the result is that "some people come here and they hate it! Some think the message is too blunt. But cowboys are pretty black and white. There's not a lot of frills."[45] With a note of realism, Mike Meeks explained that a pastor always has to tailor his message to the audience in question. "I would not use the same treaties or outline in a cowboy church that I might use in an established church," he said. "It's not that they're simple-minded, but the cowboy church does need to create identity . . . . So we will use illustrations and terms in our preaching style and words" that resonate with people of the western heritage culture.[46]

Perhaps surprisingly, politics is not strongly present as a topic in the cowboy church, even though the image of the cowboy is often closely associated with American conservatism and strong patriotism. At CCU, leaders specifically tell pastors to avoid referencing politics from the pulpit, even in passing or jest. Although at times I noted church activities that suggested particular kinds of political leanings—such as a contingent of members participating in a walk to support a local pro-life resource center, or a church hosting a workshop on earning a Concealed Carry License— it was rare that I encountered any overt political discussion in cowboy church. In the course of my research I heard only five sermons containing explicit political messages, and four of those were delivered by guest pastors. In the remaining sermon, at a church that proffers premillennial Dispensationalism, the message had to do with Christian support for the State of Israel. It is possible that political viewpoints are conveyed more strongly within small groups and activities, or during times of important elections, but in general the cowboy church cannot accurately be described as having a politicized atmosphere.[47]

When cowboy pastors discuss the Bible during services, they tend to keep the specific references brief, focusing on just a small number of verses. It is less common for a cowboy preacher to refer to a variety of biblical books in a single sermon, just as it is uncommon to hear serious discussion of any books from the Hebrew Scriptures. And it is the rare cowboy pastor who reads a long Bible passage aloud. Instead, they are more likely to read or paraphrase a couple of verses and then explicate the meaning at some length. Attendee use of Bibles during services is minimal, though of course there is variation from place to place. Many pastors explain that their pragmatic approach to using the Bible in a service is based on the assumption that members are relatively biblically illiterate, so they model an approach that examines it in very small increments. Pastor Jake Shue explained that he encourages people to pick up a Bible from a common table when they enter, and when he refers to something in it, he announces the page number from which he is reading. Naming the book and giving the chapter and verse numbers is useless information for people who are unfamiliar with the way a Bible is put together, he explained, and they might feel embarrassed about their inability to find the passage.[48]

Many cowboy churches and ministries offer free "cowboy Bibles" for visitors. The second time someone offered one to me, I foolishly turned it down saying that I "already had one." At the time I did not realize how many variations of cowboy Bible there are. Most consist of the New Testament alone or even just a portion of it, and often what makes it "cowboy" is the individualized book cover. They are typically brown or blue (considered masculine colors) and feature a drawing or photograph with a cowboy theme, such as a bucking bronc rider or a variation of the cowboy at the cross image. The cover's interior will also be personalized with something like cowboy poetry, a letter to readers from a minister, or information about a particular church. However, some cowboy Bibles are distinct because they include extra features to aid understanding. For example, the traveling entity Wild Horse Ministries gives out the "KJV Plus," a version that supplements the KJV with book summaries, frequent subheadings, and parenthetical notes to clarify word meanings; and the Fellowship of Christian Cowboys' Living Bible translation contains topical cross-referencing via simple notes inserted in headers and footers. One of the most ubiquitous cowboy Bibles, *The Way for Cowboys*, is a pocket-size book designed by the FCC that includes the NIV translation of Psalms, Proverbs, and the New Testament. The book is interspersed with glossy pages of testimony and photographs of Christian rodeo cowboys, as well as instruction about methods for effective reading. Its small size makes it easy to carry, and the photo on the cover gives it a contemporary feel.[49]

Cowboy Bibles are produced in numerous translations. Dave Harvey of Cowboys for Christ prefers to give out an easy-to-read version because "we don't have a real literate society now, and so this is something they can really read." He acknowledged that he would probably choose a different translation if he were targeting an audience that was more likely to be college educated.[50] One unusual version I came across is the SCV, or "Simplified Cowboy Version," the project of "two cowboys who have a love for the Bible and helpin' cowboys and cowgirls understand its vast beauty."[51] It is a Bible paraphrase written by cowboys for cowboys, with an emphasis on making the stories relevant to a western context. An example from the text is Matt. 4:18–20, in which Jesus meets the fishermen Peter and Andrew. The SCV reads, "When Jesus was walkin' down by the Sea of Galilee, he saw two cowboys, Peter and his brother Andrew. They were gatherin' some cattle and puttin' 'em in some pens. 'Come ride with me,' Jesus said to 'em, 'and help me gather mavericks. I'll make you gatherers of men.' They left the herd right there and rode off with him." This is a typical kind of rendering, in which fishermen are transformed into cowmen, and Jesus is a cowboy on the trail. The SCV author has cowritten three biblical paraphrase books—Proverbs, Romans, and Matthew—as well as running a nonprofit Christian ranch in Colorado, which the website calls "the world's first working ranch cowboy church."[52] Similarly, another pair of authors has written a Bible digest aimed at a cowboy audience, called *Get Your Bible Out of the Saddle Bag!* Its summaries of biblical books are interspersed with random bits of history called "Western Heritage Past." The five-page summary of Exodus, for example, includes not only the Ten Commandments, but also the ten points of Gene Autry's Cowboy Code and half a page of biography about Autry. Intended as a six-volume series covering the entirety of the Bible, after the 2011 publication of the first book no further volumes were issued.

I was surprised to find that no pastor expressed commitment to a particular Bible translation, and yet at the same time many indicated that they have a rather literal approach to reading it. Pastor Jason Taylor, for example, said, "Scripture is not interpretive. God's word is infallible and unmovable." He added, in criticism of his fellow men, "*We* are the ones who interpret and make it say what *we* want."[53] Other pastors said things that indicated issues of literary criticism, such as questions about context, authorship, and redaction, are of no concern to them, or perhaps simply not on their radar. Very typically, if I asked a specific question about a pastor's theological source material, he would say something like, "I just teach the Bible," or occasionally that "the Holy Spirit tells me what the text means." More rare were those pastors who acknowledged that there are biblical contradictions and aspects of the text that cannot be clearly understood, and for that reason, a few said, there are certain issues they avoid discussing, and in some cases particular biblical books they avoid using.

The overall vague attitude I found about the Bible may reflect the fact that many of the pastors are not formally trained. Of course, being an able pastor requires many skills, of which biblical literacy is only one. But there are those who are concerned about the large numbers of men going into ministry who do not have a firm theological education. Gary Morgan can be counted among this group. As he says, "The bottom line is, there's a whole lot of cowboy churches where the pastors are not good communicators and where the messages lack depth . . . . I think that some of our guys have wrongly gotten the impression that simple means shallow. And there's a difference. You can preach deep things and do it in a simple way, but I'm concerned at the quality, and what people are getting from the pulpits in some of our cowboy churches."[54] Rob McDonald, a Nazarene District Superintendent who works closely with cowboy churches in the Lone Star group, says that pastors who enter the ministry without training are encouraged to become licensed and ordained over time. "You want to make sure people are teaching the same things, not different things," he says. "You don't want—one pastor teaches this way, and the other that way." He adds that their denomination is extremely careful about who is allowed to pastor, because they are concerned about maintaining standards and insuring that they have trustworthy, accountable men.[55] At the AFCC, Todd Mitchell expressed only minimal concern that the lack of education is a problem. He says that programs such as the one at Baylor will foster some pastors, and he hopes that within the next few years resources will become available to develop a more cost-effective and suitable program. "Most of the guys that come from the pasture to pastor already have a family, are already pretty far down the road in life," Mitchell says, implying that financial realities prevent them from getting more education.[56] In the meantime, men like Mike Morrow, who describes himself as "not the man when it comes to preaching," advises his fellow cowboy pastors to put real time and effort into biblical study and sermon preparation and to consult multiple sources. He makes the astute point that while formal education about the Bible would be helpful for many cowboy pastors, most programs also include pedantic instruction about how to "do" church. For those in the cowboy church, who spend intensive amounts of time considering

the mechanics of church institutions, that aspect of formal education programs would surely be a deterrent.[57]

The Challenge of the Arena

According to some, arena ministry is one of the most important features
of any cowboy church, if not the most defining feature of the movement
as a whole. Certainly, no church that I have seen architecturally captures
the significance of the arena quite like the Lone Star Cowboy Church in
Red Oak, Texas. The rear wall of its sanctuary has a horizontal window at
eye level that runs nearly the length of the building. As congregants sit
through a worship service, whether watching the band or the pastor, they
cannot help but look through this window. Just outside it is the arena, and
in the distance, pens for cattle and horses. Thus at no time during the
service is a person disconnected from the presence of the arena, and this
simple choice in design speaks volumes.

And yet, the centrality of arena ministry to the cowboy church project
turns out to be a surprisingly contentious point. Many cowboy churches
have an arena on the church grounds that they use to attract and engage
people via culturally relevant activities that can be infused with religion.
For readers unfamiliar with the culture, an arena is a space where activities involving horses and livestock, such as riding and roping, take place.
It is not simply a fenced yard, though it may look like one. The arena
surface has to be graded and layered with gravel and porous materials for
proper drainage, then topped with a thick dirt/sand mix, the specifics of
which are dependent on local climate conditions as well as the activities
the arena will be used for. All of the fencing and gates must be strong
enough to safely contain animals that may run and buck. The arena typically has chutes where animals can be held, and in most cases there is
a return lane. Arenas may be indoors or outdoors, and in the latter case
they may or may not have a roof; all of these add to the building expenses,
but improvements can be made incrementally as funds become available. Other additions might include bleacher seats, judge and announcer
booths, a public address system, restrooms, a concession area, fans, and
lighting. The intricacies of building and maintaining an arena can create significant expenses, though an arena can also be used as a source of
income.[58]

The arena serves to attract the target audience. In the words of Mike
Meeks, "The cowboy finds his identity most comfortably when he's out

riding the range, trail riding, or in the arena. And so the cowboy church movement finds its identity of purpose and being within the arena."[59] For members, informal events like ropings, sortings, or play days allow people to socialize over a common activity.[60] More formal competitions can draw large numbers of new people to the grounds, and some portion of them are likely to return to try out a service. Church members who are not horse people can be made to feel included by using the arena for activities like target shooting, ATV riding, a game of horseshoes, or a herding event with dogs. One pastor says he sometimes has weeknight gatherings for members in which riders teach nonriders. "There's a lot of people who would like to be a part of this lifestyle but just never had the opportunity," he said. "So in sharing our enjoyment of horses or rodeo or whatever, we hope that they'll have a run-in with Christ."[61]

In fact, part of the reason for the arena's centrality is that every event in it should have a religious component, so that even those who do not return to the church have been touched with the gospel. Often called an arena devotional, this is a brief talk that relates a Christian message to the specific activity at hand. As a leader at CCU instructed, for maximum effectiveness the content of the devotional must connect with the arena activity, and a less-is-more approach is best. "Don't overdo it," he said bluntly. As an example, prior to one informal event I attended, the preacher gathered participants around to give a short demonstration about methods of hand release when riding a bucking animal. In his past experience riding bulls, the pastor said, sometimes his hand got stuck, and in those instances he had to trust that the bullfighter was somewhere nearby and would release the strap. It's just like in life, he continued: sometimes you have to trust that God will take care of you, even though you cannot see Him, because putting your life in His hands is your best shot at success. This devotional lasted about six or eight minutes, and almost all of it focused on the practical matter of hand release. The religious element was slipped in quite seamlessly. It did the job of getting people to think about how God relates to everyday life, particularly in the arena, without overwhelming anyone with a heavy religious message. Mike Morrow adds that different events require different approaches. "We pay attention to the subculture that's represented in the arena. So, if it's the barrel racers, primarily female, we'll have a female speaker that day. If we do a rough stock event that's got all the PBR bull riders, we're gonna usually get a guy that is connected to those guys."[62]

In general, there are many ways in which cowboy churches vary, and most of the time pastors have a live-and-let-live attitude. But when it comes to arenas, stronger positions emerge. Some pastors are adamant that the arena is a crucial part of cowboy church, while others resist it as potentially distracting. Representing one perspective, Mike Morrow has said, "I'm a purist when it comes to cowboy church. You can't separate the cow from the cowboy . . . . If you have an arena and it don't have hoof prints in it, I don't think you're doing it right." He added that if a church fails to use its own arena, "To me, that's not even a cowboy church."[63] This was echoed by Greg Horn at a cowboy church clinic, who asked rhetorically, "If you don't have an arena, are you *really* a cowboy church? Think about that." But others note that many problems can occur at arena events, from injuries to fights to drinking. It becomes impractical to police everyone, and thus unpleasant things inevitably occur. In Henrietta, the church's arena use has declined over the years. Pastor Larry Miller found that although arena events would bring new people to church, "You can have a lot of problems at horse events; people get mad and get their feelings hurt. So I think it's nearly an offset. And that's a problem I have when you want to focus everything around the arena."[64] Pastor Paul Lutz, who moved his church out of an arena, said, "If you want to go to a rope and horse show, go to a rope and horse show. If you want to talk about Christ, that's what I want." He particularly disliked the idea that some churches would waive competition entry fees for those who attended a service. In such cases, he feels the Christian message becomes subordinated to the personal benefit sought by the individual.[65] Miller echoed the sentiment; as for the centrality of the arena, he said, "I probably will disagree with the cowboy church philosophy in the Southern Baptist church . . . . At some point those things will get old, and I don't think they should ever take the place of the grounding in the Word."[66]

Speaking generally, Shane Winters has commented that not every aspect of the cowboy church model is right for every cowboy community. He cautions that a pastor has to carefully evaluate what is and is not right for his particular group. One cannot help but guess that Winters may be thinking of the emphasis some put on having an arena. When I visited his church in Mexia in the spring of 2013, a partially built arena sat just beyond the church building, grass growing in its center. Progress had clearly stalled. Coincidentally, he addressed the issue in his sermon that day. "For a while, we've been worried about this arena," he said. "That's been the end-all. 'We gotta get this arena done. All we need is this covered arena. We get that covered arena, our church'll be successful.' . . . *I thank God* that He didn't give us an arena," Winters emphasized, and then paused to let his comment saturate the silence. "We weren't ready to take care of an arena. I don't want this to be known as the 'arena church.' That's not why we're here." Winters continued with his characteristic forthrightness, reminding them to concentrate on the bigger picture. "The arena is just a light. The arena will draw the lost, but if we're not ready to take care of the lost, then we've missed that opportunity."

In reality, cowboy churches land all across the spectrum in relation to arenas, and so it is difficult to objectively call it a defining feature of the cowboy church movement as some want to do. There are cowboy churches that conduct their worship in an arena, sometimes with the chairs set right out in the dirt. There are others that neither have nor want one. In Missouri, Ginger Hayes is planning to start a cowboy ministry out of the arena-centered business she already runs. With both indoor and outdoor arenas on her ranch, she uses horses for counseling and therapy, and her next step will be to open a cowboy church at the same facility. For Hayes, the arena is absolutely central to her vision, and she is even considering preaching on horseback.[67] In contrast, Tuck Whitaker of Grapevine, Texas says that while his cowboy church will probably move to a different space someday, he has no plans to build an arena. Instead, Whitaker would prefer to have a building that is more conducive for music performances, so that the local community could be invited in. This is clearly related to the fact that his is a suburban church for people who feel a deep connection with western heritage culture, but whose lives are now city oriented. Whitaker joked, "We're a horseless cowboy church," but this reflects his realistic assessment of his target audience, their location, and what his church can potentially offer to attract them.[68]

The Challenge of New Christians

The arena presents an explicit challenge for individual cowboy churches as they determine if and how arena ministry fits into their program. A more subtle, but common, challenge is the range of issues created by new Christians. Although the actual proportions are unclear, cowboy churches do appear to be having some success drawing in people who have not recently been regular church participants. And yet, pastor after pastor confessed that new Christians can be among the most problematic parts of their work. Most of the difficulties new Christians create revolve around the basic fact that they are not used to being active and supportive members of a church organization.

One issue is the extent to which new Christians may be physically absent. One pastor, for example, said that his total membership is about three hundred people; however, most of those people come about once a month, or twice at most. So it seems that rather than thinking of church as the place they go every Sunday (and through the week for other activities), their actual commitment is much lower, although this may not have any relationship to their enthusiasm for church.[69] Sporadic attendance can make it difficult to plan and organize events that require volunteers, especially in small churches. It also makes it more difficult to evaluate whether a person might be suitable for a leadership position; in some cases, people are moved into positions of leadership prematurely. Stacy Wiley, a church elder in Texas, says new Christians can cause "train wrecks" when they are not spiritually mature enough to handle the responsibilities of leadership; and yet, this becomes a catch-22, because one of the ways the cowboy church flourishes is by engaging new people in teamwork and leadership.[70] Ron Nolen adds that another problematic aspect of new Christians becoming leaders is that people in the cowboy culture are often used to working and making decisions independently; there is "this individualistic concept that is so strong in the western culture," he says. It can be a struggle for them to adapt to a more collaborative environment like cowboy church, where work is done on teams and decisions are made by consensus.[71]

Somewhat related to peoples' physical presence is the issue of monetary support. Rarely is any collection of money taken in cowboy churches. The belief is that a focus on money makes people uncomfortable and it becomes a barrier, particularly to people who are new to churchgoing. Thus, most cowboy churches have some kind of closed container near the door where donations can be deposited. In some churches this low-key approach is quite successful and they never suffer from financial problems, but others admit that because of low giving they eventually resort to passing a collection plate—more typically a bucket or hat—to remind people that money is necessary to keep the organization going. Jon Coe, whose Texas church has over six hundred members, has said that their donation income is roughly equivalent to what would be received in a traditional church of one hundred members. "There's a huge difference in income between the two," he says of traditional versus cowboy churches.[72] It is not at all clear that the economic situations of different congregations reflect income levels of members; though this must play some part in church giving, there is also an element of educating people about Christian structures. At a clinic, Todd Mitchell advised that pastors must look at the bigger picture and "teach them to be stewards of the church, monetarily. Teach them about biblical giving."[73] In other words, people of the cowboy culture are not accustomed to donating to church, and so the churches must take it upon themselves to change that aspect of the culture. This is noteworthy because, as will be seen in the next chapter, on other issues the churches are adamant that the cowboy culture should neither be changed nor guided toward different ways of thinking.

Pastor Shane Winters says the depth of what is needed by some new Christians can be overwhelming, not only for a pastor but for the people themselves, because they lack both knowledge and acculturation. "If somebody grew up in church, and then they decide to give their life to God, they at least know the stories," he says. "They kinda understand more than just anybody who's never been to church before in their whole life . . . . So, now you're trying to teach 'em something that is huge; you know, Jesus is huge, that Bible is massive. It's easy for them to feel overwhelmed."[74] Ultimately this scenario puts a greater burden for spiritual leadership on the pastor and others who are more advanced in their religious life as they try to help the less-experienced Christians around them, especially with their religious questions and difficulties. Perhaps most importantly, a church full of new Christians means that few people have survived ups and downs of their own faith. In most cases they are not experienced with having their beliefs and/or their religious community support them through times of trouble. They are also not equipped to mentor others through recovery from behavioral backsliding. Jason Taylor explains that nurturing new Christians requires time, effort, and energy, and there is no guarantee on the investment. "When you take people that have been engaged in a life of drugs and alcohol and pornography and sex, prostitution, you name it, and you love them anyway . . . . You have to be willing to engage in their life and love them enough to become a part of their life, build a relationship, so that they can see through you that that's not how life has to be." Taylor's wife, Christie, added that she feels nourished by seeing such people make big changes in their lives, but sometimes, "Those mindsets take back over, and they slide back into that, and you feel, well, I just didn't do it good enough, there was something I didn't do." Her husband added that the stress of these situations can cause them personal anguish; he has to keep in mind that he is not responsible for other peoples' decisions.[75]

As discussed previously, it is difficult to determine with certainty the demographics of cowboy churches, and that includes precisely what is meant when people are referred to as "new Christians." Cowboy pastors do describe situations in which large clusters of the membership have little to no adult experience of being fully participating church members with all the responsibilities that entails, which suggests they should be considered first-generation members. Sociologist of religion Eileen Barker, who has considered the particular strengths and weaknesses of first-generation members, refers to such people as needing "secondary socialization," a process whereby they internalize beliefs and practices and incorporate them into their lives. In the groups Barker studied, this was often accomplished partly through social or geographic separation; however, isolation is by no means part of the cowboy church approach. Therefore, perhaps to pastors' dismay, it is reasonable to expect that fluctuations in commitment and challenges to ideas and authority will continue among the membership for as long as the cowboy church continues pulling in large numbers of unchurched people.[76] From the perspective of sociologists, the dynamic can only shift when the membership predominantly consists of people who have been a part of the faith group for an extended period of time, a situation that very few cowboy churches have reached because of their young age.

The Challenge of "Keeping it Cowboy"

While new Christians may not know how to be part of a church, a different sort of challenge is brought by those who believe they know precisely how best to "do" church. Sometimes referred to as "traditional church folks," these are people who have joined on the heels of leaving a more mainstream body. Mike Morrow describes them as "the folks that will come to your church and think it's really cool they get to wear jeans in church, or think it's really cool that you can drink coffee in church, and so they join your church, but their heart is still deeply rooted [in] traditional church. And they'll come in and they'll get on one of your leadership teams, and all of a sudden they want to go back to the way they used to do it."[77] Some have deemed them "the enemy of the cowboy church" because they stir up trouble trying to change how things are done. When they fail, they often return to the churches they left; for that reason, some call them "go-backers." Even though they represent a very small portion of cowboy church membership, fighting their influence and preserving a cowboy-centric mission is something that a surprising number of pastors say occupies much of their time. At the end of the day, this challenge is all about what Mike Morrow calls "keeping it cowboy."

Many pastors have listed examples of what traditional church folks want to change—ideas that typically only emerge once the newcomer has become fully embedded in the church community. For instance, they will say the cost of the arena makes it impractical, and the same goals could be accomplished with a less expensive facility such as a gymnasium. Pastors counter that while an arena can be very expensive, a gym is not its equivalent for horse people, and that's the point. Church folks may suggest that the music should include more traditional songs or more group singing. They may dislike the structures of leadership, or the infrequent business meetings, or the lack of an altar call, or they may think the attire has become too casual. An exasperated Shane Winters said, "I have to constantly reiterate our mission, our vision, and why we do things this way" to the people who come in with a "church mentality."[78] Larry Miller echoed the sentiment: "And you've got to deal with that constantly! And I'm kinda amazed . . . . We are comfortable in what we're doing. We're not going to come in and change what we're doing because someone wants a new fad, or this or that."[79] It is not the case that "churched" people are unwelcome in cowboy church, but rather that they become unwelcome when they try to subvert the model. In fact, as people who are usually more advanced in their Christian faith, they are needed, but only if they are able to adjust their expectations and align with the whole concept. As Greg Horn advised in a clinic, "They can't change the church; they have to adapt to it. But there can be a place for them, too. They can be missionaries to the cowboy."[80]

Ron Nolen has said this problem has been present since nearly the beginning of the modern movement. There was a time when he felt the cowboy church "got heavily weighted with some church culture people, who wanted to see what they had seen before replicated in the cowboy church . . . . If you *have* to have it done that way, there are twenty other churches down the road here, you may just have to go join one of them. We're not going to do a thousand other things that the existing churches do and do well."[81] AFCC director Todd Mitchell agrees that this is an ongoing problem, though it varies from place to place. In his estimation, "The greatest risk that cowboy church faces is the church folks that want to come in and bring their church plan into this fellowship." Mitchell, trying to find a more illustrative way to express it, recalled a scene from the film

Shawshank Redemption in which a long-term prisoner offers his wisdom to other inmates. The essence of the character's message was that becoming comfortable within the confines of an institution can make a person terrified of ever trying anything different, even though what is different may be better. That same risk exists within the cowboy church, Mitchell implied, particularly via people who come in with an extensive background in the traditional church. In his role leading the AFCC, Mitchell prioritizes working on unity of vision in order to help stabilize the movement overall, thus decreasing any threats to their nontraditional church approach—an approach that, though Mitchell did not say so, is itself becoming more and more of its own defined tradition.[82]

The Challenge of Morality

A particular approach to sin and sinners is, ideally, one of the distinguishing characteristics of cowboy church. The precept is that barriers are erected when visitors feel judged; therefore acceptance of others, as they are, is of utmost importance. However, I observed numerous inconsistencies related to behavior and acceptance, which is somewhat surprising given the nature of my status as an outside observer just passing through. It leads me to conclude that consistency on issues of morality introduces another major challenge for the cowboy church. According to Seventh-day Adventist Bunny Reid, the crux of any cowboy church is that it's about "love and acceptance. We accept anyone who comes through the door," she said, and they avoid being "critical and judgmental about behavior." Echoing the same phrase uttered by countless other cowboy church pastors, Reid said that while the church members are the fishermen, "It's God's job to clean the fish, not ours."[83] Ideally, cowboy churches welcome and embrace people whose lives may be quite marked by sin, and rather than expecting them to instantly stop sinful behavior, the idea is that they will change over time as they grow spiritually. Gary Morgan boiled this approach down in technical terms: "You gotta be justified before you can have sanctification. And I think that the mistake that the [traditional] church has made theologically, is that in a lot of cases they have tried to put the sanctification in front of the justification . . . . When you get saved, that's justification. You're made right with the Lord. And then once you're set right, *then* you go through the process of discipleship, and the Lord begins to take out of your life those things that are displeasing to him. That's sanctification."[84] Thus, in seminars they teach that while congregants may engage in many behaviors that pastors would like to eliminate, much of that should be overlooked. They tell preachers to avoid getting caught up in micromanaging petty "religious rules" or "doctrinal sins," and if they feel compelled to preach about sin, they should stick with those discussed explicitly in the Bible. Beyond that, the task of getting "right" with God must be worked out on an individual basis, perhaps with encouragement and counsel from one's pastor, but ultimately as a matter that lies between the person and God.

The question is how this lofty goal translates into actual practice, and the answer is that while some cowboy church pastors stick closely to the ideal, others seem to have a much lower bar of toleration and therefore struggle to enact low barrier style acceptance. Admittedly, embracing sinners is not an easy goal, and acrimonious relationships can readily develop among members if they forget to keep acceptance as a priority. As Jon Coe said in a CCU session, your church may be filled with adulterers, drinkers, homosexuals, outlaws, and on and on; but keeping *those* people in church should be the priority, rather than assuaging more well-behaved members of the congregation who are offended by them. Coe recalled when church members complained to him about a regular attendee because the giant soda cup she always brought to church was full of liquor. Overruling their concerns, he said to them, "I'd rather she be drunk in church than drunk at a bar. At least she's here listening to the Word." In fact, he explained, he would be happy to baptize that woman if she was ready to commit to the process of making changes in her life, and by no means would he expect her to stop drinking overnight, or even any time soon. Compared with many mainline denominations, Coe's position is a radical stance that is in keeping with the cowboy church ideal. Similarly, Gary Morgan gave the example that some of his members were upset that people in the congregation were "shacking up," and so they wanted him to preach against living together outside the bounds of marriage. However, he refused to moralize from the pulpit, and said only that if the opportunity arose with individuals, he would offer counsel. In instances like these, cowboy church leaders are being true to the vision of creating a place where people are welcomed in and allowed to be themselves, gradually working on improvement but not being pressured with the threat of church condemnation.

But it is not hard to find instances in which the lived religion conflicts with the cowboy church ideal of love and acceptance. One of the first examples that stood out to me was when two different pastors discussed a particular moral situation they sometimes deal with: the scantily clad female church attendee. Gary Morgan was the first pastor who mentioned it to me, saying, "You come around here on a Thursday night, it'll burn your eyeballs out what some of these girls come up here wearing . . . . Maybe she's wearing a spaghetti strap top with nothing under it, and maybe her shorts or her skirt or whatever it is she's wearing are too short . . . . Or maybe her language is coarse, you know." Morgan went on to say that the appropriate response is to welcome her and love her and hope that she keeps coming back. In this, Morgan stays true to the ideal that people cannot be expected to be sanctified before justification.[85] Strikingly, in an AFCC clinic a few months later, another leader spoke from the podium about this very same issue. Advising others, the pastor said that he keeps a few sweaters and jackets on hand at his church, so that any time a woman comes in dressed inappropriately, someone offers her one to put on. What surprised me was that no one in the room seemed to object this approach; no one raised a hand and pointed out that such a response only serves to shame the woman, rather than to love and accept her as she is, and that it goes against the ethos of the cowboy church approach. This advice was allowed to stand, unchallenged, in a place where leaders were being trained in best practices.[86]

Like this latter cowboy pastor, there are many others who turn themselves into arbiters of morality, and although they continue to claim that they welcome everyone, their standards for appropriate moral behavior are so strict as to be indistinguishable from the traditional churches they eschew. For example, in a sermon by one Oklahoma pastor, he condemned both drinking and swearing, rhetorically asking, If Jesus were to walk in the room while you were doing one of those things, wouldn't you be ashamed?[87] This type of higher-level policing also creates questions and discrepancies about how sin affects a person's ability to participate in church. Almost all cowboy pastors say that major sin present in a person's life prevents them from being able to serve in leadership positions. Major sin is somewhat subjectively defined, although there is consistency that sins of a sexual nature are usually classified in the "major" category. But surprisingly, there are all sorts of different positions taken by pastors regarding whether people who have sin present in their lives are able to be baptized, or to become members of the church, or to participate visibly in church life. Mike Morrow, for example, says that such a person is not ready to be "a good servant of

Jesus," which means that he or she can be an active church participant but not a member.[88] Others hold the reins of church participation even more tightly: consider the example of a woman in Henrietta, Texas who was not allowed to sing on the stage at church because she works as a waitress in a bar. From the pulpit, that same pastor mentioned that he boycotts a particular television channel because he feels the programming is anti-Christian and normalizes homosexuality, comments that certainly would have been received by some people in the room as admonitions, even though he said that was merely his personal choice. It becomes difficult to reconcile examples like these with statements from the very same people indicating that "everyone is welcome" and "we're not going to force you to believe [a particular] doctrine."[89] As Ron Nolen put it, "This judgmental spirit is prevalent in Christianity," and it is a difficult behavior to break.[90]

A striking exception to the complicated parsing of sin was pastor Shane Winters, who said God has taught him that sin is sin, and there are not "worse" and "better" sins. Sin is a great equalizer, Winters said, and thus no one has the right to sit in judgment of others. He illustrated with the example of homosexuality, which some people speak openly against in cowboy church circles. He said, "The reason people pick on gay people is that they can see their sin; it's out in the open. They're an easy target. But if I have a drinking problem, or a pornography problem, or something else that's easy to hide, it's no different. It's no better or worse, it's still sin . . . . [And that] doesn't give me a right to hate that person." Winters added that he will certainly preach against any and every sin that is in the Bible, and as a pastor he feels an obligation to be the best person he can. Nonetheless, he does not lose sight of his own past and present sins, and the way those make him just like everyone else in the room. Jon Coe echoes this sentiment, saying that he thinks it is important for pastors to publicly admit their own shortcomings, because it sets a realistic tone for the congregation and equips people to admit their own mistakes. "I can't keep something from somebody that God has freely given," Coe says, "which is salvation. If they're saved, then they can be baptized. If they're saved, they can be involved in the church. If they're saved, it just opens a whole new set of doors. Now, are they Christ-like? Not yet. But neither are any of us. I want my church to understand that and embrace that."[91] In the meantime, as they work on a long-term process of eliminating sinful impulses and behaviors, ideally all such people are welcomed into cowboy church.

Cowboy Churches and Mainstream Evangelicalism

Many "distinctive" aspects of the cowboy church structure and worship are surely familiar to any historian of North American religion. Rather than being an entirely new invention, cowboy church must be understood as one more in a historic line of churches that focus on making the Christian experience relevant to peoples' lives while maintaining certain core principles—or what sociologist Donald Miller has classified as "new paradigm" churches. Using a broad view, we see that cowboy churches readily parallel styles of worship that emerged full force in evangelical circles in the 1970s. From the dressed-down buildings to casual attire, to culturally relevant music and sermons that use innovative language and techniques, the entire concept is like a thumbnail portrait of what was happening in the Jesus movement circa 1971. Instead of baptisms in the Pacific Ocean, we see baptisms in stock tanks; instead of hippies wearing tie-dye, we see people in cowboy hats; and for most other ways that the Jesus movement brought innovation to conservative Christian churches, there is a parallel to be found within today's cowboy church movement.[92] Likewise, cowboy churches are reminiscent of the megachurch approach, such as what Lee Strobel said about his first experiences at Willow Creek in 1980. Strobel, an atheist dragged to church by his wife, found the music modern, the multimedia services interesting, and he was "captivated by the message," which was delivered in "a sincere conversational tone" that he could respect. Pastor Bill Hybels did not force particular beliefs on people, but instead suggested that people should investigate Christianity for themselves.[93] Strobel was initially made comfortable by the tactile aspects of church and became engaged with learning and debating Christian history, all of which ultimately led to his own conversion. Many aspects of the cowboy church approach are obviously in line with this, from pulling people in via the arena, to the approaches in worship, to the concept of letting the gospel stand on its own for evaluation. Thus, cowboy church has numerous close cousins, including churches that grew as a result of the Jesus People movement like Calvary Chapel and its Vineyard Church offshoot, and the related megachurch movement that includes such behemoths as Saddleback and Willow Creek.[94] While the size of the cowboy church will never rival the aforementioned groups, they may serve as useful points of comparison, indicating that the cowboy church movement could have a robust future ahead. And yet, because it is situated within a society that continues to evolve, something that may stunt its potential is the one barrier that it refuses to lower: that against the full participation of women. As explored in the next chapter, significant restrictions on women within the cowboy church largely relegate them to submissive roles defined by archaic ideas of "women's work." Yet dissatisfaction and disagreement with this situation, brewing in numerous corners of the cowboy church world, suggest that this point of tension may be the cowboy church's biggest hindrance to long-term growth and success.

5

The Cowboy Church as a Man's Church

THE SPEAKER WITH the slightly raspy voice sways gently from side to side, almost imperceptibly. The wife of a Texas cowboy pastor, she has been addressing the Cowboy Church Clinic audience for several minutes on the topic of "The Role of Women in Cowboy Church." There is not much to say about it; therefore her presentation is shorter than most.

The woman tells audience members that she spent much of her life in traditional religious institutions, and when she and her husband first started attending a cowboy church, she did not care for it. For many reasons, it did not feel like "real" church to her.

Initially, she said, "It rubbed me the wrong way when somebody said women aren't supposed to be in leadership. It truly rubbed me the wrong way." For a time, she adopted a sour grapes attitude, attending church without immersing herself in it. But eventually she had a change of heart. "God showed me, through my husband, that *it wasn't about me* . . . . As he showed me that, I changed."[1] Now, she serves as a teacher to other women, encouraging them to accept that it is not about them, either.

Quite simply, the "it" to which she refers is cowboy church: cowboy church is not about women. But more broadly, the "it" is the hand of God working among men of the western heritage culture, leading them toward a life of active faith. As a kind of neomuscularism, cowboy church is focused on men's faith and men's salvation vis-à-vis activities, structures, and an ethos designed to appeal to men of the cowboy culture. It is rooted in the same set of assumptions about what people of cowboy culture like and dislike, and leaders take the approach that cowboys are unwilling to submit to women's leadership.

In her clinic presentation, the speaker explains that women have very limited church roles because of biblical teachings. Eliding the content of Genesis 1, she refers to the creation story of Genesis 2, saying, "We are designed as women to be helpers. There may be times that there are teams that need a woman to step up and lead. But at any time that that team finds a man with the same passion as that woman . . . it is my true belief that it is our job to step aside and help that man. That's in all areas. We are not called to be elders. We are not called to be pastors. We are called to help." Helping men, she emphasizes, is what women do all throughout the Bible, and she names the New Testament books of Romans, Colossians, and Philippians as evidence of this. Of course, she is not wrong in identifying relationships of assistance in the Bible, but her selective reading also ignores named women who served in positions of religious leadership as both peers and superiors to men, some of whom are found in those very same biblical books. In a subsequent version of her presentation, the woman added this tagline, ostensibly for inspiration: "The day I realized that I wasn't important was the day my ministry was rewarded by God."[2]

Unlike all of the other clinic sessions, no time is set aside for questions or discussion at the end; therefore any dissent is silenced. There is no acknowledgement that not all cowboy Christians agree with this teaching, and that some pastors speak openly against it, or that the issue is not nearly as simple as this woman has painted it. And most certainly the clinic does not encourage resistance, or even independence. Instead, the law having been laid down, a man immediately rises and shifts focus to the next topic. It plays out this way every time I attend the clinic.

Across time and space at the parallel entity Cowboy Church University, the message about women's roles is much the same, and delivered by a man. At CCU there is little reliance on the Bible to justify male leadership and female submission; instead the focus is on the cultural norms of cowboy essentialism. Though most of the time they speak generally about cowboy culture people, when it comes to discussing leadership roles, a different nuance emerges. "We are there to attract the male, unchurched cowboy," leaders say. Lowering the barriers to appeal to him includes making the entire institution male-centric, which includes having only men as pastors, elders, and in any other visible leadership role. Furthermore, they say that women of cowboy culture *want* men to lead them and are relieved when they do so. Thus, in Nazarene cowboy churches, women are permitted to lead ministry areas designated for females (such as the kitchen, children's Sunday School, or a women's group), and occasionally they can share facilitation duties with a man (such as over a youth group). But they are prevented from serving in any position that would give them decision-making power over a man. Without any sense of irony, leaders say that allowing women to take leadership roles "excludes" men and prevents them from fulfilling what God wants them to do. This is "not chauvinistic," they add; it is "just part of the culture."[3]

Naming it *cowboy* church is thus extremely accurate, because it is the male cowboy on which the church centers. As demonstrated earlier, conscious effort is invested in making the physical space of cowboy church a casual environment, often akin to a barn atmosphere. This is not only referred to as a way to lower barriers, but also as "masculinizing" the space. As one pastor explained, cowboys "don't feel comfortable in a building that they perceive as designed by and for women . . . . The flowers everywhere, and the nice pictures and paintings everywhere. The color schemes, and all of that." Said another, "The environment here is about a man cave. You keep your 'man card' and come to church here." Ideas about masculinization reach beyond the space itself. One pastor explained that the "feminine characteristics" of church include hand-holding, hugs, sentimental songs like "Kumbayah," and an atmosphere in which people prioritize getting along over challenging one another. Even tiny things can make a difference, they say. One CCU speaker discussed using collectibles and advertising items to help market individual churches, such as hats, cups, or bumper stickers. But when making these decisions, "make sure you have a man in charge," the speaker emphasized, because otherwise women might choose items that men would not want. Without another word, he held up a bright yellow t-shirt with a church logo on it and rolled his eyes.[4]

Whether cowboy church leaders are framing a conversation about who qualifies for leadership, what the space feels like, or how people relate to one another, at the heart of this approach we repeatedly find gender essentialism. Also called "radical" essentialism by some, this idea basically blurs the boundaries between sex and gender, using them interchangeably to refer to categories leaders purport are natural: specifically, women are born feminine, men are born masculine, everyone is heterosexual, and anything that falls outside of these expectations is an aberration. Within Christian circles, a variety of sources have been used to support this idea, including the Bible ("biblical essentialism," as discussed in the introductory chapter), conservative Christian commentary (such as from James Dobson and Gary Smalley), pop psychology (books such as *Men Are from*

Mars, Women Are from Venus), and outdated biological ideas (such as found in writings by Tim LaHaye). In his study of evangelical families, sociologist John P. Bartkowski found that belief in radical essentialism tends to impact both church life and home life. He observed, "Proponents of a patriarchal family structure view masculinity and femininity as radically different from one another and argue that distinctively masculine traits— including logic, strength, assertiveness, and instrumentalism—uniquely qualify men for familial leadership and for the burden of responsibility that accompanies this superordinate position." Similarly, they believe the innate nature of women "predispose[s] them to submit willingly to their husband's leadership."[5] For cowboy church leaders, this acts as a guiding principle, and so a wide range of behaviors, characteristics, and material goods is classified as feminine—that is, inherently related to women but not to men—and therefore regarded as being in opposition to the cowboy church project. That is why, for instance, no one needs to actually discuss whether the yellow t-shirt is appropriate: yellow is regarded as a feminine color, end of story. In this context, gender essentialism fosters negative regard for those who do not conform to its stark limits, and it is therefore alienating and potentially insulting to many people. In the real day-to-day world, even in cowboy country, there are women who are not "nurturing," and there are men who are not "risky." There are women who prefer concrete floors to plush carpet, and there are men who like the color yellow. And there are women who are consistently level-headed, and men who readily become very emotional, as the tears during numerous pastor interviews demonstrate. In this age of advanced knowledge about human biology and the social construction of gender, cowboy church ideology attempts to reify outdated notions of gender as biologically determined and fixed, rather than performative and malleable.

Of course, the cowboy church is by no means unique in its embrace of gender essentialism. The cyclical resurgence of muscular Christianity has been a particularly fertile ground for this idea. After a period of dormancy following World War I, muscular Christianity expressed itself anew in the mid-twentieth century through athletic organizations for men that had an overt religious component, such as the Sports Ambassadors, the Athletes in Action (an affiliate of Campus Crusade for Christ), and the Fellowship of Christian Athletes. These groups advocated engagement with team sports and Christian service in order to achieve both moral and physical health, and they promoted this specific combination of traits as the new masculine ideal. As with their predecessors many decades earlier, these neomuscular Christians seemed to be reacting against what they perceived as the "feminization" of Protestantism as well as societal changes that increasingly accepted female leadership in the public sphere. By uniting Christianity with "manly" activities, they not only sought to make religious participation and evangelical morality more appealing to men; they also wanted to mesh the adjectives "masculine" and "Christian" in peoples' minds. As documented by Ladd and Mathisen, neomuscularism set the stage for a variety of more specialized sports ministries to ultimately grow out of it, including the elder siblings of cowboy church: racetrack chaplaincy and rodeo ministry.[6]

What might be called a third wave of muscular Christianity emerged in the 1990s, with organizations such as the Promise Keepers and mythopoetic groups bringing national media attention to male religiosity.[7] Athleticism was present, but not as central, to the message of these groups; instead the emphasis shifted to the masculinity aspect of the muscular Christian ideology. These ministries promoted distinct gender roles, particularly in the domestic setting, and encouraged men to embrace qualities like assertiveness and decisiveness. As summarized by Robert Cole, Promise Keepers taught that men's lives were being compromised by "assaults on their manhood and forced abdication of their proper role. Conditions conspire to prevent men from achieving their Christlike potential . . . . Compounding the problem for men, PK says, are many women's attempts to feminize the world, making it over in their own image rather than in the godly image of men."[8] Cowboy churches also emerged as part of this third wave of muscular Christianity, appealing to men with a similar message but using approaches tailored to a more culturally specific audience. Cowboy churches veered away from the tender, emotionally vulnerable male imagery occasionally employed by Promise Keepers, as did several other groups founded during this period, such as Church for Men and GodMen (now defunct). But, as a movement that is clearly concerned with manly Christian men reclaiming the church and shaking off its feminine cloak, cowboy church should readily be understood as part of the most recent cycle of muscular Christianity.

The Debate about Women's Leadership

Despite the pervasive rhetoric about masculinizing the cowboy church, not everyone agrees with the prohibitions on women's leadership, and the variations in opinion come from every corner of the movement. In my time spent mingling with cowboy Christians, I have talked with both male and female church members who have little regard for this teaching and consider it out of step with modern society. I have been to cowboy churches where women serve in visible lay pastor roles, and not just over "women's" areas; I have been to a cowboy church where the pastor's wife preaches the sermon twice a month; and I have met a woman who plans to become the first female pastor of a cowboy church.[9] Beyond the bounds of cowboy churches themselves, women have long served as ministers in various parts of the horse world, and none of these women are jumping up to give their spot to men, nor are they embracing a mantra that they are unimportant. To be sure, all of these exceptions are tiny blips on the radar, but they also serve as reminders that in any religion, lived practices are not always in line with official teachings.

Early in my research, I was taken by surprise during an interview when the pastor mentioned something about his time off. He said, "I go, every now and then, to a little ol' church where a woman pastor is, and she does a great work. I love her." I then asked where he stood on issues of women's leadership in his own church, a question that he seemed to find odd. Though he had been a cowboy pastor for several years and had worked in racetrack chaplaincy prior to that, his church was independent and unaffiliated, and he was not aware that cowboy churches often institute gender limits. He quickly responded that such a practice did not seem like following the example of Jesus, saying, "I'm not against women like that." The youth pastor and his wife, who were sitting with us, also expressed confusion about my question, and they attested that their church had never prevented women from serving in any way that God called them. The young woman commented that she thought such a mentality reflected "a different generation, different times and everything."[10]

Rather than seeing it as changing societal norms, Jeff Copenhaver characterized the argument about women's leadership as being a "denominational angle." Copenhaver is not opposed to women serving as pastors. "You can grab these scriptures and make one argument, or take some others and make the other argument," he said. "To me, scripture says there's neither Jew nor Greek, male nor female. We all have an eternal spirit. I just believe God is looking and he says, go into all the world. And he's talking to *all* his disciples. Men and women." From Copenhaver's perspective, people have different gifts, and the best way to honor God is to create a church atmosphere "where everybody can shine." Though Copenhaver neither named nor blamed the Baptist denomination specifically, many cowboy

Christians I encountered readily did so. For instance, several Nazarene men indicated that they think the cowboy church stance on women comes from Southern Baptist influence, particularly the emphasis on "male headship" that has burgeoned in recent decades.[11] Standing around the arena one evening at CCU, a member of a Texas church commented that he disagreed with the stance on women's roles. "That's Baptist," he said, spitting out the words in marked disgust, and explaining that no one has a right to prevent what God calls another person to do. Similarly, in a break-out discussion another man expressed discomfort about women being barred from cowboy church ministry because it "feels more like Southern Baptist tradition." Even Rob McDonald, a district superintendent with the Nazarene church, admits that on this and other issues in cowboy church, "What we're trying to figure out is, are we dealing with the fact that we're in a Baptist culture and we're doing it because that's the way Baptists do it? Or is it a biblical thing?"[12] McDonald's honesty is somewhat refreshing when so many other leaders are reluctant to admit there may even be a problem. However, though their past influence makes them an easy scapegoat, today there are far more than just Baptists involved in the cowboy church movement, and leaders are drawing on a wider range of thinkers and writers than those in Baptist circles.

There are some pastors who consider prohibitions on women's church leadership rooted in biblical misinterpretation. One man who might be classified this way is Randy Reasoner of Oklahoma. When we met, he spoke at length about the dangers of adding human ideas to the biblical text. "I'm serious about the biblical things. Don't got room to be adding 'man stuff' into it. It tends to mess God's recipe up." Among such revisionist additions would be preventing women from holding positions of leadership, including preaching and serving as elders. "So many great women did so many great things for God!" Reasoner says. Thus, his church supports women in all aspects of ministry. However, he also believes the Bible clearly mandates male spiritual leadership in the home. "When you've got the husband in the right place, and the wife in her place, then the whole atmosphere of the home changes . . . . And a strong healthy family from a scriptural standpoint makes a great church." Reasoner's position, then, is that families are meant to have God-given spiritual hierarchies, and supporting that does not include broadening it to an institutional level that he does not see evident in the Bible.[13]

Most surprising were the people who do not necessarily think the Bible prohibits women from being church leaders, yet they are willing to go along with that teaching for what they consider a greater good. In other words, they personally believe one thing, but allow a different worldview to guide the church structure. Gary Morgan, for instance, calls women's leadership a "tricky" issue. Emphasizing that he knows his opinion is out of sync with the cowboy church movement as a whole, Morgan said, "I don't see a theological reason why women can't serve at almost any level of the church that they feel so called to serve in. I'm one of the people that believes you see women deacons in the scripture."[14] And yet, because Morgan also believes in the mission of the cowboy church, in his congregation only men are permitted to occupy the most visible positions that would be observable to the random visitor, and he tacitly supports the party line on the question. I inferred a similar stance from Todd Mitchell, the executive director of the AFCC. When I directly asked him if he thinks the Bible teaches that women should not be pastors, he answered, "It's not for me to judge. I'm not going to interpret." However, he followed this with a protracted lament, if not a jeremiad, about the breakdown of American society. He emphasized that the presence of both a male and female parent in families is crucial for societal restoration, and thus the cowboy church has a role to play in that greater project by helping men aspire to spiritual and familial leadership.[15] In other words, Mitchell appears to take the same position as Morgan: the Bible may not forbid women in ministry, but because the male-centric cowboy church is a positive force in society, he supports its position on limiting what women can do.

An even darker version of this stance was represented by an anonymous interviewee from Oklahoma. This pastor, whose church is independent, said that although the Bible only mentions male pastors and elders, we should not necessarily assume that women are prohibited from taking those roles. And yet, when I asked him if any women serve as elders in his church, he admitted that they do not and never will. Confused, I asked him to clarify. Lowering his voice, he sheepishly admitted that pastors from other churches had advised him that women are not level-headed enough to serve in important leadership roles, and they "cause drama." So he took that under advisement when delineating his church structure, and supports it in public by noting that the only named elders in the Bible are male. In other words, he deliberately uses a particular interpretation of the Bible to support what is essentially a personal preference about leadership, even though he does not think that is the correct reading of the biblical texts.[16]

As the years passed and information from my interviews accumulated, I continued to learn new perspectives on the question of women's leadership in cowboy church. What became fascinatingly evident is that the reasoning used to prevent it is utterly inconsistent from church to church and pastor to pastor. Among their defenses one finds biblical ideas, generalizations about cowboy culture people, statistics, popular writings about men and masculinity, and often unique combinations of any or all of these. Though all of these ideas can be made to intertwine, my encounters with cowboy church leaders have shown me that on the question of women's leadership, there is no brief, direct answer that reflects the general ethos of the churches, or on which they would all agree. When one looks at the big picture, it appears that cowboy churches are often grasping at any idea that will stick in order to justify a patriarchal religious structure and perpetuate female subordination. Yet they frequently deny that that is the case.

The Defense of Women's Subordination

A biblical defense of the stance on gender relations is commonly found among cowboy Christians, who sincerely believe the scripture contains a clear and consistent message on this issue. In conversations with people who hold this perspective, they usually apply their biblical interpretation to both church and home environments. A response of this sort was demonstrated by the interviewee who said, "Don't take this as a slam on ladies, but God gave men and women different roles, and we've rejected that." Men are to be leaders in the home and in church, he asserted, and as an outgrowth of our increasing disregard for scripture on this and other issues, we are "suffering as a society."[17] Many pastors echoed this point, which dovetails with the "male headship" ideal mentioned earlier and relies on essentialist notions of gender. For those congregants who do not want to pore over the Bible in focused study, a trustworthy pastor's biblical answers about why only men can serve in leadership are often acceptable. For instance, pastor Mike Morrow said, "I believe there's a biblical order, and when people start talking about women's roles in the church, they're thinking about America and American democracy . . . . People need to get all that out of their mind. We're talking about church, and I believe there are principles from Genesis to Revelation that indicate that men need to be primary leaders in church. And what we've done is we have reimplemented that, we have reactivated that. Cowboy church is a lot about a renaissance of old school, fundamental beliefs."[18] This kind of vague answer may suffice for people if they find the task of reading the entire Bible daunting, as some cowboy Christians surely would, because it is easier to accept the sage guidance of the pastor about what the Bible says than it is to read from Genesis to Revelation looking for general principles.

Occasionally in conversation, pastors would refer to more specific scriptural passages on this point, which at least serves to narrow the conversation. Jason Taylor, a minister in east Texas, alluded to Genesis 2 to explain man's inherent role as leader, and referred to the Pastoral Epistles—the books of Timothy and Titus—to say that the roles of pastor and elder are limited to men.[19] These particular New Testament books are problematic for understanding leadership roles, partly because they have internal inconsistencies. For instance, although 1 Timothy 3 indicates that both men and women can serve as deacons in the church, other parts of Timothy and Titus proscribe limits for women in the church that appear to impede any kind of leadership, including as deacons. Perhaps more importantly, scholars generally agree that the Pastorals are pseudepigrapha, written much later than authentic Pauline letters but ultimately canonized in the New Testament. The unknown authors' purpose was to address questions about church structure, an issue with which Paul had little concern. As such, the limits these books set for women stand in conflict with earlier Pauline teachings that recognized the equality of all people in Christ and did not indicate any sex-based restrictions in the church. Even if the Pastorals are regarded as equivalent in authority to the Pauline Epistles, it is selective reading to see in them only a message that women should be subordinate to men in both home and church.[20]

One of the more shocking biblical defenses of this point became evident when I was reviewing transcripts of interviews conducted years earlier, and read something I did not remember hearing. A pastor suggested that one might look at New Testament examples of slavery to understand the issue of power dynamics in cowboy church. According to the pastor, rather than Jesus saying that slavery is wrong, Jesus basically tells enslaved people to emulate his example of goodness by being content with their lot in life. "Is he trying to say, 'Be the best you can within the culture you are, and be like me'?" the pastor asked, rhetorically. If that is case, he reasoned, this biblical teaching suggests that women should not challenge the norms of cowboy culture, and instead should just be the best subservient cowgirls they can be. In other words, women should be *like good slaves*. The pastor was not necessarily convinced by this particular interpretation and considered it to be only one among several possibilities. Nonetheless, he was unique among those I interviewed in drawing parallels between women and enslaved people, and furthermore coming away with what he considered a potentially useful instruction for gender roles in the cowboy church.[21]

At other times, the subjugation of women is upheld through ideas about cultural norms, particularly what I call "cowboy essentialism." Paralleling and building upon ideas of gender essentialism, cowboy essentialism posits that cowboys are defined by a narrow slate of unchanging behavioral traits, as are the women who marry them. A hierarchy of leadership—men over women in both home and church—is thus classified as part of the cowboy package; the only difference in this kind of defense is that it is justified through a reliance on cultural norms rather than biblical texts. Jon Coe, for instance, emphasized that he is not against women serving as preachers in general and does not think it is biblically forbidden; nonetheless, he sees male leadership as essential to cowboy culture. "I think you have to deal with what the culture accepts and embraces. And our culture does not embrace women in that role, nor will it," he said. Similarly, Mike Morrow said, "In a cowboy church, in our culture, [even] if we *wanted* to have women preachers and women elders, it wouldn't work." More succinctly, when asked about allowing a female pastor in cowboy church, Gary Morgan simply said, "I just wouldn't see that as something that our audience would respond to."[22] By basing church policy on broad, sweeping statements about what cowboy culture universally accepts and rejects, leaders not only affirm cowboy essentialist notions: they bring them to life and perpetuate them.

Furthermore, cowboy essentialism appears to work dialectically: authentic cowboys are assumed to demonstrate stereotypically masculine traits, and by demonstrating such traits, a man can reinforce his cowboy credibility. In contrast, men referred to as "sissies"—references that I heard in both private interviews and public settings—were uniformly disparaged and considered to be incongruent with the culture. This concept of unacceptable men seemed to be applied primarily to men who do not appear to have a dominant relationship over women in general. For instance, one CCU speaker stated, "Most men *that are men* don't want to be told what to do by a woman, other than their wives."[23] In other words, if men allow women to tell them what to do, their masculinity is implicitly called into question. Among the many problematic implications of this statement is that a man is not fully human in the way God intended if he so much as takes instruction from a woman. Real cowboys, who are "men," would never do such a thing, as I was frequently reminded. "A man will hit the road if he sees a woman is calling the shots," said an AFCC clinic instructor. "The culture is still male dominant," elaborated a CCU speaker, and "women in leadership is one of the things that deters men."[24] It becomes rather unclear in all of this whether leaders actually believe cowboy culture people only respond to male leaders, or if they are simply trying to limit the church population to people who agree with this division of power.

At other times, the reason for women's subjugation is cast as a confusing combination of both biblical origins and cowboy essentialism. For instance, during a CCU session, one speaker advised that women "have a place where God intends them to be in ministry"; he then listed various jobs in the church associated with cooking and the care of children. But a few sentences later, the same man said "it's the world" that made this separation of duties, not God. Yet, because challenging core ideas within cowboy culture might drive men away from church, women must be relegated to roles that are culturally acceptable to cowboys.[25] That night, sitting by the arena, a pastor's wife expressed to me that she was uncomfortable with that message. "Just because some men in the cowboy culture won't take orders from a woman, that shouldn't stand in the way of women being able to hold those roles," she said. She added that the distinction between women's roles being God-given and being culturally constructed is significant, and leaders' attempts to blur that distinction are disingenuous, making their reasoning appear insincere.

Another way the focus on men is supported is through a variety of outside sources, especially those that speak to issues of gender and church attendance and that appear to provide objective validation to their approach. One of the most commonly referenced books among cowboy church leaders is *Why Men Hate Going to Church*, written by television producer/professional speaker David Murrow. In fact, leaders not only refer to it: they lavish praise upon it. The book is "phenomenal," gushed one pastor at a seminar before reading a passage aloud, adding, "it changed my life."[26] Murrow accurately observes that while Christian church leadership in North America has been dominated by men, its actual membership has been numerically dominated by women. Rehashing the muscular Christian argument and framing it with plenty of gender essentialism, Murrow says that women have caused the church institution to become feminine, or perhaps effeminate, over time. Churches now typically focus on nurturing relationships, sensitive expression, humility, safety, and predictability, all of which he classifies as being core feminine values and therefore deterrents to all men except "soft men." According to Murrow, if churches focus on masculine values like challenge, action, risk, danger, independence, and fun, they would attract more masculine men, and according to Murrow, masculine men attract masculine men.[27] Although cowboy church leaders regard Murrow's book as unbiased research proving an effective church growth strategy, technically it is more akin to pop psychology because its content is essentially based on Murrow's personal observations and opinions. At times he pulls in secondary sources to support points of observation, such as polls from the Barna Group or references from writers such as Leon J. Podles or James Dobson, but a careful read of the book demonstrates that his prescriptive ideas about the connection between gender and church attendance are based on his own musings.[28] Nonetheless, the cowboy audience inexplicably treats it as an important and original study, perhaps because it aligns so well with their approach and therefore creates external validation. As Mike Morrow put it, "It's a great book. But it's cowboy church, is all it was."[29]

The Use and Misuse of Statistics

A seemingly more reliable way that cowboy church leaders use outside sources is by referencing statistics related to church attendance and gender. Pastor after pastor repeated to me that studies have proven that if a church can find a way to engage men, then those men will also bring their wives and children, thus building the church membership and making it a family-centered space. This is partly rooted in cowboy essentialism, which frames the typical cowboy family as a heterosexual married couple with children who all want to spend time together in culturally specific endeavors, such as arena activities. "If we get cowboy Bob, cowgirl Jane and cowgirl Shirley are going to follow," said one CCU instructor, echoing a point I heard often. The opposite approach does not work, they always added: if a church works to attract women, there will be little impact on whether their husbands or children will attend. Leaders frequently offered statistics on this point, eager to show that their approach is rooted in something objective and verifiable. For instance, one pastor told me, "If you get the man to come to the church, you get the family in a high percentage of the time. It's like 80 percent."[30] This impressive statistic varied a bit depending on the source: for example, the CCU handbook claims that families will follow the father into church 88 percent of the time, and the AFCC handbook says the statistic is actually 95 percent.

As a person who appreciates solid research studies, I was eager to read and evaluate the information for myself. Therefore, when pastors mentioned it, I often asked for more information. But despite their expertise on the findings, no one, it seemed, could tell me what the study was called, who had done the research, or where I could get a copy. Instead, they said things like "it's broadly available," and "you can find them online." From this, I inferred that it was likely they had not actually read the findings, perhaps only being told about them or seeing some kind of summary. And in fact, when I tried finding a study of this sort in databases of academic research, I came up empty. Even the vast online resources of the Barna Group, whose findings are sometimes cited by cowboy pastors, did not reveal any studies of this kind, nor did related books they have produced such as *Churchless* and *Grow Your Church from the Outside In*. "Widely available" turned out to be only the first of the overstatements regarding this study.

It was a thesis footnote that led me to the apparent source. In 2003, Robbie Low, a former Anglican vicar who later converted to Catholicism, published an article called "The Truth About Men & Church" in an online Christian magazine; it was subsequently reposted on numerous websites. Low writes that he "whiled away the long winter evenings" reading an obscure book about various minorities in European countries, and that some of the findings about Switzerland, in particular, were revelatory for him.[31] The book's chapter on Switzerland is predominantly an analysis of its 1990 census, but also incorporates data from other sources, including a large international study known as the FFS, or Fertility and Family Survey, the Swiss leg of which was conducted in 1994–1995. Two paragraphs and a table about generational religious continuity, which rely on the FFS data, indicate that in Switzerland, between 33–44 percent of people who had religious fathers were themselves religious as adults, which is an interesting statistic but not nearly as dramatic as the 80+ percent that cowboy church leaders claim.[32] Based on this, Low concludes, "It is the religious practice of the father of the family that, above all, determines the future attendance at or absence from church of the children." Low's article then ruminates and elaborates on this idea, imploring men to take back their proper leadership roles in society and church. He dramatically writes, "You cannot buck the biology of the created order. Father's influence, from the determination of a child's sex by the implantation of his seed to the funerary rites surrounding his passing, is out of all proportion to his allotted, and severely diminished role, in Western liberal society . . . . You cannot keep the children if you do not keep the men." Although Low is correct in the way he reports the numbers about religious participation, his conclusions seem premature. Without more information about the particulars of the Swiss version of the study, such as the phrasing of questions and the demographics of respondents, we cannot know whether there is actually a causal relationship between the father's religiosity and the adult child's, or simply a correlation that is rooted in another unidentified factor. The obscure book he read includes none of this information, as the two relevant paragraphs within it are actually focused on whether adults remain in the same denomination as their parents.[33] To assume this study's findings can be directly applied to families within the cowboy culture, then, is an intellectual stretch.

And yet, considering the emphasis that cowboy church leaders place on this statistical point, we must consider whether this information is at all applicable to the United States. Although Low claims that the Swiss context is readily comparable to that of both the United Kingdom and the United States, he provides no defense for such an assertion. Switzerland is a small, wealthy country defined by its worldwide political neutrality. Most of the Swiss cantons, which are akin to states, are quite religiously homogenous as well as defined by the dominance of one of four nationally recognized languages. Unlike the Protestant majority of the United States, Switzerland has almost equal numbers of Catholics and Protestants, and nearly a quarter of its population declines to identify with any particular form of institutional religion.[34] For many people, the social and cultural differences between the two countries would make it evident that comparisons of religious patterns between them could be considered weak, at best. Furthermore, studies on Americans have shown that the influence of family behavior on the religious participation of their offspring is particularly different in Catholic and Protestant families, with the children of one or more Catholic parents exhibiting much higher rates of involvement.[35] If that same tendency is found among the Swiss—and it is unclear that it is—then the likelihood of a high number of Catholic respondents in the Swiss survey is surely one important factor in interpreting its results.

Religious patterns in the United States are best considered on their own, without comparison to other countries with such different social compositions. Unfortunately, very few longitudinal American studies that relate to parental influence on religious involvement actually track religious changes from childhood to adulthood, and therefore relevant results must be culled from research focused on other issues. After extensive searching, I located three small studies that supported the assertion that a father's church participation is particularly influential on the religiosity of his children, though one was focused only on Lutherans and another was focused only on African American men.[36] But, counterbalancing these were four studies that indicated a mother's religious influence is more important than the father's, and five studies that indicated neither the mother nor the father is particularly dominant in religious influence.[37] None of this adds up to overwhelming evidence that shows a father predominates in influencing the religiosity of his offspring. The significance of these results for cowboy churches is that if they genuinely believe a particular statistic is true, and then they observe that their member families do not bear that out, they will think they are failing in some way. The real problem is that the statistic they are starting with is not correct for the American context, and expecting that more than 80 percent of families will follow a man to cowboy church sets these churches up for deep disappointment in the long term.

While all of the defenses for the myopic focus on men in cowboy church are problematic, it also seems that the concern about male attenuation may be overblown. Despite the hundreds of articles written about the disparity among male and female religious participation rates in the United States, the actual gap is not huge. Pew Forum statistics from 2014 indicate that 45 percent of evangelical Protestants were male and 55 percent were female; the United States census for that same year showed men made up 49 percent of the general population. Thus, the different ratio reflected in churches was in fact quite small. Even the Barna Group points out that the gender gap in active church involvement "is not huge and has been steadily closing," implying that a focus on men among evangelicals should not be a particular priority.[38] As indicated earlier, precise statistics about male and female religious participation in cowboy churches are not available. During my five years of observation, I always attempted headcounts in the churches I visited. Most of the time, my rough counts of those present in the service mirrored the national church attendance statistic of 45 percent male, 55 percent female, although there were a couple of exceptions where the number seemed quite close to 50/50.[39] Even if my rough estimates are wrong, they are not wildly wrong, which ultimately leads me to conclude that cowboy churches are not necessarily closing the gender gap in religious attendance; instead, their membership is comparable in gender proportions to that found in other conservative Protestant churches. All of the talk about needing to be male-centric and male led is having little discernable impact on how many men actually attend.

The Nazarene Double Standard

Perhaps nowhere is the tension about women's leadership more keenly felt than in Nazarene circles. The Church of the Nazarene licenses and ordains women for ministry and has done so since its founding, with its 1898 constitutional statement reading, "We recognize the equal right of both men and women to all offices of the Church of the Nazarene, including ministry." Although the number of women pastoring Nazarene churches fell during the mid-twentieth century and remained low for several decades, in recent years that number has been increasing.[40] And yet, the Nazarene cowboy churches do not actively support women in ministry, discouraging it so heavily in seminars that one would almost think there is a specific policy against it. In fact, some pastors do think it is a rule, and were surprised when I would point out that it is not.

At higher levels of denominational leadership, some Nazarenes have expressed concerns about what it means to limit women's participation in one aspect of the church, and they indicate that it remains an ongoing conversation. A man who works in new church development worried that, even as an unofficial policy, its consequences might cut short the life of the cowboy church project. Not only will women be turned off by it, he said, but eventually there may be a retention issue with youth and young adults because the policy will conflict with American values of gender equality being enacted all around them. When I raised the issue with district superintendent Rob McDonald, he agreed that what cowboy churches teach to children should be part of the conversation. "We need to be careful about that," he said, and indicated that it would not be right to pass off a cultural practice as being biblical, especially to impressionable children.[41] And yet some members feel that is already happening. One man attending a CCU pointed out that in the arena the night before, men had clearly treated the women as equals. Why, then, should they suddenly be unequal the moment everyone steps from the arena into the church? Furthermore, what if his granddaughter were to say she wants to grow up to be a minister: how would he explain that limitation to her? As another man put it, it seems that in lowering barriers for men, the church has raised new barriers against women.[42] All of these aspects of the issue fester under the surface, making the long-term Nazarene commitment to the full cowboy church ideology a serious question. Though cowboy churches are creating new growth for the denomination, it will likely have to decide whether a doctrinal compromise is worth that trade-off. Their only other option is to support and encourage any woman who feels called to pastor a cowboy church, which would also require lesson and language changes at CCU seminars, as well as attitudinal shifts among Nazarene colleagues in ministry.

Ginger Hayes may be the first woman to put the issue to the test, because she intends to prove incorrect the idea that cowboys will not respond to a female pastor. When we first met in Colorado, Hayes tipped her hat back, looked me straight in the eye, and calmly said she does not need any man's permission to start a cowboy church. "And I won't get it anyway," she added.[43] Hayes is a cowgirl who grew up ranching in Montana. She is licensed for ministry by the Church of the Nazarene, and for the past few years she has been preparing to launch a ministry that involves horses and arena activities. The cowboy church emphasis on active engagement and challenge is something she is particularly invested in. "This is good for women too!" she says. "This isn't just men. This is learning for adults, because adults seem to need a kinesthetic type approach." Rooted as she is in cowboy culture, Hayes does not believe that the gender of a pastor is crucial to cowboys; rather, what matters are the person's credentials, character, and skills. Every person has a range of abilities, she says, so limiting women's contributions in the church is shortsighted. "I'm not gifted in the kitchen," she says, but she can ride a horse alongside someone and help that person talk through problems, whether they are male or female. She anticipates being flexible about responsibilities within her church in order to best respond to the needs of congregants, which will mean that positions of leadership will be open to both men and women. Thus far, Hayes has not met any other women who are planning to go into cowboy ministry, and she does not think that very many would want to. But it should be God's decision, not man's, she explains, and that means they should not be told that ministry is closed to them.

I asked Hayes to tell me about her ministerial path, which included years spent in the Southern Baptist faith and various forms of lay ministry, as well as endeavors in visual art and equine-assisted therapy. "God created me this way," she stated. "I am a cowboy. I grew up a cowboy. This is my home and this is my culture." Hayes feels called by God to open a cowboy church on her land at the Rocking H Ranch in Missouri, a plan that cowboy church leaders have not encouraged. At CCU in 2012, both

Hayes and her husband made it clear that they did not appreciate leaders' attitude toward her aspirations, especially considering the Nazarene doctrine affirming female ministers. But ultimately she will not allow them to dissuade her. If necessary, she will open her church independently, and she is steeled for criticism, knowing she will have to prove herself.

Jon Coe, one of the leading figures within Nazarene cowboy churches, thinks the present cowboy culture is not ready for female leadership, but he admits that most things change over time. Using a business example, he pointed out that people who sold cassettes and vinyl and refused to adapt their products to changing times eventually went out of business. Somewhat reluctantly, Coe then said, "Who knows who God will use. I might bite my tongue on this, but if a lady came to me and said, 'God has called me to start a cowboy church, and I feel led of it,' who am I to say that God didn't call you to do that? I'm going to support her and help her, and tell her what I see as the fallacies of it all, and leave that up to her and God. But if she's successful and has twelve people there, then it would be twelve people that I woulda never reached." Coe echoed this sentiment at several points in our conversation, explaining that God is his ultimate authority and there may be a time when God sends a woman to minister to cowboys, in which case he would obey God and offer his support.[44] Coe has not yet had to prove his sincerity on this point, but Hayes or another woman may force the issue in the near future.

Surveying Women about their Views

The perplexing cornucopia of male rhetoric about women's roles is only one side of the story. The views of female cowboy church members tell a different story, and their perceptions about their roles in the church diverge from and correspond with men's ideas in interesting ways. Based on passing comments made by pastors in interviews, I discerned that cases of women objecting to limited roles in church arise regularly. But pastors never seemed concerned about it, describing the situations matter-of-factly. "I had one lady running around in here who was furious, *furious*, about it!" Shane Winters said with a smirk, and he noted that at least one had left his church over the issue. Mike Morrow commented, "About once a year we'll have somebody who wants to buck, wants to know why they can't preach, or why we don't have women elders. But every single time, number one, they leave, and number two, they came from a church background that had female pastors, and 90 percent of them was charismatic." And, exuding his trademark individualism, Jason Taylor said, "We tell 'em, there's probably seventy-five churches you just drove past that women can run all the time. Go there! . . . We say, 'I love you, goodbye.'" Taylor, however, demonstrated equal nonchalance about men who have left his church for any reason, adding, "I mean, I've made so many people mad that left here, it ain't even funny."[45]

An opportunity for me to learn about women's thoughts on the matter arose through the Cowgirl Get Together, a conference for women held annually in Tyler, Texas. The idea for the conference formulated when two pastors' wives approached musician and cowboy church member Michelle Carson about starting an event for women. They each felt that there were too few opportunities for women to shine in cowboy church. As Carson summarized it, a decade ago "there really wasn't anything for women to do in the cowboy church, except to cook and clean up, unless they were participating in rodeo events."[46] Additionally, from her time spent traveling to churches playing music, she had seen many women whom she described as "broken," who might benefit from learning more about the concept of God's grace. Carson, a lifelong Southern Baptist who identified more as a tomboy than a frilly female, had always recoiled at the idea of women's ministry, and generally tried to avoid it. But suddenly, she felt like she might be able to offer something "real" to women, providing an environment in which they could be themselves, "hoot and holler," and perhaps hear someone speak who would give them a new spiritual perspective. Thus was the Cowgirl Get Together born.

Carson held the first event in 2007 at her own church in Athens, Texas. Although the building only had seating for three hundred, nearly four hundred and fifty women showed up. She recalled people cramming into every free spot, sitting atop bales of hay at the back and on blankets on the floor. Since then, the event has moved and grown, though its format has remained essentially the same: female speakers give talks that focus on God's grace and Christian empowerment, interspersed with a live band. The speakers do not come from cowboy churches; rather, they come from all over the country and are renowned for their books, speaking tours, and radio shows. When I asked Carson about this, she said that she seeks speakers who are theologically sound, convey authenticity, and are experienced in their faith journey; cowboy church women are more often new to their faith, so not appropriate for the job. In addition, she tries to bring in people who can speak about issues that are different from what is typically discussed in the women's home churches.

I attended the annual Cowgirl Get Together in 2014, which was a sold-out event with over two thousand attendees. It is essentially two half-days, during which bands play and speakers present in the large ballroom of a conference center. In the hallways and other rooms around the building, dozens of vendors set up shop. That year, the program included professional speakers/authors Michele Cushatt, Lurna Cumby, Shellie Rushing Tomlinson, and audience favorite Laura Petherbridge, all of whom imbued their talks with explicit Christian messages in addition to offering secular wisdom. The conference is billed as a gathering of faithful women, and each speaker seeks to empower and inspire listeners both as Christians and as women living in a challenging world. The event does not include a structure for women to meet and mingle in smaller groups, and it would be quite easy for someone to come and go without ever engaging with others. Thus, while many women are motivated anew by the speakers and some even have salvation experiences, it is much more of a personal event than one that fosters networking or leadership development.

At the conference, I set up a vendor table that was nestled in among booths selling jewelry, religious paraphernalia, and purses with handgun compartments. My table, decorated with pink and cowprint tablecloths, invited anyone who attended cowboy church to fill out a survey form. There were periodic lulls in the conference program, and for those women who had already explored the shopping options, spending a few minutes at my table was a way to pass the time. Some came in church groups, wearing matching t-shirts and roaming around in clusters. Others came in pairs with a friend or family member. As women filled out the survey, I was often able to chat with them about some of the questions, or about their church. However, I was disappointed that few women demonstrated serious interest in what I was doing, and almost no one took the project information sheet I offered. The survey itself asked ten questions plus voluntary demographic data, and one of my main goals was to find out women's perspectives on their limited leadership roles within cowboy church. I ultimately came away with two hundred and sixty-five usable forms, on which the following discussion and statistics are based.[47] While this number represents just a small portion of cowboy church attendees, to date it is the only survey of its type and thus an appropriate starting point for inquiry.

Demographically, the survey respondents were diverse in a number of ways. Their ages were spread surprisingly evenly among ten-year brackets from thirty to sixty-nine, with far fewer respondents in the eighteen to twenty-nine and seventy-plus categories. They represented approximately sixty-five different cowboy churches primarily located in East, Central, and North Texas; fewer than 3 percent of respondents attended a church in another state. Sixty-seven percent of the women indicated they had lived most of their lives in Texas, but the real number may actually be higher: 17 percent left the question blank, and among the remaining 16 percent were nonspecific answers such as "the West" or "South," either of which might also refer to Texas. In terms of education, 28 percent indicated completion of some college and/or trade school, and an additional 27 percent had earned a college or graduate degree. However, each of those categories was dwarfed by those who had only a high school diploma or less, at 38 percent.[48] One interesting factor was that 63 percent of the respondents had been attending a cowboy church for three or more years, and many for upwards of five; fewer than 10 percent had been attending less than one year. This is a good indication that the overall responses represent attitudes of people who are committed and experienced cowboy church members, as well as coming from a range of ages and education levels.

From my perspective, the two most important questions on the survey were the following: (1) Do you think that women have enough opportunities for leadership in cowboy church? And (2) Do you think it would be good for women to be able to serve as elders and/or pastors in cowboy church? For each of these questions, women could mark yes, no, or uncertain, and there was also a space inviting written comments. My expectation was that individuals would give congruent answers to the two questions: that is, I anticipated that people who thought women should be able to serve as pastors would also think that there were not enough leadership opportunities. However, that turned out not to be the case; a great number of women had varied answers on the two questions, and sometimes wrote in comments that helped to explain.

In response to the first question about having enough leadership opportunities, a large majority agreed that they do, at 72 percent. The second-largest group, at 17 percent, was uncertain, and only a little over 11 percent answered no. Regardless of whether they answered this question in the affirmative or negative, many women chose to use the comments section to list areas in which they are able to lead, and these lists mirrored each other. Thus, women who agreed that there are enough opportunities for leadership wrote things such as: "teach children," "chuck wagon team," and "we have a women's ministry," and women who said they do not have enough opportunities wrote comments such as "unless it's with youth or kitchen" and "only in children's programs at our church." This question did not elicit as many written comments as the next, but based on the limited answers, those who are in favor of the status quo expressed that it is important for men to have most leadership positions, with some indicating that the "biblical place" of women is as helpers. Comments supporting the opposite perspective included "women are not given opportunities to serve at higher levels," and "I believe there is an awesome outcry for women to be used in the ministry." In sum, this data shows that women agree about what types of leadership opportunities are available to them in cowboy church—things related to children, other women, and food—and it indicates that although there is a small percentage who hold a bitter distaste for this situation, the vast majority feels satisfied about the opportunities open to them.

Considering this level of satisfaction, I was surprised at the responses on the question of whether women should be permitted to serve as pastors and/or elders in cowboy church. Thirty percent of the women said "yes," with another 23 percent indicating uncertainty on the issue. Less than half, at 46 percent, definitively said "no," which is significantly different from what cowboy church leaders maintain about women's beliefs.[49] As with the varied defenses cowboy church leaders give for prohibiting women's leadership, women's reasoning for agreeing or disagreeing with the policy also spanned several different types of answers.

Some women, for instance, clearly consider this a straightforward issue of modernity and gender equality. Agreeing that women should be able to serve as pastors and elders, their comments about it included "equal opportunity," "broaden the view," "women are just as important as men," and "times are changing." With aspiration, one of the younger women wrote, "In our day, maybe more likely." Though many of the comments appeared to reflect secular values of equality, there were also those who framed it religiously, writing things such as "God loves us women as much as the men," and "I feel God calls everyone to preach." One surprising comment came from a woman who identified herself as the wife of a cowboy church pastor, who wrote, "If they're called, we're open to it." This provides further evidence that individual cowboy churches may in fact approach the issue quite differently from one another. The numerous written comments related to equality stand in contrast with leaders' rhetoric, which generalizes that cowboy Christian women are "traditional" and want men to step up and lead so that they are relieved of the burden.

Because cowboy church leaders rarely address this question from the per-spective of gender equality, they fail to engage with the actual concerns of a large number of female members, which is likely to exacerbate the conflict over time.

The Bible was another source that women relied on for understand-ing this issue. Unlike the equality argument, biblical teachings are dis-cussed by both men and women and can be used to provide support for those on either side of the question. In alignment with what some pastors espouse, many women's comments indicated belief that the Bible states that women are not supposed to serve in the roles of pastor and elder. "It's not biblical," wrote a number of women; or as one said, "Bible is clear about women pastors—they aren't." In a similar vein, others commented that men should be spiritual heads of both the home and the church. These comments are in alignment with what cowboy church leaders say women think, and are similarly vague in identifying the precise biblical source material. Perhaps the most unintentionally honest comment came from the woman who wrote, "*I was told* that in the Bible women aren't to do that."[50] Demonstrating the malleability of the text, the Bible is also the basis for other respondents' belief that women should be allowed to serve as pastors and elders. As one wrote, "There was a female disciple at one point, and if Jesus could ask her to speak for him, then we should be able to speak." Said another, "God used women in the Bible so what's the dif-ference today. I think we need to realize that they are just as valuable and God wants to use them." And one other simply wrote, "This is man's law, not God's."

A small number of women gave reasons for male-only ministry that related to maintaining the status quo of their church, but their answers did not particularly reveal where they stood on the concept of cowboy essentialism. For instance, a few comments explicitly stated that the point of cowboy church is to get men involved, so if male leadership helps achieve that, then it is acceptable to them. Comments like this one—"I think cowboys relate best to elders if they're men"—implicitly suggest that the respondent is concerned about what makes men of the cowboy cul-ture most comfortable, and perhaps implies ideas of cowboy essentialism. Other respondents were in the same ballpark of thought, though they did not mention cowboy culture specifically. "If women had say, some men wouldn't come," wrote one, and therefore she disagreed that it would be good to let women serve. Said another, "Men are kind-of babies. If they don't feel like they run things, they won't participate"; the same woman, however, also checked the "yes" box that women should in fact be allowed to pastor. One woman, who was uncertain about this question on the original survey form, was leaning toward "no" two years later. In a follow-up interview, she explained that there is a palpable gender bias among the men in her congregation, who "take the Bible to say men are the head of the household and church."[51] Because of the social disruption that women's leadership might cause in her particular church, she was coming to see that it might not be a good thing in that context; but, she wrote, "I certainly believe women are capable." She and others implied that they do not believe that men are superior in the realm of spiritual leadership, but that the women basically humor them to keep them in church.

To understand the survey responses more thoroughly, I looked for other patterns. For instance, though I expected there might be a relationship, I found that the duration of a woman's membership in cowboy church was not correlated with belief patterns about female leadership roles. I also anticipated there might be a relationship between geography and beliefs; specifically, I wondered if women who had spent the majority of their lives living somewhere other than Texas might be more likely to believe that all roles of leadership should be open to women. However, the statistics on women from outside of Texas were not dramatically different from the overall survey results, and no single state had a large enough numeric representation to tabulate it individually. On the other hand, parsing the data by age and by education did reveal interesting points for consideration.

Age appears to be an important factor when it comes to opinions about women being able to serve as pastors and elders; in general, younger people were more likely to say that women should be able to do these things, whereas older women were more likely to say the opposite. Thirty-four percent of survey respondents under age forty said women should be able to serve as pastors; 28 percent said they were uncertain; and only 38 percent said no. This may be an important consideration as the cowboy church moves forward, because it is possible that the larger ratio of liberal attitudes among younger women represents generational differences in thinking. If these women continue to be dissatisfied with the situation, it may become a sticking point to which leaders are forced to respond. In contrast, older female attendees were more likely to agree with the principle of male ministry. Among women ages fifty to sixty-nine, more than half—54 percent—said that these roles should be restricted to men, and only 24 percent said women should also be able to serve as pastors and elders.[52] The statistics for women in the forty to forty-nine age group were extremely close to the overall survey averages, and therefore did not offer any particular insight.

Education also appears to have some correlation with the question of women being able to serve as pastors and elders, but it was in a direction that I found surprising. I expected that women with more formal education would be more likely to say that women should be allowed to pastor, but this was not the case. In the overall survey, we recall that 30 percent of respondents said women should be allowed to serve as pastors/elders, and 23 percent were uncertain about it. Among those respondents with at least a college degree, only 19 percent said yes to this question; 36 percent of women with some college or trade school said yes; and 32 percent of those with a high school diploma or less said yes. That last point is especially significant because women in that educational category make up a much larger percentage of respondents; thus, in raw numbers they represent many more church members. In terms of uncertainty on this question, 26 percent of college graduates were uncertain, 19 percent of those with some college or trade school were uncertain, and 25 percent of women with a diploma or less were uncertain. Of course, neither age nor education are fixed. All women will grow older, and many women will continue their formal education, and both factors may potentially cause attitudinal shifts.

It must also be noted that the very large group of "uncertain" women is a crucial factor in the long run. It is nearly impossible to predict what might make them decide one way or the other about this question, as well as how important that answer will be to them. People are rarely fully satisfied with any church; therefore, if they are generally comfortable, they can often overlook things that bother them. An example of this emerged in follow-up, when one woman who strongly believed women should be able to pastor said that she will be unlikely to leave the church even without expanded roles for women, because "sometimes you can't fight the system." There are also women who have no strong feelings on the issue in either direction. They do not aspire to leadership of any kind, and are not bothered that men have decided the positions are not open to them. In conversation, one woman in this group said that as a lifelong Baptist she had never been exposed to a female pastor, so she had never really thought about it. Then she turned to her friend, standing nearby, and asked, "Isn't there a verse in the Bible that says women are not to lead men?" Neither of them could not remember where it was, but they nodded in agreement that they thought it was in there somewhere. However, she essentially shrugged off the issue as unimportant to her. Certainly, her blasé attitude about the question represents the views of a portion of woman in the cowboy church, though it had not occurred to me to list "don't care" as an answer option on the survey form.

Other parts of the survey asked women open-ended questions about why they first attended, what makes them continue attending, what they like best about cowboy church, and what they think could be improved. Not a single person wrote in an answer suggesting that it is a relief to have men lead, or that they are glad men are finally in charge because it frees them from an unwanted responsibility. Women did not refer to statistics about male attendance, or indicate that their children happily go to church because the father does, or say anything about the church reinforcing their family unit. Women said nothing to suggest a belief in unchanging cowboy essentialist qualities or that all cowboys are inherently incapable of responding to a female leader. There were only two comments that suggested respondents' belief in gender essentialism was a reason to limit women's roles: "Women tend to get too emotional," said one; "women are too judgmental," said the other. All of this stands in marked contrast to what leaders say women believe. The overall findings from this survey show that while leaders think the vast majority of cowboy church women believe in and support a male-only ministry, the actual proportion seems to be much smaller than they think, at less than half. Furthermore, the men and the women are not in harmony about the reasoning for their positions. While total uniformity of belief and practice should never be expected, it appears that male leaders and average women in the cowboy church are significantly out of sync on this issue, which does not bode well for future church stability.

Female Leadership in Rodeo and Racetrack Ministry

From my observations, gender distinctions appear to be a less contested issue in the greater cowboy Christian world beyond organized cowboy churches, though there may still be hidden or unspoken disparities. The ethos of rodeo church, for example, seems to contrast with that of the cowboy church; through site visits I observed that many rodeo ministries include women in visible leadership roles, which is particularly surprising considering the male domination within the sport itself. Rodeo church services are attended predominantly by fans with only small numbers of rodeo participants and their families present; nonetheless, one would expect that the rodeo-attending audience has a great degree of overlap with the target audience(s) defined by cowboy church leaders. Rodeo organizations do not typically contract with religious groups, nor does any single organization control rodeo ministry; thus, many ministries voluntarily offer services in a decentralized way based on their own networks. Cowboys for Christ continues to be active on various rodeo circuits, and there are many independent ministries that offer services at rodeos small and large, amateur and professional. A majority of cowboy pastors I spoke with had been involved in rodeo ministry at some point during their career, even if only briefly.

One place where gender divisions in leadership seem minimal is in the Cowboys for Christ organization. In an interview with current president Dave Harvey, his inclusive language stood out to me; I observed that every time he mentioned cowboys, he also included cowgirls in the same phrase. For example, he listed questions he is likely to ask when speaking with a person who feels called to cowboy ministry: "How are you involved with the livestock industry, and do you feel comfortable in ministering to cowboys and cowgirls?" He also named both when specifying what kind of testimony he prefers to publish in the *Christian Ranchman*: "Because we're cowgirls and cowboys, and we want to relate to them. They relate to real people. It makes a lot of difference."[53] In these and other instances, his automatic inclusion of both men and women seemed to be a natural reflection of his train of thought about whom he is serving. He noted that CFC has always allowed for female pastors and licenses and ordains them, and he spoke positively about several women who had started and/or led chapters over the years. Recent directories show that there continue to be CFC chapters all across the country with female presidents. It therefore does not appear that gender inequality has been an issue within CFC as a national organization, though one cannot rule out the possibility of exceptions on regional or chapter levels.

Although Harvey mentioned that there have been ebbs and flows in women's interest in cowboy ministry over the years, he did not offer thoughts on possible causes. Through our conversations, I inferred that gender parity is simply not an issue on the CFC radar; if inequality is present, there is a chance it would not be noticed except by those affected. For instance, I tried to ask Harvey about a CFC brochure entitled "5 Things a Cowgirl Should Know." Written in approximately 1975 by volunteer Cecilia

Bowling of Fort Worth, it remains available both in print and online. At the time of its first publication, some women were already feeling ignored within the cowboy Christian world, evidenced by one who wrote in to the *Christian Ranchman* praising them for it, saying, "It's about time we women got a tract."[54] The brochure instructs women on "how to look like a girl; how to act like a lady; how to think like a man; how to work like a dog; and how to live like a Christian." Biblical verses are used as evidence for God's wishes regarding women's attire and behavior. Women are also advised to work tirelessly without gratitude and, in competitive situations, "choose to win or lose like a lady." When I asked Harvey what he thought about this brochure, he said it was written by an individual cowboy Christian, as many CFC tracts were. Characterizing the content of a number of different brochures they have published, he said, it is "almost like their personal testimony." He did not seem to digest my suggestion that the content might be problematic and paternalistic, especially considering there is no similar tract for men. Harvey jumped up from his chair and dug through a filing cabinet, emerging with what he considered a parallel brochure, "Five Complete Steps in How to Become a Top Hand," and then said he appreciates it when members contribute this way. The five steps for men are all points of religious faith, such as "believe Jesus died for your sin," and "admit you can't save yourself from sin." Thus, this brochure offers no parallel instructions about gendered behavior in the everyday world. In fact, none of the many other brochures I acquired from CFC enumerated suggestions about behavior or appearance directed toward men. In the vast territory of CFC outreach ministries, it is easy to understand why the content of one decades-old brochure would seem irrelevant. And yet, its continued availability undermines the wider inclusion of women that distinguishes CFC as an organization in the cowboy Christian world.

In the other closely related network, racetrack chaplaincy, the record of gender equality has been somewhat mixed. From its inception, both the national board of the RTCA as well its regional subcouncils have had women actively involved in the organization. In the 1990s, after many years on the board, Tanna Dawson served as RTCA board president, during which time she opened up its meetings to any spouses—most of them female—who wished to attend.[55] During the 1980s and '90s, Carol White Marino served first as an officer on the board and then as the acting Executive Director (ED) of RTCA for two different stretches of time. It is noteworthy that she worked as the administrator during a period when financial troubles prevented the organization from hiring an ED, because it implies that her work was not fully compensated, if at all. And yet, despite women like these working at high levels in the RTCA, women becoming actual racetrack chaplains seems to have been a different kind of hurdle. As early as 1974, Beatrice Price, who was credentialed as a chaplain, was considered for a position at Liberty Bell Race Track by the local RTCA committee. But it was not to be, because "race trackers said they were just getting use [*sic*] to a 'chaplain' and were not ready for a woman as yet."[56] Over the years, numerous women served as racetrack co-chaplains with their husbands, usually in an unofficial capacity, and there are records of solo female chaplains working at tracks in Kentucky in the 1980s and New York in the 1990s. Rose Salios recalled that she enjoyed working as a ministry team with her husband at two tracks in the 1980s. She took care of chaplaincy needs at one track while her husband traveled out of town to the second several days a week. But the job came with challenges, such as learning to ignore those who admonished her that "the race track is no place for a woman."[57] Although one can search for and find records of women such as these working in racetrack chaplaincy and in higher levels of the RTCA, none of their stories are easily obtained. Their relative absence from the history may be another indication that racetrack ministry has not been a particularly welcoming environment for them.

Like Salios, longtime track chaplain Lee Alphen has made a practice of ignoring people who think racetrack ministry is not appropriate for women. "I don't have time for that foolishness," she says, explaining that she has always shrugged off gender-based criticism and just focused on the ministry tasks in front of her.[58] Alphen, who grew up in the world of horse racing, worked on the backside of various race tracks through her college years, and she later earned a master's degree in theology. In 1975, Alphen was invited to assist when a Baptist pastor affiliated with the RTCA founded a ministry at Rockingham Park in New Hampshire, where she was working as a veterinary assistant. Although she did not say it outright, Alphen implied that their relationship was somewhat contentious due to theological differences. The pastor departed after a year and, after a brief stint by a second RTCA-affiliated minister, Alphen became the sole chaplain at Rockingham Park. It was her impression that the RTCA was not keen on her chaplaincy, both because she was female and also because she was Catholic. Undaunted, she proceeded without them, serving as the Rockingham Park chaplain for thirty-five years and expanding her work to nearby tracks, including Suffolk Downs.

Over the phone, Alphen's voice reveals no sentimentality toward the RTCA, though she does describe it as "a good organization." In approximately 2001, RTCA director Enrique Torres visited her to learn about the scope of her track chaplaincy. In addition to charitable programs and ministerial services, under Alphen's direction Rockingham Park had created an on-site day-care facility for workers' children, and had also built a chapel on the grounds. She had constructed a strong network of community support for the track chaplaincy, with many local churches regularly participating in ministry events on site. Torres, impressed by her work, wanted Alphen to become involved with the RTCA, and invited her to speak at a conference. She recalls, "I sort-of thought to myself, 'What do I need them for?'" Nonetheless, she agreed. But she implied the event was disappointing, and from her perspective her gender still caused her to be a marginal figure in racetrack ministry, if not also her religion.

In the days when Salty Roberts was walking the shedrows, racetracks were primarily male environments, with women rarely working as trainers, grooms, or jockeys. That is no longer the case, and today women occupy all levels of work on both front and back sides of the track. Alphen is probably not the only one who experienced gender prejudice within the RTCA, although she makes it clear that it was individuals, rather than the organization as a whole, who marginalized her. Over time, she learned to confront people head-on when they suggested women had no place in ministry, but ultimately, she says, "It's their problem, not mine." Because the RTCA's record appears to be somewhat mixed on gender equality, one might say it exists as a midpoint between the stringency of cowboy church pastors who deplore the idea of women pastors, and the more carefree nature of rodeo church, where both men and women serve in ministry roles.

One of the best conversations I had about this issue was with Larry Miller, whose cowboy church in Henrietta, Texas is among the oldest. When I visited in 2013, prior to the worship service I attended the adult Bible study, which has been taught by a woman for many years. To me, her lesson was nearly identical to a sermon, and in conversation she also spoke about leading devotionals at barrel racing events. Yet, when I referred to her work as a "ministry," she laughed and quickly demurred that she is merely a teacher of the gospel, not a minister. Intrigued, later that afternoon I raised the issue of women in cowboy church leadership with Miller, whose comments revealed a different stance on the question. Referring to people who use the Bible to defend limitations on women's roles, he explained that "sometimes I think we take things out of the Bible and make a doctrine out of it, and take them out of context."[59] Miller said that while he knows about varying biblical interpretations regarding the role of women in church, from his reading, he believes it is fine for women to serve as both pastors and teachers over men. But he also admitted that in practice, he prefers to only have male elders at his church. I stopped him in his tracks and asked him to explain.

"I'm gonna be honest with you," Miller said. "And you can call me sexist, or whatever. I think there are certain things men are better at, or have more authority, than women." Men, he went on to explain, are better at rational decision-making, and therefore are better suited to the tasks required of church elders. And yet, framed against his own understanding of the Bible, he then admitted that his view "doesn't make sense . . . . I don't think it's biblical that they can't be those things. And yet, sitting here, I just told you I don't know about [permitting women to be] deacons and elders. I didn't give you a biblical answer. And that tells me my feelings towards that is probably just 'tradition.'" Miller and I had already shared several hearty guffaws about religious "traditions" that have little relationship to the Bible, but now his tone was more serious. Although his overall position was reminiscent of other people I had spoken with, by the end of our conversation he recognized his own inconsistency and said he had more thinking to do on the issue, which I respected. At the very least, his admission that his position is based not on the Bible but on "sexist" ideas about women's abilities puts him on the same page with many women, who argue the same point. This sets him apart from those pastors who refuse to seriously engage with women's actual concerns.

Although many leaders within the cowboy church movement would like to believe that there are comfortable and consistent policies about men's and women's roles in the church, in fact there is disparity that goes much deeper than quaint academic distinctions between ideal and lived religion. Rather, what we see is a rupture in the discourse. Because the cowboy church is multidenominational, the defense of patriarchal practices within it is reconstructed individually in each church that dots the landscape. The result is inconsistency of reasoning, and disharmony about the core issue itself. Over time, I came to feel that the variant answers evinced flailing among cowboy church leaders to preserve a social order they simply like better, much like what sociologist Bartkowski felt among evangelicals when he "began to wonder if these qualified defenses of gender difference were merely a cover for this organization's seemingly sexist practice of not allowing women to hold the pastorship or an elder's position."[60] Female leaders remain a tiny minority in the world of cowboy Christianity, and for many people the issue of gender roles is a point of serious underlying tension. But in the long term, as more women stand up to question the policy or claim that God is leading them to cowboy ministry, the policy of exclusion stands a good chance of becoming increasingly problematic on a broad level, especially because the teaching is fraught with inconsistency.

The Wider World of the 21st-Century Cowboy Christian

I KNEW THE exact moment that my project had come to its end. Although technically I still had a few research tasks remaining, something happened in January 2016 that made me realize, instantaneously, that my personal journey among cowboy Christians was finished. This was not my deal, as the cowboys would say, and so it was time to move along.

It began when I made a connection with former bull rider Cody Custer, who had served as the unofficial chaplain of the Professional Bull Riders (PBR) for many years. After Custer and I spoke on the phone, he invited me to attend an upcoming PBR competition in Oklahoma City, where he would be working as a chute boss. Custer gave me a behind-the-scenes tour before the event started, and he introduced me to others involved with PBR chaplaincy. The media pass he obtained provided me with a front-row seat near the chutes from which riders and bulls emerged. That night I experienced sensory overload, uncertain where to focus my attention because everything was so new and thrilling. As arena events go, the PBR was far more exciting than just a rodeo. I was so close to the action that I could hear the men yell and the bulls snort, and at times a rampaging animal would crash into the steel fencing two feet in front of my seat. Mud flung in all directions, pelting my face and landing in blobs in my purse. Far above me in the stands, friends who were longtime PBR fans could not believe my dumb luck in getting such an incredible seat; as I joked with them over drinks afterwards, the PBR was ruined for me, because how could I ever attend again and sit somewhere lesser?

The following morning, I returned to the arena for cowboy church. Led by Todd Pierce of Riding High Ministries, the service centered on a lengthy testimony given by Frank Newsom. Newsom is a bullfighter, a job in which he distracts angry bulls so that they do not gore riders after flinging them from their backs, and through which he has earned the nickname "Fearless Frank." Newsom's testimony included the usual trajectory of early, unbridled life successes followed by massive personal failures, then a slow rebuilding of his life through the salvific power of Jesus. His wife, Dea, joined him onstage to add details to the story, and they smiled sweetly as they finished each other's thoughts.

Later, I went to the final round of PBR competition. I took my seat on the front row and waved hello to Custer; chaplain Pierce nodded to me as he made his way through the crowd. No longer overwhelmed by the spectacle of it all, my plan that day was to focus on the riders so that I could begin to appreciate the sport's technical and athletic elements. Things proceeded as normal for the first hour, and I was enjoying myself and accomplishing my goals. Another rider mounted his bull, it bucked wildly out of the chute, and eight seconds later the buzzer sounded as he dove off and ran for safety. The bull then spun in circles, still bucking, and almost crashed into the fence near me as the bullfighters moved in. In a flash, the bull kicked its hind legs, hitting Frank Newsom in the face and lifting him off the ground. Newsom slammed into the arena dirt, lying on his back about a dozen feet in front of me. A quick cry of horror rose up from the crowd as the bull turned around in an attempt to trample him, but it was chased off. The thousands of spectators fell silent as officials and medics ran toward Newsom. Within a few seconds he began to let out a haunting wail, and I saw a trickle of blood gurgle up from his mouth. Though officials moved in to shield him from public view, I was too close not to see. More blood came. Tears were streaming down my face, and I realized I was grabbing the knee of the stranger next to me, a teenage boy. I pulled my hand away and choked out an apology.

Newsom was taken out on a stretcher and the PBR resumed. It only took a few moments for the crowd to relax and get back into the spirit of cheering on the riders. But I could not join them in that spirit. I felt strangely cold, and a little weepy, and terribly sad that this man I did not know—whom I had been studying as he gave his testimony that morning—had just been critically injured right in front of me.[1] Chaplain Pierce, who had exited with the medical team, reappeared and made his way over to speak with Newsom's family, still seated in the arena. The fact that they had waited in the stands, rather than rushing to be by his side, signaled to me that they were accustomed to this environment of danger and injury.

I felt like a child who had just touched the hot stove burner. The rodeo, the racetrack, the cowboy church—this was not my world, I realized, and it was time for me to go. I had gotten burned by getting too close to it all. Though the PBR competition had at least another hour left, I gathered my things and left the arena, knowing my research had just reached its end.

Cowboy Christian Entertainment

Cowboy church is the most visible and identifiable part of the cowboy Christian world, but it is not the entirety of that world. A vast marketplace exists to support it, harmoniously integrating religion and entertainment for all types of horse people. Although evangelicals used to shun anything reeking of worldliness, over the past several decades their purchasing power has legitimated the practice of using material goods to make religion more omnipresent in peoples' lives. Conservative Christian attitudes toward secular entertainment have softened, and concurrently, entertainment has become more religion-friendly. Music, television and film, clothing, toys, clubs and slogans, and even hobby stores and restaurants have become sites for Christian expression and commerce, making it easier for those who want to immerse themselves or their children in a world permeated with religious reminders.[2] So too is this affecting the realm of the cowboy Christian, where options abound for people to proudly display their particular flavor of religious identity. Bumper stickers and t-shirts with the image of the cowboy kneeling at the cross with his horse have become ubiquitous. Online companies, like Cowboy Christian Living, meld western design with crosses and other religious iconography on products including home décor, children's games, luggage, and even "cowboy cell phone holders." The Cowboys for Christ organization raises funds through products bearing its name and symbols, including belt buckles, flags, pins, and a limited-edition rifle. Cowboy Christian books and magazines are available for every reading level, and inevitably every form of cowboy culture entertainment is sacralized with a religious option. As those with entrepreneurial interests find new ways to tap into the cowboy Christian market, there are also people who attempt to shape it by offering free or nonprofit religious products, and they continue to add ministry elements to secular events. All of these entities serve as the backdrop of cowboy church, sometimes acting as feeders into formal churches, other times being alternatives to it, and in many cases simply reinforcing it by facilitating material, cultural, and social connections among cowboy Christians.

In arena environments, chaplaincies provide a bridge from the secular to the sacred. As discussed earlier, the rodeo and racetrack were simultaneous starting points for the modern wave of cowboy Christian ministry. Since then, they have taken divergent paths, with rodeo ministry staying decentralized and racetrack ministry becoming highly structured, and the PBR offshoot landing somewhere in between. The formal chaplaincies of the latter two industries primarily serve employees, but they have also expanded to include some forms of outreach ministry. Public worship services and opportunities to meet competitors who identify as Christian help support the idea that these sporting environments are not out of sync with a Christian lifestyle. Thus, despite the presence of things like alcohol consumption, tobacco ads, and gambling, the cowboy Christian can comfortably attend leisure events in arenas or at the track, knowing that there is a chaplain on the grounds who serves the religious needs of riders, other workers, and even the public. While these chaplaincies were started internally by Christians who merely desired fellowship, there is no denying that today their existence also benefits the formal sports organizations by providing a religious veneer, at least for those who wish to see it, thereby making it an unquestionably wholesome entertainment environment.

Cody Custer was one of PBR's founders, as well as an avid Christian, and the existence of the PBR chaplaincy seems to begin with him. The PBR is a spinoff of rodeo, focusing on the single event of bull riding through touring competitions. In approximately 1990, an investor started a similar organization called Bull Riders Only (BRO), but riders were quickly dissatisfied with many of its regulations, including that it contractually forbade them from competing on any other rodeo circuits. Disgruntled, in 1992 a group of riders that included Custer pooled their money and founded the PBR as an event that promised to give primacy to rider concerns. Economically, it prospered by gaining corporate sponsors and obtaining contracts for cable television broadcasts. From the rider perspective it was preferential because rather than having to pay for all of their own expenses, PBR riders were salaried in addition to competing for prize money. Although PBR is now owned by a large corporation, insiders attest that it remains committed to rider satisfaction.[3]

Much like the start of other rodeo ministries, Custer describes the chaplaincy's beginnings as "not a glamorous thing. It was just a bunch of believers, getting together and discipling each other." He elaborates that for a long time a handful of riders simply met in a motel room for Bible study. The scope of their religious fellowship developed organically as different cowboy Christians moved in and out of the PBR, and various people took on leadership roles. Custer describes a bit of a hiccup in 1998, when they began to hold public cowboy church services at which fans were welcome and which some of the riders did not like. Nonetheless, that aspect of the chaplaincy has remained. Although Custer was the de facto chaplain for about the first decade of the PBR, he says most of it was very informal, and his focus was always on riding first and ministry second. Custer and other well-known riders who worked with him, like Adriano Moraes, Brian Herman, and Wiley Peterson, had an inside track because of the fact that they were riders themselves. Just as with cowboys on the range in the 1800s who decided they wanted to evangelize to other cowboys, being an insider to the profession provided PBR Christians with a social advantage that could be parlayed into a religious advantage, should the right moment arise. Though Custer did not specifically say it, he implied that chaplains for the PBR have a bigger challenge if they are not professional riders, which has been the case for some in recent years.

Custer moved into other jobs with the PBR after sustaining an injury in 2001, and he recruited a Christian cowboy from Idaho named Todd Pierce to help with chaplaincy. Pierce, and others who have worked with him through the nonprofit organization Riding High Ministries, eventually took full responsibility for the PBR chaplaincy. The job includes a few formal tasks, such as organizing a public cowboy church service and providing facility tours to a children's charity, but it is primarily a ministry of presence. As described by Winnifred Fallers Sullivan, who has studied numerous forms of chaplaincy, presence "seems to be a practice that is defined and takes place in opposition to a range of possible secular and sectarian modes of human interaction that are seen as undesirable or impossible . . . . [The chaplain] is not trying to improve or constrain your life, but rather simply to be there."[4] The essence of the PBR chaplain's activities are very much in line with this description of chaplaincies found in other unusual environments: on competition weekends, he makes himself available to PBR employees and their families for counseling, prayer, and general life coaching, and during the down time he may also socialize with them. Before and during competitions, he roams the arena and can be quickly summoned to any part of it by cell phone, ready to respond to religious needs.

I was able to witness Pierce in action on various occasions when visiting cowboy church services, and in informal conversations he told me about his work there. But it was in the moment that Frank Newsom was injured that the greater relevance of the chaplain's position became clear to me. After Newsom was kicked, when the audience had fallen silent and medics were still rushing in to tend to him, Pierce sprang into action. He climbed through the first level of the arena, stepping over heads onto armrests and empty seats, creating his own path to the injured man. He leapt over the fence into the dirt and knelt behind the medics, praying. In the period that followed, he was able to be with Newsom as he was being assessed, and then he returned to comfort the family with first-hand information about Newsom's condition. If he had not been there to assume those responsibilities, there was no one else clearly designated to do so. On the other hand, I also observed that there were two other riders who sustained injuries during the first hour that day, and Pierce had not rushed in to help either of them. Whether that was because their injuries were less severe or because they were not part of the Christian PBR contingent was not clear, but regardless of the reason, it may indicate a certain kind of fissure in the chaplaincy.

Despite the calming relevance of the chaplain during emergencies, his job remains an unofficial entity; leaders gingerly described it as being permitted by the PBR albeit not fully supported by it. For instance, although PBR provides space and staffing for cowboy church services, chaplains are paid only by donations from the public. This is not unlike the structure of chaplaincies found in many other sports organizations, including baseball, hockey, and NASCAR. If the PBR chaplaincy were to become more formalized, its ministers would likely need to embrace a wider range of faiths than just conservative evangelical Christianity; that would bring it in line with other modern workplace chaplaincies, which are typically designed to positively affirm and support all faiths while also conveying doctrinal neutrality.[5] As it stands, the PBR chaplaincy remains comfortably in the shadows. Those fans who listen carefully will hear an announcement inviting them to attend the public cowboy church service, and people in the know will recognize the chaplain as he wanders through the arena, speaking with as many people as possible. His presence pleases the religious people who recognize him, and he is completely unobtrusive to everyone else, just another cowboy in the crowd.

Meanwhile, at the racetrack, the cowboy hat-wearing chaplain engages in a similar range of activities, including being there to help in emergency situations while also trying not to get in the way. Carl Crisswell, the chaplain at Remington Park in Oklahoma City, says that injuries and death are a stark reality at any racetrack, and that applies to both humans and animals.[6] For that reason, Crisswell considers himself on call twenty-four hours a day, seven days a week, ready to be of service to any tracker regardless of that person's religious background or whether he has ever met them before. When live racing meets are on, and approximately five hundred people and two thousand horses reside on the backside, he has an intensive schedule that puts him on the grounds six days a week, in the morning and the evening, as well as two late nights for extra activities. In addition, Crisswell is regularly enlisted for hospital visitation, funeral planning, personal counseling, and collecting benevolence funds. But he prefers the more average days, during which he walks the shedrows and makes himself visible and available to workers on both the back and front sides of the track, pausing in his rounds to give short devotionals and pray with workers in the maintenance barn, the jockeys' lounge, and at the starting gate prior to the first race.

As with the situation at other large racetracks, and even more developed than what is found at the PBR, Crisswell's chaplaincy serves a wider community of people through outreach. For instance, one outreach arm is a farm ministry, in which an RTCA-licensed minister acting under Crisswell's supervision visits horse breeding and training farms to offer counsel and worship services to the workers. Because he also spends time at the track, that person's presence reinforces the spiritual continuity between the farms and the track. Another form of outreach is Sunday morning worship service on the backside, attended not only by track workers but by members of the local community. Just as the barn-like environment of cowboy church deliberately mutes distinctions between sacred and secular space, worship at the track plasticizes the environment for those who engage in multiple activities there. In fact, when I spent an afternoon shadowing Crisswell at the racetrack, we bumped into one of his church members and her young son, who were eagerly anticipating a race in which one of their horses was competing. Shortly thereafter, while walking through the casino, Crisswell pointed out another church member who was busy at the slot machines. This time, we did not stop to say hello; some people do not like running into their pastor while gambling, he said, adding, "it's more uncomfortable for them than it is for me." Unlike

PBR chaplains who blend into the crowd, Crisswell's button-down shirt has embroidered logos and text to publicly identify him as the racetrack chaplain. "We've got to be visible," he says. "I've got to have some type of label on me." It does happen that, while walking through the grandstand, a patron will see that he's the chaplain and pull him aside to talk. Though Crisswell's presence is primarily for workers, he will attend to anyone in need, and thus he acts as a bridge among all Christians whose lives coincide in the racetrack environment.

In addition to cowboy pastors who have experience working in racetrack or rodeo ministry are those who engage in Christian horse whispering, an entertainment-religion hybrid. Horse whispering is the skill of training an unruly horse with gentle means, and it is generally considered specialized work that requires psychological insight into horse behavior. As one observer has written, whisperers are people "who have an almost mystical affinity with horses, able to tame even the most cantankerous animals through sympathetic handling" and a quiet communication style; this contrasts with practices of breaking horses through more aggressive or forceful means.[7] Though horse training is generally done in private, the public performance of secular horse whispering dates to the late 1850s when one whisperer determined he could make more money from public demonstrations than by serving individuals.[8] That performance tradition trickled along through the ensuing years and, today, has begotten a religious variant.

In an attempt to understand the essence of Christian horse whispering, in 2013 and 2014 I attended demonstration events led by three independent ministries: Todd Pierce's "Born Wild, Created to Be Free," Paul Daily's "Wild Horse Breaking," and Lew Sterrett's "Sermon on the Mount." By attending, I was hoping to get a sense of how horse whispering can be approached from a Christian standpoint. Former rodeo cowboy Michael Johnson, for instance, has written that horse training can be a "spiritual assignment," in which the human helps the horse do "what the Lord had made him to do in the first place."[9] Rather than bringing in a genuinely wild horse that has already proven resistant to training, the more modest goal of these demonstrations was that a previously untrained horse would, by the end, tolerate being saddled and ridden in the ring. As it turned out, much to my disappointment, there is no use of specifically Christian principles in the training. Rather, a Christian horse whispering is just a visual sermon involving an extended analogy. The untrained horse is like the person who has not yet found God: erratic, defensive, obstinate, and unfulfilled. In contrast, we are told that trained horses, like good Christians, are calm and obedient, and as a result they feel fulfilled and at peace. What is needed to bridge the two states of being is the horse trainer, who is analagous to God.[10]

In these events, each man spent about an hour on actual horse training, and music and other speakers rounded out the evening. A brochure given out by Daily, which is mirrored by his presentation, makes explicit that his lesson is analogic. It lists ten points for contemplation, each of which has a line related to horse training and a counterpart idea for human obedience to God. For instance, point two reads, "Horse: I do not expect this horse to be any more than what he is right now, an untrained wild horse. Man: God does not expect us to be or do more than we are capable of." Subsequent points relate to the process of incrementally coaxing the horse into submission to the trainer, with parallel statements about human submission to God. Taking a similar approach, Pierce begins his demonstration by describing it as "representational," and inviting people to relate to the horse while listening to his message. Pierce spoke as he worked the animal, and after each major segment of teaching, the band kicked in with a song, allowing him to focus entirely on the horse training for a few minutes. The crux of his message was that humans have been given a loving and patient savior to help them with their sinful nature. Assuming God's persona, Pierce spoke to the horse: "I gotta tell you something sweetheart. I love you . . . . There's an instinct that's inside of you that's causing you to be afraid of me. But I'll wait for you." Pierce encouraged people to enter into a relationship with God, boldly cautioning them against the trappings of churches. He even likened organized religion to the horse breaker who confines the animal and trains it by using fear and aggression. "Jesus didn't create us to be controlled," he said; "he created us to be inhabited."[11] Pierce speaks a radical anti-institutional message, even though his events are often sponsored and/or supported by cowboy churches. Based on my observations, audiences appeared to be a mixture of random local people and members of various churches, possibly including some cowboy churches through which the whisperings had been advertised. How people respond to his critique of institutional religion is unknown, but an educated guess is that, at the very least, they would regard cowboy churches as existing outside of typical institutional confines and therefore not part of what he decries.

Each of the horse whisperings included elements of entertainment, and in this they bear recognizable similarities to the entertainment cowboy preachers of the mid-twentieth century. Like Leonard Eilers or Gene Autry, these men allude to romantic ideas about inherent cowboy values and the eternal nature of the horse as the cowboy's working animal, contextualizing it all within Christianity. Their presentations also offer other ways for people to become engaged. Sterrett, for instance, who is very personable, makes himself available before and afterwards, chatting with people and inviting children to pet his horse and take photographs. Sterrett's message, both in its language and theological content, is a bit more sophisticated than the others and contains the fewest explicit comparisons between humans and horses. His overall package is also more developed, as he promotes and sells books, videos, horse clinics, and leadership training seminars. In contrast, Daily's event was low key, book-ended by extensive Americana at the start and lengthy testimony from his daughter to close. At Todd Pierce's demonstration, the entertainment included a live band and the horse world equivalent of guest stars: speakers Mike Lee and Elsie Frost.[12] Mike Lee, an accomplished bull rider who identifies as Christian, had also accompanied Pierce that morning to a cowboy church in Cleburne, Texas, where he spoke about the dangers of allowing material things to replace God. Onstage during the horse whispering, Lee recalled a childhood during which he'd been "hard-minded" and "tried to run from God," but through his salvation he was now on a path of purpose and fulfillment. After giving his testimony, Lee sat near the door to sign autographs, give out Bibles, and accept donations on behalf of the ministry.

Elsie Frost, the other special guest, opened the event by giving a lengthy testimony about her late son, Lane. If the cowboy Christian world has a single martyr, it is Lane Frost, and his parents are beloved figures of the cowboy Christian circuit. Lane's story gets retold publicly at special events, and the 1994 major motion picture *8 Seconds* was made about his life. Frost aspired to be a bull rider from his earliest years and worked his way up the ranks, winning the PRCA World Championship in 1987 at age twenty-four. He was known as an all-around nice guy, always willing to stop and sign autographs and talk to fans. However, as his professional success took off, his personal life was in turmoil, particularly his marriage to barrel racer Kellie Kyle. It is unclear exactly what caused his personal suffering; on the website maintained by his parents, they indicate it was his difficult travel schedule. However, in her public presentation, Elsie Frost enigmatically said that the devil was wreaking havoc in Lane's life, and that she pleaded with him to accept Jesus as his personal savior and prove to his wife that he was a changed person. He assented and, as Elsie Frost has said, "God worked a miracle in their life." In the year that followed, things improved significantly for the couple, which made it all the more tragic when Frost was killed during a 1989 bull ride in Cheyenne after what looked like a minor accident. "When Lane hit the dirt in Cheyenne," his mother said, "this [PRCA Championship] belt buckle meant absolutely nothing. The only thing that meant anything is that decision he'd made for Jesus. And I'm just so thankful he did that."

When, a few years later, the Frosts agreed to assist with the movie about Lane's life, they hoped the opportunity would allow them to "talk about his salvation and it would bring glory to God." However, each version of the script was unsatisfactory to them, not only because it was "full of foul language," but also because they considered the climax of Lane's story to be his salvation experience, and the director had no intention of including that in the film. The Frosts were unhappy with the final version, which his mother said contained numerous misrepresentations. Few films, cowboy-theme or otherwise, make religious conversion a focal point; therefore the narrative structure of *8 Seconds* is not surprising even though it may have been disappointing to a small portion of viewers. When recounting her experience, Elsie Frost dwelled for several minutes on the theme of secular entertainment being devoid of God, and she implied that her time in Hollywood taught her that many people working in the entertainment profession will probably end up in hell. She described people in Los Angeles as "a whole different breed," elaborating that "they had no idea who created them or where they came from! I guess they believe they came from a monkey." Invoking differences in perspective that she framed as both regional and religious, Frost then abruptly concluded her cautionary tale by emphasizing the importance of accepting Jesus so that one does not land in hell after suffering an early, unexpected death. In this instance, the cowboy Christian entertainment ended on an atypically heavy note.

Multimedia Cowboy Christians

Beyond live entertainment, today some cowboy Christians attempt to reach their target audience through culturally themed television shows that broadcast on RFD-TV, a cable channel with programming crafted to appeal to rural Americans. For example, *Cowboy Church*, a thirty-minute show cohosted by pastor Russ Weaver and singer Susie McEntire, has remained on the air for nearly a decade despite content that can best be described as disjointed. Episodes are a hodgepodge of things such as interviews with people at stock shows and arena events; sermon excepts or short Bible lessons given by Weaver; testimonies, especially from people who lead ministry organizations; musical performances by McEntire or special guests; and conversations between the cohosts. The exact format varies each week, and the religious message frequently gets divided across two episodes that comprise a "part 1" and "part 2." In reruns, the shows are not necessarily broadcast in order, so the episode partitions feel even more erratic.

In contrast, the more coherent program *Cowboy Authentic* was cancelled after only one season. Advertised on its own website as "family entertainment with a moral" that served as an "alternative to 'made for mature audience' [sic] programming," *Cowboy Authentic* blended documentary of the cowboy world with religion. John Riggs, the pastor of a cowboy church in Texas, served as host. The show's high-quality filming and artistic shots of landscapes and working ranches made it visually engaging, but that was offset by unscripted narration and interviews that were often stilted. Each episode focused on a concept that could be framed both within cowboy culture and Christian life, such as episode 115, entitled "Chronic." A "chronic" is a cow that fails to thrive and does not respond to typical medicinal treatment. In the episode, Riggs makes the parallel that, like cows growing larger for consumption, humans are meant to grow and thrive in their faith, though they do not always do so. Fortunately, Riggs says, "The truth is that we have a God who loves chronics . . . . He has a remedy for the things that keep reoccurring in our life." The episode's lesson is that if humans spend time "in God's feedbunk," that is, reading the Bible, they will grow to become more like Jesus and will excel. In addition to weaving religion into ranch scenarios, Riggs also found ways to raise political topics, emphasizing his stance that America is troubled due to a decentering of Christianity in the public sphere.

Capitalizing on this same theme, Riggs received significant regional news coverage when, in October 2015, he undertook a 104-mile ride on horseback from Texas to Oklahoma. At the time, tempers were flaring about the removal of a Ten Commandments monument from outside of the Oklahoma state capitol: after nearly three years of legal wrangling, it had been declared in violation of the state constitution and was removed. Riggs stepped into this cultural war on behalf of cowboy Christians. As posted on the show's Facebook page, Riggs claimed he was inspired to deliver a message "to the church in America today. To say wake up . . . to stand up . . . to speak up. To speak up for the things we hold to be true and dear." Elsewhere, he elaborated that it was America's Christian foundations that needed defending. With that intent, a small group of men set out on horseback from Wichita Falls, Texas, riding north on back roads to Oklahoma City, where they arrived three days later.[13] With them they carried a small stone tablet listing the Ten Commandments, which they publicly presented to Oklahoma governor Mary Fallin at the capitol. Fallin, who had consistently voiced support for the presence of the monument, graciously accepted the plaque and indicated she would put it in her office. This event has been one of the rare incidents providing cowboy church with anything more than localized media coverage, and so in that sense it was an effective publicity tool for cowboy church in general. However, it is difficult to believe it was concocted entirely as a symbolic religio-political gesture, as Riggs publicly claimed. Unfortunately, because *Cowboy Authentic* was cancelled before its second season was broadcast, there is no way to know how much the Ten Commandments ride would have been featured and what wider impact(s) it might have had for the cowboy church movement.

Like RFD-TV shows, most forms of cowboy Christian media primarily reach community insiders rather than serving as outreach. If one knows to seek them out, numerous cowboy ministry organizations, as well as a few individual churches, have active websites with regular devotional blog posts and sermons that can be watched online. Although some churches use Facebook to announce events or post concerns, it is not unusual for them to become dormant pages with infrequent updating. On the other hand, there is an active market for print media, most of which aims for a generic multiregional western heritage culture audience. One can readily find religious books with cowboy-themed titles and covers, but which lack any specific cowboy content; an example of this is the *Trail Guide for the Christian Woman's Journey*, an adaptation from a book series by Christian counselor and radio host June Hunt, who has no connection with cowboy culture. Somewhat more substantive are devotional books written by those who work in cowboy ministry and who have a specific cowboy culture subgroup in mind. Kevin Landis, for instance, the pastor of a cowboy church in Texas, has self-published two books that weave together biblical commentary, stories, and life advice in short thematic chapters. The back cover of his first volume, *The Cowboy Steward*, describes the content as biblical teaching "in an understandable format. We don't need to use big fancy words at The Cowboy Church." The book also promotes cowboy exceptionalism, frequently emphasizing the uniqueness of the cowboy's outlook. Likewise, racetrack chaplain Sam Ed Spence has written two books of daily devotionals. Peppered with plenty of references to horses and riding, these paperbacks contain reproductions of cowboy-themed art by noteworthy western artists such as Chuck DeHaan and Tom Chapman, and they include references that speak to different racing audiences.[14] And Jeff Copenhaver, the founder of the cowboy church in Fort Worth, has written three books in a series of "devotionals for champions," in which he recounts anecdotes oriented around the theme of achievement, and reflects on Bible verses. Copenhaver's books have been republished numerous times and translated into several languages, and he attributes their success to the widespread appeal of cowboy imagery. Part of their popularity is also likely due to the fact that they are given free of charge, as well as the detailed personal stories he recounts from his days competing as a calf roper.

Many of these cowboy Christian publications intrinsically reinforce connections among different sectors of the horse world. For instance, the continued overlap is well demonstrated by *Trail Ride*, a thick magazine that puts present-day cowboy culture in conversation with the "Old West" and the Bible. Its first issue, in 2012, included individual profiles of diverse figures including independent cowboy church pastor Terry Hill, AFCC executive director Todd Mitchell, and Christian horse whisperer Lew Sterrett, as well as an obituary for Ted Pressley of Cowboys for Christ. Subsequent issues have maintained inclusion of various parts of the cowboy Christian world through pieces such as devotional essays focusing on rodeo, advertisements for the Fellowship of Christian Cowboys (the FCA offshoot), and a profile of Western Harvest, a ministry that claims to be "impacting lives through extreme sports and God's love." By emphasizing athleticism as intrinsic to cowboy culture, this magazine also consistently makes ideological links with muscular Christianity. The notes at the bottom of its masthead even include this statement: "We believe in cowboys as athletes who maintain a vital role in our nation." From an entrepreneurial standpoint, the inclusion of elements that appeal to different slices of the cowboy Christian audience ensures that this periodical, and others like it, will have relevance and marketability in many different horse-oriented settings.

One thing that remains relatively absent from the print and online cowboy Christian media is a public forum for serious discussion of charged issues, and that includes space for dissenting views. Although it is still young, the cowboy church has not been immune to scandals, most of which have been related to sex and/or money.[15] Throughout my travels, various people told me stories about such things, though it was often conveyed as gossip. The approach of cowboy church member Sonny Spurger was one exception, in that he believes it is important to have a forum to address and resolve serious issues. Through his former work with the Baptist General Convention of Texas, Spurger has experience teaching classes in cowboy church ethics, as well as serving as a mediator in situations of pastoral misconduct. He emphasized that, in the particular situation of Baptists, tracking problematic pastors is difficult because of the denomination's structural decentralization. If a congregation fails to do its due diligence, it might enlist a pastor with a sordid or even criminal past. Spurger implied that this is even more likely to occur in the cowboy church context where, broadly speaking, the culture emphasizes personal trust and de-emphasizes paperwork. Furthermore, many cowboy church pastors are independent founders of their own church, which means no one has vetted their background.[16] A history of sexual misconduct, or even sexual abuse, can slip under the radar and manifest itself again. Similarly, in interviews, various pastors identified monetary accountability as one of the most important things their denomination provides for them, and yet several of the independent pastors I spoke with said financial independence is a primary reason they prefer to have no affiliation. This, too, may be a potential point of concern. None of the cowboy Christian websites I have found, nor any of the publications, offer a venue through which average members can openly express concerns about internal problems and communicate about ethics with a wider audience of their peers. People are, however, willing to whisper about rumors and mumble about dissatisfaction; when they told me sordid stories, I often sensed that what they really wanted was answers, or at least clarity about the resolution. Providing a safe space for such conversation may be an important internal checkpoint for cowboy churches as they look toward the future. Admitting to failures, certainly, opens them up for outside criticism, but not making safe spaces for such conversations will inevitably shape the culture in unhealthy ways.

Conclusion

Cowboy Christians are no longer a disparate group of people who occasionally find each other in the arena or at the racetrack, coming together only briefly before dispersing again. They are more organized than their initial forms, decades ago—a single congregation, or a radio program, or an impressive speaker. Today they have a self-conscious identity through which they are building a movement. Cowboy church is the most visible and uniting force of that movement, but undergirding it are organizations that provide ministry in numerous horse-oriented environments. Cowboys for Christ, in particular, has often served as a point of first contact for both potential Christians and aspiring ministers, and hindsight allows us to recognize it as an important networking hub within this community. Furthermore, many chaplaincies at rodeos and racetracks, which predate cowboy church itself, continue to be relevant for that same reason.

Calling cowboy church a movement, which I believe is most appropriate, identifies it as an organizational form and also suggests its potential for influence. Cowboy Christianity involves hundreds of churches that cross denominational lines, as well as numerous parachurch organizations. Leadership comes from multiple sources and includes scrappy grassroots actions as well as sophisticated strategic maneuverings. Its momentum, at times unfocused, continues to drive changes in approach and structure. If a singular voice can be discerned, we hear the cowboy church critiquing many formal elements of Protestant tradition, opposing heavy-handedness about sin, and articulating a conservative perspective on gender roles and family structures; as such, it is both progressive and regressive at the same time. Because the cowboy church and its related arms are primarily striving to change Christianity from within, sociologically it would be classified as an endogenous religious movement. However, cowboy Christianity also shares traits with exogenous religious movements because, secondarily, it envisions bringing about wider societal change. At present, having external influence is more of what it aspires to than what it actually does; forming coalitions with other specific social movements that hold similar ideology would increase its potential to influence a wider sphere, but it has not yet done this.[17] While it remains primarily inwardly focused, it is succeeding in forging a new breed of evangelical church: something that tastes and sounds like mainstream evangelicalism, even though it does not look or feel like mainstream evangelicalism. It is a church for people who do not like church, which ironically is something evangelicals are known for saying.

The range of cowboy Christianity—from churches, to rodeos, to racetracks, and in popular entertainment arenas—demonstrates that it is a culturally based religious innovation that is likely to be more than just a footnote in American religious history. Its international reach is still in its infancy, but people all over the world are responsive to cowboy imagery and mythos; therefore some of its most interesting developments and adaptations may lie in the future as it spreads geographically. In the United States, we should expect that this revivalist movement will continue to prosper among people who have been disillusioned by traditional church and who self-identify with the cowboy culture. Increasingly, we can expect that it will be viewed as a normal Protestant variation, especially since evangelicalism has proven to be accommodating to new things as long as a core theological message remains consistent. In recent decades, evangelicalism has accepted modernizations from youth culture, it has embraced technology, it has expanded its internal social vision, and it has found space for charismatic expression. There is every reason to believe, then, that it will also accept expressions of cowboy culture in a religious context, so long as those expressions contribute to evangelical vitality. In the meantime, aspects of cowboy church structure, ideology, and institutional development can provide deeper understanding of the historical trajectory of evangelicalism.

Despite the dominance of cowboy culture in Texas and parts of the West, class prejudice and elitism allow many Americans to regard it as relatively insignificant, and so too goes its cowboy Christian subculture. The fact that this growing group has largely been—as Gary Morgan put it—"left behind," has allowed it to flourish beneath the radar, developing something fresh and unique that may someday be seen as having had an important impact on American Christian practice. It is easy to be dismissive of a new religious form when its constituents are perceived as having only marginal social power, but that can also mean that its potential is underestimated. A prime example of this same social dynamic was seen in the Jesus movement of the 1960s–1970s, in which young Americans embraced a theologically conservative version of Christianity and married it to burgeoning elements of youth culture that included music, attire, lingo, and social relations. Although some historians remain skeptical of that movement's impact, others insist the Jesus movement was absolutely critical for a resurgence in evangelicalism that today allows it to be an incredibly influential body in the United States. Larry Eskridge has argued that a spate of churches grew out of, and because of, the movement, and "while no longer associated in the public mind with the Jesus Revolution, [they have] continued to reflect its style and values."[18] It is not since the Jesus movement that we have seen an America subcultural group, identified primarily by material characteristics and an idealized system of values, engage anew with Christianity and build itself into an institution, but the cowboy church is just such a phenomenon. Like a revival or an awakening, it is pulling inactive people into Christian practice, and they are forging new ways of being a Christian community.

What most clearly distinguishes cowboy church from mainstream Protestantism is how it *feels* as a place of worship and as an organization. It offers a relational approach to church, rather than striving to engage people on intellectual or emotional levels. Its mood is culturally comfortable, and sometimes that may be all that is needed to get a person's foot in the door. All of this was also true of the Jesus movement, especially in its early years. Churches whose growth was dependent on that movement, including such behemoths as Calvary Chapel and its offshoot, the Vineyard Fellowship, today target middle class suburban families. By maintaining a youthful vitality in their church cultures, they have preserved some of the building blocks that initially vaulted them into prominence, even as they have in other ways become more mainstream. It would not be entirely surprising to see a similar shift in the cowboy church over time, especially considering that pastors already indicate that growing proportions of new members are coming from an audience that is not at the center of their target, and sometimes not on the target at all. If they are to weather that change, their vast program may need to be condensed into a core identity, though it is not yet evident whether that would be based on theology, practice, mission, materiality, or something else. If the Jesus movement is to be any guide, then cultural and relational aspects of cowboy church would be its most obvious defining features.

In addition to its Jesus movement parallels, cowboy churches can also readily be classified within the new paradigm church family as defined by Donald Miller, and this measure allows us to see its alignment with a wider trend in American evangelical practice that developed in the late twentieth century. Miller delineated a dozen traits of new paradigm churches, many of which can be summarized as the use of modern approaches to lighten the overall mood of church without diluting the message. It includes aspects such as a down-to-earth pastor, Bible-focused lessons instead of sermons, and an informal atmosphere. He elaborated that such churches emphasize "internal transformation as opposed to change in external appearance."[19] The centrality of cultural comfort and the improvement of one's interior spiritual life, among other aspects that Miller lists, are similarly defining points of cowboy church. As an iteration of this evangelical development, then, cowboy church is already somewhat more mainstream than both its detractors and its adherents would like to admit. Miller's work is not without minor flaws, including an overestimation of the extent to which new paradigm churches would transform the practice of Christianity in America. However, he rightly identified that intricacies of theology and doctrine seem to be less important concerns for those attracted to these churches, and he anticipated that new movements would spring from this overall impulse.

As should be evident, the idea of the new paradigm church shares much in common with the Jesus movement. Although Miller acknowledges a minor influence of the Jesus movement on the new paradigm, he interprets them as separate developments. Eskridge has responded in critique, saying that Miller "failed to grasp that the new paradigm he described had in fact been the Jesus People movement," and that the structure of churches like Calvary Chapel should be recognized as "the ecclesiastical legacy of the new paradigm, not its fount."[20] Yet other evidence indicates that this new approach to church was already being discussed in higher echelons of evangelical leadership concurrent with the Jesus movement, if not prior to it.[21] In other words, the question remains whether the Jesus movement, new paradigm churches, and cowboy church are three separate developments, or if they have a significant historical relationship. Such academic debates do not, from my perspective, actually require a winner or a solution. They are all valuable ways of thinking about historical antecedents to new church developments, and each offers a different window into the process of religious change. Cowboy church has many parallels with the Jesus movement, so there is value in what that pairing can demonstrate about religious revivals in the modern day. Cowboy church is also in harmony with the new paradigm church structure that Miller identified, and recognizing that helps us see it as a normal, perhaps even predictable, development within mainstream evangelicalism. By highlighting its relationship to various revivalist trends, the cowboy church aids us in more fully understanding the scope of American evangelicalism.

When we shift to consider the content of the cowboy Christian message, rather than church structure and method, what stands out is its alignment with other forms of men's ministry. A variety of groups and institutions in the nineteenth and twentieth centuries, including fraternal lodges, the Young Men's Christian Association, the Men and Religion Forward movement, the Fellowship of Christian Athletes, and many others all articulated a particular relationship among masculinity, athleticism, and Christianity. Their theological commonality, muscular Christianity, posits that athleticism and masculinity are crucial aspects of the Christian man; thus Christian practice should help those attributes thrive. That translated into boosting male leadership to insure that churches remained devoid of sentimentality and emotionalism, as well as emphasizing team sports to build both health and moral character. While historians of religion have primarily discussed muscular Christianity as an older phenomenon, it is becoming apparent that it is more of a cyclical ideology than a fleeting historical one. Cowboy Christianity is one of its newest expressions, echoing its assertions about ideal Christian men vis-à-vis cowboy essentialist ideas of gender roles and the centrality of arena sports to its identity.

Sports-focused ministries, as well as ministries tailored to men, can be valuable community-building entities, but those whose ideology simply reifies muscular Christianity appear to be stuck in time. Instead of finding modes of Christian thought and practice suitable for new social circumstances, muscular Christian ideology resists modernity and attempts to stand as a stalwart against social change, particularly changes related to gender and sexuality. Regardless of this theological stasis, in practical terms the boundaries between male and female are becoming ever more fluid, and by extension gender roles and sexual identities are also more porous. It will not be surprising if, in response, a wider swath of conservative Christians increasingly emphasizes gender divisions that are informed by a conservative reading of the Bible, possibly invoking muscular Christian ideals. As cowboy church pastors are already rooted in this perspective, a few may be poised to become prominent voices among those who prefer that gender remains fixed, which would also bring a new surge of attention to their religious project. For historians, the fact that muscular Christian ideology periodically reappears should prompt us to reconsider its role as a religious response to cultural change, and to consider the spectrum of fears it seeks to allay. What is interesting is that although the muscular Christian ideology is cyclical, its newer iterations—like Promise Keepers or cowboy church—do not self-consciously model themselves on previous men's ministry endeavors, instead appearing to consider themselves brand-new solutions to a perceived problem. It is only this broader view that allows us to observe the theological pattern uniting these groups and to tease out the connections among them.

Pulling the evaluative lens back even further permits us to consider aspects of the institutional development of cowboy church, and to evaluate it as a new religious movement (NRM). For the most part, individual cowboy churches are still in their first generation: members have joined as adults rather than growing up in them, and a great many are led by their founding pastor. Leadership is often populated by people who have been members from the start. For a little over a decade there have been attempts to unify the churches in various ways, many of which have involved organizational fluctuations. Thus, although insiders often regard the cowboy church as a solid and fully established institution, relatively speaking it is still a young religious movement that should be expected to have more changes ahead. If sociological modeling of successful new religions can be a guide, one of the developmental strengths of the cowboy church is its alignment with the cowboy culture and with evangelical Christianity, both of which are identifiable norms in many parts of the United States, especially the Southern Great Plains. People are able to enter the churches with a high degree of familiarity and comfort, and joining should feel relatively easy—easier, that is, than joining a religion that is culturally foreign. In addition, the churches are also generally successful in engaging voluntary labor to make everything happen, and their members' enthusiasm readily draws new people in to see what all the fuss is about. All of these are important attributes of successful new religious movements.[22]

On the other hand, the same modeling tool also reveals potential weaknesses in the cowboy church movement, particularly in areas related to authority, prophecy, and societal tension. According to sociologist Rodney Stark, successful religions require that members buy into and validate the leadership structures and processes. As we have seen, there appears to be a high number of women, as well as some men, who do not fully agree with the cowboy church leadership plan. Additionally, many do not consider the present structure to be biblically supported. When doctrinal authority for leadership is lacking and members do not feel included in decision-making processes, structural breakdowns are nearly inevitable, and therefore it is a recipe for schism and/or movement failure. A second potential weakness relates to prophecy, because failure of prophecy can cause rupture. For the most part, cowboy church beliefs are based on non-empirical doctrine and therefore cannot be disproven; according to the modeling, that is a strength. However, the Smith Wigglesworth prophecy regarding the last great revival beginning among cowboys still lingers as a presence in this movement. Although only a minority of people seems to put a high value on its importance, many people are aware of and refer to it. This prophecy seems to be at best a miscommunication and at worst a deliberate hoax—and possibly both—and awareness of that fact might dampen the enthusiasm of some cowboy Christians, were it to become more well known. Additionally, its loping presence also indicates that the cowboy church is open to and potentially accepting of prophecy, which as a general characteristic translates into a heightened risk for movement failure.

The most complex potential problem point relates to preserving boundaries between cowboy church and the rest of society, and particularly what Stark refers to as eliminating the free rider problem. Successful new religions typically require a commitment to behavioral or lifestyle codes that are more strict than what average people are doing. Having these restrictions in common serves to bond members, to provide them with a sense of distinction, and to deepen their overall commitment to the religious group. People with a lax attitude or an unwillingness to commit to expectations will negatively impact the group psyche if they are allowed to stay. According to the model, if these free riders remain in the group, it will lead to either a watering down of the overall expectations such that its difference from the alternatives becomes negligible, or it will cause the more deeply committed members to leave, which means the church will only be populated by marginally committed people. Either one would be considered a developmental failure. The reason this issue is particularly complex for cowboy church is that the church's only defining theological feature is the de-emphasis of behavioral perfection. Sanctification is considered gradual, often full of setbacks, and in the long period of spiritual growth members' rough behavior is to be tolerated. Recall, for instance, the example of the woman drinking alcohol from a large cup while sitting in church. Her pastor refused to heed member requests that he tell her to leave, saying, "Christ accepts her where she is, and I've gotta do the same thing."[23] In a sense, the entire idea of cowboy church erases the behavioral boundaries between members and nonmembers from the start, and free riders are always allowed to tarry. Stark's work would indicate that such a religious group will fail because the requisite feelings of distinction and unity cannot not be sustained under such circumstances.

If, however, the model is altered slightly such that the boundaries cowboy church creates between its members and the rest of society have to do with worship style and church structure, rather than with lifestyle and morality, then this characteristic actually becomes more predictive of success. The maintenance of appropriate boundaries around worship style and church structure is immediately recognizable as a point of concern many pastors have spoken of, as some feel their group is being infiltrated by "church people" who are initially entranced with the church but ultimately want to turn it into something more mainstream. In adapting Stark's model for this circumstance, the church people are akin to free riders, and their presence will dilute the cowboy church vision and chase away the "real" cowboy Christians if their attitude is allowed to become dominant. Whether such a modification to the model is appropriate is its own question, unanswerable without more widespread data. But perhaps the cowboy church gives us a new way of thinking about different types of boundaries a religion can set, and how such boundaries are both challenged and maintained.

As demonstrated throughout this volume, the question of *what is authentically cowboy* continues to thrive as a tension beneath the surface of everyday niceties in cowboy church. It is not a new issue. Debates about authenticity were seen in the late 1800s, when range cowboys like Will James disparaged "that class of young preachers who covet the appellation," claiming to be cowboys without having the necessary experience.[24] A few decades later, notorious itinerants capitalized on the concept of the honest cowboy by calling themselves cowboy preachers to gain attention and trust. All throughout the twentieth century, nostalgia caused a whitewashing of cowboy history, repainting the average working men as heroes and ridding their song lyrics of indecency, and in turn provoking disagreements about which version of their history was most accurate. Today, living cowboy cultures are ideological conglomerations, including real history and imagined history, ideas taken from country song lyrics, imagery from film and television, and patterns of social life in suburban and rural communities in varying regions. Distinguishing the real from the mythos is as fleeting and subjective as it ever was. Within the church, the question of authenticity is closely intertwined with the issue of independence versus control. The independent spirit of the cowboy, a romanticized quality believed to be embedded in the culture, is often promoted. Team leaders and lay pastors are encouraged to come up with new ideas, and they are empowered to bring their ideas to fruition. Internally there is plenty of self-congratulatory rhetoric about cowboy church being different from the mainstream. But among the highest echelon of cowboy church leaders are very intelligent men who are extremely strategic about church design. Too much independence, leaders think, can cause a church to stray from the established model and the carefully crafted vision. They prefer that cowboy churches appear to be free-form while actually being tightly controlled, and they have succeeded in enacting this sleight of hand. As such, their predetermined version of cowboy authenticity is kept intact.

Despite its pastiche nature, many cowboy Christians are still deeply concerned with preserving the culture's integrity, however that may be construed. Over the years I have heard numerous negative judgments about a church's level of authenticity based on things like the pastor's cowboy credentials, the presence of charismatic worship, the lack of an arena, the way members dress, the use of praise music, a woman in a high position of leadership, or members who are disconnected from cowboy culture. At times, I too was affected by this bug of authenticity. I have walked into a few churches that did not feel like "real" cowboy church to me, and I struggled to figure out why I reacted that way, and what "real" even meant. There is no single correct answer. Today, there continue to be working cowboys—people who tend cattle and engage in other ranch work from atop a horse—but they are few in number and often somewhat geographically isolated. Cowboy culture is a moving target, with most of its constituents peripheral to the characteristic they consider its core.

As Romano and Potter's edited volume *Doing Recent History* has reminded me, historians participate in the construction of the histories they write, and this is certainly true herein. I do not merely refer to the discussions of my own experiences alongside those of cowboy Christians; what I mean is that the story I tell is a curated one, and if another scholar were to tell it, it might look dramatically different. In my decision to choose the starting point of 1865, I implicitly invoke notions of the romanticized Anglo cowboy of the open range, and I ultimately use that image as a measuring device for what is occurring in the present. Someone else, however, might argue that this story rightly begins only in the 1990s, and that all cowboy religion prior to that time belongs in a different analysis. That would, certainly, change how ideas like *cowboy* and *authenticity* are perceived and defined. Similarly, by choosing comparison points in American religion such as muscular Christianity and Jesus movement revivalism, I highlight particular aspects of the cowboy Christian enterprise that resonate with my own interests in religious history. Others might encounter this religious movement and see entirely different trends and nuances. And, were I writing several decades hence, it is unlikely that I would choose 2016 as a stopping point in the exploration.

Like the research projects of many who write recent history, it is only for practical reasons that this project concludes at this moment in time, and that fact has no relationship to whether the cowboy church is itself concluding, or plateauing, or has become substantially developed such that it is ready to be assessed in a way that I pass off as authoritative. Cowboy church is a thriving and changing entity, and cowboy Christians continue to remake their world every day.

A Note on Sources

The fieldwork on which this book is based was conducted between 2011 and 2016. During that time, I attended services at cowboy churches in Oklahoma and Texas, attempting to have a diverse array of experiences in terms of location, congregation size, and denomination. I was able to visit some churches more than once over the course of the project. In addition, I attended Nazarene Cowboy Church University twice, and I attended AFCC Cowboy Church Clinics (formerly Ranchhouse School) three times. I also attended a handful of rodeo churches and several other special events of a cowboy Christian nature.

It is difficult to pinpoint the precise number of visits I made. For example, if I attended a worship service that took place as part of a cowboy church training seminar, should it be counted as an individual service visit? Or if a church was so large that it had multiple service times, and I attended more than one service on a given day, did that count for multiple visits? These and other intricacies make the number approximate, so I generally say that the research is based on more than fifty service visits. My original intention was to visit a larger number, but after a few years I found that I was seeing the same thing over and over with little variation, and the investments of time and money to travel for the visits were giving diminishing returns.

Initially, I chose the sites somewhat randomly, picking places that were within a three-hour drive from my home in central Oklahoma. But I soon turned to a snowball approach, in which I asked pastors to recommend other churches to visit, and this method guided the rest of my research process without dictating it. Whenever possible, I informed pastors in advance of my visit, and with each person I met I made a point to identify myself as a researcher as soon as I had any opportunity to do so.

The most significant sources for this project were the dozens of people who generously gave of their time by allowing me to interview them. In the bibliographic entries I have distinguished "interviews" from "personal communications." Interviews were formal question-and-answer sessions that were audio recorded and typically lasted one to two hours. Almost all of these were conducted in person, except where noted in the bibliography. In many cases, a pastor's wife would be present during an interview but did not speak; I have listed the wife's name in the bibliography only when she actively participated in the conversation. In contrast, things labeled as personal communications were relatively informal conversations in which I made it clear that I was conducting research—so they were distinct from the casual chitchat one might make with church members before or after a service, for example—but they were not guided by the same formal question structure, and they were not typically audio recorded. A location is included in the reference if a personal communication was face to face; all others were by telephone or email.

Interviewees had the option of remaining anonymous, and a few chose complete anonymity. In some instances, people said only one or two things that they specifically did not want associated with their identity; in cases where I used that information, I rendered the speaker anonymous. What that means is that some interviews are technically listed twice in the bibliography, once by their name and a second time as "anonymous" with a random number assignation. There are also several cases in which the speaker did not ask for anonymity but, in an effort at protection, I classified him as anonymous because I thought he might regret something he had said on the record. Lastly, when drawing on information that was spoken as part of a public appearance, I have tried to indicate that fact in the text.

A number of archival sources, especially papers related to church histories, were loaned to me by individuals. These are listed in the bibliography with as much specificity as possible, but in general these items are not publicly available. A few rare publications were purchases that I made online from used book sellers.

Notes

1. This short introduction is a composite portrait, meant to be illustrative of cowboy church in general. It pulls in descriptive elements from various churches I have visited.

2. Following the lead of my subjects, in this book I use the terms *western heritage culture* and *cowboy culture* interchangeably. In some ways, "western heritage culture" is a particularly problematic term, because it suggests that modern-day people are consciously attempting to preserve or recreate something of the past, but it is a relatively nebulous "something" that gets labeled as "western." Nonetheless, I appreciate that people sometimes choose this term because they are hesitant to identify as cowboy, perceiving *that* word to be about an even more specific laboring culture that they are not necessarily part of.

3. This was the Horse & Bible Fellowship held at Celtic Cross Equestrian Center. Though they had some aspirations of becoming a church someday, at the time of my visit in 2012, it consisted of a handful of people meeting in the stables for Bible study.

4. Limerick, in *The Legacy of Conquest*, emphasizes that many thematic and temporal divisions made by historians of the American West, as well as mythologies about the western ethos, have prevented us from recognizing historical continuity as well as actual patterns of change and development. See esp. chap. 10. My interest in the concept of "the unbroken past" corresponds with her approach.

5. As with anything, scholarly opinion delineating subregions is varied. Some place Oklahoma and Texas in the Southern Great Plains; others have called it the western South; and others would distinguish the two as not being part of the same subregion at all. These are only a few examples from among the many possibilities.

6. Steiner and Wrobel, "Many Wests," 3; see also Meinig, "American Wests."

7. Some colleagues have expressed that this term sounds derogatory. However, "horse people" is a neutral phrase commonly used within my subject community, and I have adopted it as another way to reference a broad swath of people who identify with aspects of cowboy culture by virtue of their interest in horses. This also extends to many people in the racing industry.

8. Savage, *Cowboy Life*, 209.

9. Information and quotations related to the target audience come from official handbooks and lectures given at cowboy church training seminars.

10. "American Fellowship of Cowboy Churches," 1. Elaborations on these categories are based on field notes from Cowboy Church Clinics.

11. As stated at Cowboy Church Clinic, 23 May 2015.

12. Stacy Wiley, personal communication. No pseudonyms are used in this text; interviewees who preferred to remain anonymous are identified by number only.

13. Jon Coe, interview with author.

14. Gary Morgan, interview with author.

15. Ibid.

16. Several pastors I interviewed made a point of mentioning that they have a contingent of bikers in their church. Most seemed pleased by it but also regard the bikers as being outside of their target group.

17. Todd Mitchell, interview with author.

18. Michael Meeks, interview with author.

19. Lynn Walker, personal communication.

20. Coe, interview with author.

21. Lawrence, *Rodeo*, 84.

22. Lone Star Cowboy Churches follow a particular model for organization and ministry. It began as an independent group under the leadership of Jon Coe and was gradually absorbed by the Church of the Nazarene, which is now the parent denomination. However, cowboy churches within the Nazarene denomination are not required to be part of the Lone Star group, which members refer to as a franchise.

23. There are cowboy churches that exist internationally, including but not limited to missions of American cowboy churches. These are beyond the research scope of this book.

24. Similarly, AFCC executive director Todd Mitchell said that when he first began, a large part of his job was investigating the status of all the churches that were supposedly a part of the organization. He explained that because of the movement's explosive growth, he needed to "stabilize . . . what had already been started," which included determining when churches were no longer following the model.

25. Terry Hill, interview with author; John Spencer, as stated at Cowboy Church University, 26 Apr. 2014.

26. Dan O'Daniel, personal communication.

27. Anonymous interview 008.

28. For examples and discussion of these terms, see Perry et al., "Toward a Typology"; Roozen, "Church Dropouts"; Marler and Hadaway, "Toward a Typology"; Cragun and Hammer, "'One Person's Apostate'"; Tamney, Powell, and Johnson, "Innovation Theory"; and Lim, MacGregor, and Putnam, "Secular and Liminal." Individual researchers typically use terminology in consistent ways from study to study, but as a whole, the social science world employs many different words, making it difficult to compare studies. From 1984–2008, the Barna Group, a Christian-based research company that conducts public opinion polls, used the term "unchurched" to refer to those who had not attended a religious service in the six months immediately prior. In 2008, Barna stopped using "unchurched" and introduced new terminology, ostensibly for the sake of precision.

29. This survey was taken voluntarily by women attending a conference loosely affiliated with the cowboy church. A total of 265 usable forms were completed.

30. More detailed statistics on prior denominational affiliation are not possible, because some people left the question blank and others answered it in ways that were not classifiable, such as "Christian" or "Bible-based church."

31. However, a portion of these people might claim they are new Christians in a theological sense. I expect that most cowboy church leaders will say that demographics about women are irrelevant to them, because they are primarily concerned with the religious status of men.

32. Pew Research Center, *Religious Landscape Study*, "Gender Composition" and "The Unaffiliated by State," 2014, http://www.pewforum.org/religious-landscape-study/. The same study found that, nationwide, 27 percent of men and 19 percent of women were religiously unaffiliated; in Texas the percentage of unaffiliated men was just under 11 percent.

33. See Aihoshi, "The Best Place," 116–19; Bendixsen, "Pastoralist Ethic," chap. 3; and McAdams, "Can I Get a Yee-Haw," chap. 2.

34. J. Williams, "Historicizing the Breakbeat," 135n10; 147.

35. Aihoshi, "The Best Place," 115.

36. J. Williams, "Historicizing the Breakbeat," 163.

37. For more on this, see Aihoshi, "The Best Place," who writes about cowboy identity as related to place. In chap. 5, she explores the way history of other groups, such as Native peoples, is erased and invalidated when people claim that cowboys and ranchers were the first caretakers of the land. Also interesting is Bendixsen, in "Pastoralist Ethic," who actively delves into contradictions within cowboy images and self-perceptions. He writes that while the cowboy is a "folk hero" associated with taming the frontier and a host of other positively-conceived American actions, he also represents "chauvinism, homophobia, racism, religious intolerance, and anti-intellectualism" (5).

38. George Spurger, interview with author.

39. Mike Morrow, interview with author.

40. Ron Nolen, interview with author.

41. Anonymous interview 001.

42. Mitchell, interview with author.

43. Barker, "What Are We Studying," 94–99.

44. Ibid., 96.

45. Ibid., 96–98.

46. This definition comes from David Bebbington, *Evangelicalism in Modern Britain*, 2–3. There are also cowboy Christians, and some cowboy churches, that lean more toward fundamentalism.

47. Putney, *Muscular Christianity*, 1–5, 11, 98.

48. Ladd and Mathisen, *Muscular Christianity*, chap. 5.

49. Ibid., 203–7.

50. Messner, *Politics of Masculinities*, 24–32.

51. Miller, in *Reinventing American Protestantism*, uses the term "new paradigm" to describe a particular kind of church body, which differs from its earlier usage as a lens through which the American religious landscape could be understood, 13–16. For discussion of its use as a lens, see Warner, "Work in Progress."

52. Miller claims all twelve *must* be present to make it a new paradigm church, an insistence with which I disagree. In the case of the cowboy church, the remaining two factors—extensive small group ministries, and worship serving as a vehicle for deep emotional connections with God—do describe some churches, but are not broadly characteristic of them. Miller, *Reinventing American Protestantism*, 20.

53. Ibid., 11.

54. For instance, in 1983–1984, an exhibition entitled "The American Cowboy" toured five North American cities, stirring up controversy in some circles because it depicted late 1800s working cowboys as common laborers engaged in a brutal lifestyle, rather than as heroic and noble men engaged in adventure. The National Cowboy Hall of Fame in Oklahoma City (now the National Cowboy and Western Heritage Museum) was so offended by this depiction that it demanded the premature return of an object loaned for exhibit. William Savage has referred to similar reactions after the publication of Forbis, *The Cowboys*, in 1973. See further discussion in Savage, *Cowboy Hero*, 15–18.

55. Westermeier, "The Cowboy and Religion"; and Westermeier, *Trailing the Cowboy*, chap. 6.

56. Szasz, *The Protestant Clergy Clergy in the Great Plains and Mountain West, 1865–1915*; and Szasz, *Religion in the Modern American West*.

57. These include Homann, "Contemporary Cowboy Culture"; McAdams, "Can I Get a Yee-Haw"; Moczygemba, "Rounding Up Christian Cowboys"; Williford, "Ethereal Cowboy Way"; and K. F. Williams, "The Land-Grant Mission."

58. I also conducted a small number of formal interviews with people who held a leadership role in cowboy church but were not pastors. On a related note,

I occasionally encountered people who distinguish between ministers and pastors; in this text, I use the two words as interchangeable titles.

59. There were a couple of notable exceptions in which people affiliated with the AFCC demonstrated a high degree of concern about who I was interviewing and how the church would be officially represented, but these were definitely the exceptions rather than the rule.

60. Anonymous interview 002.

61. Cody Custer, personal communication. As demonstrated in Annie Blazer's work, the "witnessing without words" approach is increasingly common among those who serve in sports ministry; see *Playing for God*, chap. 1.

62. The survey form filled out by women is an exception to this. I was not able to balance it with a survey for men because there is no comparable event that draws large numbers of average male cowboy church members. There are some small men's ministry events, like the Testicle Festival and Horse Gate, but as a woman I would not be welcome to attend. In her master's thesis, Moczygemba discusses facing the same challenges regarding paperwork, data collection, and trust in cowboy church fieldwork; "Rounding Up Christian Cowboys," 18.

63. There were several points—race and ethnicity among them—that were not part of my original question set for pastors. Over time, that question set developed based on issues I observed. For instance, though I did not initially ask pastors about the role of women in cowboy church, I added that to my line of questioning once I observed it was a point of tension. Similarly, although I do refer to a few pastors' comments about sexuality, I also chose not to pursue questions about homosexuality within the cowboy church. There are small numbers of gay and lesbian cowboy church members and participants, but as with race and ethnicity, the issue of homosexuality in the cowboy church movement deserves its own specialized study with parameters and lines of inquiry that are different from this study's design.

64. Coe, interview with author. However, a high volume of seasonal transience was identified as a hindrance to sustaining churches among this community.

65. There have been several attempts to start cowboy ministries targeting African Americans in Texas. Northeast Texas Cowboy Church, located in Big Sandy, was founded in 2011 as an African American cowboy church. It has a core of about fifty members, and to date it is the only African American cowboy church that has achieved a level of stability, though other church starts are underway in Goliad, Joppa, and Bedias.

66. Ezard Charles Thomas, personal communication. Thomas is careful to note that although his congregation is racially mixed, as an institution it deliberately maintains a strong African American cultural identity.

67. There was also one instance when the pastor pulled in a male chaperone. Retrospectively, I see that my only interviews conducted completely in private were with older, more experienced pastors.

68. Interview transcripts are available online through the catalog of East Texas Research Center, R. W. Steen Library, Stephen F. Austin State University. In personal communication with Jake McAdams, April 2016, I confirmed that crying had not been edited out of his interview transcripts.

CHAPTER 2

1. Adams, *Old-Time Cowhand*, 47–56, 61.
2. My summary of western life and work in this section is based on and synthesized from several excellent sources: Clayton, Hoy, and Underwood, *Vaqueros, Cowboys, and Buckaroos*; Forbis, *The Cowboys*; Slatta, *Cowboys of the Americas*; and Taylor and Maar, *American Cowboy*. Unique pieces of information and quoted material are cited to precise sources.
3. Fussell, *Raising Steaks*, chap. 2; *Oxford Encyclopedia of Food and Drink in America*, s.v. "meat."
4. Carlson, "Myth and the Modern Cowboy," 3–5; Jordan, "Pistol Packin' Cowboy," 62–63. For a deconstruction of the gendered term "cow," see Lawrence, *Rodeo*, 173, 195–97.
5. Richard Slatta has said that cowboys may have also used "Christian" as a label for white men working the range, in contrast with nonwhite cowboys; Slatta, *Cowboys of the Americas*, 227. Some people have used "cowmen" as a generic reference for anyone who worked in the industry, whether or not they were a power holder.
6. Sheepherders were also present on the open range in the postbellum period, but they were quite distinct from cowboys. They spent much time on foot and the rest riding a wagon, which made their job very different. Cowboys and sheepherders were not usually on good terms, with each finding the other to be a nuisance. Demographically, the sheepherders were typically older Mexican men. Carlson, "Cowboys and Sheepherders," 109–11.
7. Hine, *American West*, 128; Skaggs, *Cattle-Trailing Industry*, 89–91; Forbis, *The Cowboys*, 183.
8. See discussions in Slatta, *Cowboy Encyclopedia*, 393–94; Fussell, *Raising Steaks*, 75; WPA Federal Writers' Project Collection, interviews with Georgia B. Redfield, New Mexico, 28 July 1939, and J. J. Woody, Texas, n.d.
9. Historians do not agree on an end date of this era, and therefore various interpretations are widely available.
10. Scholars have used several terms for this same idea, including the "cowboy hero," the "iconic cowboy," or the "cowboy myth." It did not become the prevailing idea of the cowboy until after the golden era of cowboy work had concluded.
11. Moore, *Cow Boys*, 11–13.
12. Examples include Baptist missionary Z. N. Morrell, Catholic monk P. F. Parisot, and Episcopalian archdeacon Cyrus Brady. See Morrell, *Flowers and Fruits*, 385;

Parisot, *Reminiscences*, 9; Brady, *Recollections*, 119; and Szasz, *Protestant Clergy*, chap. 2.

13. Diary of Sam Newcomb, quoted in Rister, *Southern Plainsmen*, 178.

14. *The Tascosa Pioneer*, 12 June 1886, quoted in Haley, *The XIT*, 199.

15. *Texas Livestock Journal*, 21 January 1888, quoted in Slatta, *Cowboy Encyclopedia*, 307.

16. "Personal Intelligence," *Washington Post*, 18 January 1888; "Personals," *Chicago Daily Tribune*, 4 February 1888.

17. For examples, see Moore, *Cow Boys*; Szasz, *Protestant Clergy*; Taylor and Maar, *American Cowboy*; and Westermeier, "The Cowboy and Religion." This same sentiment is expressed today as the idea that cowboys are natural believers in God even though they may not yet *know* God.

18. Adams, *Old-Time Cowhand*, 47–48; Westermeier, "The Cowboy and Religion," 32–33; Szasz, *Protestant Clergy*, 84; Slatta, *Cowboy Encyclopedia*, x.

19. James, *Cow-Boy Life in Texas*, 153–54; "Educators, Churchmen," *Los Angeles Times*, 26 September 1915; "Was a Fighting Parson," *Washington Post*, 17 October 1915; Rollins, *The Cowboy*, 84; Abbott and Smith, *We Pointed Them North*, 79. I was unable to identify the Bible parody referred to by Rollins.

20. Haley, *The XIT*, 114–16.

21. Graves, *Reminiscences*, 75; Szasz, *Protestant Clergy*, 81; J. M. Evans, *Bloys Cowboy Camp Meeting*, 18; James, *Cow-Boy Life in Texas*, 156–60.

22. This phrase, "from the pasture to the pastorate," is commonly used today among cowboy church leaders to describe the ideal cowboy church pastor.

23. J. W. Anderson, *From the Plains*, 16–20, 80–81, 184–85, 257, 147–52.

24. James, *Cow-Boy Life in Texas*, 14, 28.

25. Ibid., 28–29.

26. Ibid., 194–96, 50–51. An interesting discussion of the cowboy idiom in relation to religion is found in Fife and Fife, *Heaven on Horseback*, 1–6.

27. J. W. Anderson, *From the Plains*, 60.

28. Hart, *History*, 6–7, 76; J. M. Evans, *Bloys Cowboy Camp Meeting*, 4–14. Evans explicitly states that it was typical for the meeting to be attended by whole families and their entire staff, save for one or two people left behind to tend the ranch, and that preparing for this kind of sojourn was an intense undertaking.

29. Letter from Sam F. Means, quoted in J. M. Evans, *Bloys Cowboy Camp Meeting*, 80, 7, 1; Bennett, "Bloys Camp Meeting," 179; J. M. Evans, *Cowboys' Hitchin' Post*, 12. The WPA Federal Writers' Project transcribes the first name of Mrs. Means as Eva, rather than Exa.

30. Bennett, "Bloys Camp Meeting," chap. 3; J. M. Evans, *Bloys Cowboy Camp Meeting*, 36; J. M. Evans, *Cowboys' Hitchin' Post*, 23–26; Hall, *Main Trail*, 163–65.

31. The event was originally called the Cowboy Camp Meeting; it was formally given the Bloys name as an honorific after his death in 1917. For a more detailed discussion of Bloys Camp Meeting history and development, see Bennett, "Bloys Camp Meeting," chap. 4.

32. Forbis, *The Cowboys*, 212, 83–86; Taylor and Maar, *American Cowboy*, 17–20; Fussel *Raising Steaks*, 92; Skaggs, *Cattle-Trailing*, 103.

33. Cranfill, *Dr. J. B. Cranfill's Chronicle*, 66; *The Value of a Dollar 1860–2009*, 4th ed.

34. Slatta, *Cowboy Encyclopedia*, 253; see also Savage, *Cowboy Hero*, chap. 3; Fredriksson, *American Rodeo*, chap. 10; and Carlson, "Cowboys and Sheepherders."

35. Erickson, *Modern Cowboy*, 34–37.

36. Sweeney, "Racism," 67; see also Hassrick, *Remington*.

37. Lawrence, *Rodeo*, 44–45; Taylor and Maar, *American Cowboy*, 67–68; Moses, *Wild West Shows*, 22–23; program book of *Cody's Wild West*, 1888, quoted in Savage, *Cowboy Hero*, 109–12; D. Russell, "The Cowboy," 10–12.

38. Savage, *Cowboy Hero*, 137–40; D. Russell, "The Cowboy," 12–13.

39. Fussell, *Raising Steaks*, 75; Taylor and Maar, *American Cowboy*, 63, 73; see also Hine, *American West*, 134–38; and Lawrence, *Rodeo*, 48.

40. Articles about Mulcahy can be found in the *Los Angeles Times*, 1895–1897; articles about Bettes can be found in the *Washington Post, Indianapolis Journal*, and *Los Angeles Times*, 1898–1909; articles about the Rice couple can be found in the *Chicago Daily Tribune, New York Times*, and *Los Angeles Times*, 1893–1901. There are variant name spellings for all of them.

41. For examples, see Clayton, "John A. Lomax"; Dorson, *American Folklore*; Szasz, *Protestant Clergy*; and Westermeier, "The Cowboy and Religion."

42. Thorp, *Songs of the Cowboys*; see also Logsdon, "The Cowboy's Bawdy Music," 127–31; and Logsdon, *Whorehouse Bells*, 296–302.

43. Logsdon, "The Cowboy's Bawdy Music," 132.

44. For examples of critiques of Lomax, see Taylor and Maar, *American Cowboy*; Slatta, *Cowboy Encyclopedia*; Porterfield, *Last Cavalier*; and Bartis, "A History." Many people have characterized Lomax's method of cowboy song collection as careless, even as they recognize that his later projects were of a high quality.

45. Lomax, *Songs of the Cattle Trail*, xi.

46. Porterfield, *Last Cavalier*, 152–55; Taylor and Maar, *American Cowboy*, 75–76; Lomax, *Cowboy Songs*, 59.

47. Logsdon, "The Cowboy's Bawdy Music," 130–34; Logsdon, *Whorehouse Bells*, 283–87; Tinsley, *He Was Singin'*, xiii; McCoy, *Historic Sketches*, 101.

48. Fredriksson, *American Rodeo*, 13–18, 29–33. Historians do not all agree about the precise definition and time period of the B-Western film; I am influenced by the scholarship of Rainey, "The Reel Cowboy." See also Stanfield, *Horse Opera*, 78–84; and McGillis, *He Was Some Kind of a Man*, chap. 1.

49. Taylor and Maar, *American Cowboy*, 76–77; Fenster, "Preparing the Audience," 271–72; Rainey, "Reel Cowboy," 52–53; George-Warren, *Public Cowboy*, 184; Stanfield, *Horse Opera*, 60–61, 83–85.

50. Wedel, "Permission to Dissent," 32.

51. Stuart Hamblen interview transcripts, 1974 and 1986; Fry and Lee, *Texas Country Singers*, 27–29; Hamblen, *The Cowboy Church*, liner notes. There are considerable conflicts in the historical record regarding *Cowboy Church of the Air*. The text represents my best effort at reconstructing some of the show's history.

52. George-Warren, *Public Cowboy*, 184–93, 256. Savage offers an interesting feminist critique of one of the "Commandments," in Savage, *Cowboy Hero*, 100–104.

53. The present-day cowboy church's incarnation of the Cowboy Ten Commandments, while perhaps conceptually inspired by these early lists, is actually a cowboy-lingo version of the biblical Ten Commandments.

54. Information about Leonard Eilers in this section comes from Eilers, *Breaking Into the Movies*, and numerous articles and advertisements found in the *Los Angeles Times*, 1940–1988.

55. Information about Kellogg is based on autobiographical sermons in Kellogg, *Broncho Buster*, and articles in the *Chicago Daily Tribune* 1931–1932, *Los Angeles Times* 1932–1936, *Pentecostal Evangel* 1934–1935, and *The Latter Rain Evangel* 1932 and 1934.

56. Hall, *Main Trail*, 47–50. Szasz erroneously suggests that Hall sometimes worked as a ranch hand because his missionary salary was too low. However, Hall's autobiography more clearly indicates that this was a deliberate strategy for proselytism to a group that would be unlikely to welcome a preacher.

57. Ibid., 24, 103, 87, 83.

58. Erickson, *Modern Cowboy*, 25–26; see also Lawrence, *Rodeo*, 117.

CHAPTER 3

1. The following is summarized from author interview with Dave Harvey. The headquarters of CFC is no longer in the same location.

2. My summary of rodeo history in this chapter is based on and synthesized from several excellent sources: Fredriksson, *American Rodeo*; Lawrence, *Rodeo*; and LeCompte, *Cowgirls of the Rodeo*. Unique pieces of information and quoted material are cited to precise sources.

3. Both the RAA and CTA later changed names; the CTA still exists today as the Professional Rodeo Cowboys' Association, or PRCA.

4. For examples and discussion of this sentiment, see Lawrence, *Rodeo*, 106–14.

5. Fredriksson, *American Rodeo*, 92.

6. Lawrence, *Rodeo*, 85–88; Thor, "Realities of Rodeo," S52–53.

7. See discussions in Rainey, "Reel Cowboy"; Savage, *Cowboy Hero*, chap. 8; and Wooden and Ehringer, *Rodeo*, chap. 12.

8. Letter from L. Morris Eiffert, *Christian Ranchman*, v. 2 n. 4, 1975–1976.

9. McGill et al., "Personality Characteristics," 147–48.

10. K. D. Tucker Whitaker, interview with author.

11. Smith, *Apostle, Cowboy Style*, 10.

12. St. John, *On Down the Road*, 14–27, 54–56, 121, 147–50; Wooden and Ehringer, *Rodeo in America*, 102–3.

13. Thor, "Realities of Rodeo," S53.

14. Whitaker, interview with author.

15. References to Sam Ed Spence in this section come from interview with author.

16. Spence, interview with author; Hillhouse, *Horses, Hoofbeats, and Halos*, chap. 2. A different version of Roberts's story is found in a 2010 ESPN.com article written by Claire Novak, but the essential trajectory is the same as that told by Spence.

17. J. Woodrow Fuller, quoted in Hillhouse, *Horses, Hoofbeats, and Halos*, 9.

18. Hillhouse, *Horses, Hoofbeats, and Halos*, 9, 11–14, 20, 86; N. Evans, *Muddy Shoes*, xix, 32. Dawson and Roberts both quoted in Hillhouse.

19. Hillhouse, *Horses, Hoofbeats, and Halos*, 4, 14–16; Spence, interview with author; Carl Crisswell, interview with author.

20. See further discussion in Sullivan, *A Ministry of Presence*, chap. 5.

21. Quoted in Hillhouse, *Horses, Hoofbeats, and Halos*, 21.

22. Evans quoted in Hillhouse, *Horses, Hoofbeats, and Halos*, 23; also recounted in N. Evans, *Muddy Shoes*, 173–76.

23. Tapes loaned to author by the Cowboys for Christ archive.

24. Spence, interview with author; Steve Womack, personal communication; Harvey, interview with author.

25. Except where noted, biographical information about Ted Pressley and direct quotes from him come from transcripts of unpublished interviews conducted by Becca Cox Schilinski, formerly Becca Doe Cox, in 1999.

26. Spence, interview with author; Womack, personal communication.

27. Letters numbered 1 through 7, and newsletters from vol. 2, 1975 and 1976, Cowboys for Christ archives.

28. *Christian Ranchman*, v. 3 n. 1 1977, v. 7 n. 5 1981, v. 10 n. 8 1984.

29. Dunn, *Sharing the Victory*.

30. Lynne Schricker, personal communication; Hurley, "Christian Cowboys"; McCaffrey, "God Does."

31. Sheler, *Believers*, 104–7; Schricker, personal communication; Spencer, "Christian Cowboys."

32. "News Worthy," *Christian Ranchman* v. 2 n. 4 1975–1976; Pressley, interview transcripts. Steve Womack, who worked with both FCC and CFC in the 1970s, recalls there was occasionally some competitiveness between the organizations; he also felt the FCC was not as welcoming to preachers like himself who were weekend rodeoers rather than full-time professionals.

33. FUMC-CS archives; Rocky Mountain Conference . . . Collection.

34. FUMC-CS archives; Rocky Mountain Conference . . . Collection.

35. Larry Miller, interview with author.

36. Except where noted, all information in this section comes from Jeff and Sherry Copenhaver, interview with author; Jeff Copenhaver personal communication; and Jeff Copenhaver personal papers.

37. Denton and Morris, *The Money*, 31; Swanson, *Blood Aces*, 2.

38. Deborah Copenhaver-Fellows is the artist who created the well-known sculpture of Benny Binion, originally installed at the Horseshoe Club but later relocated several times. In *The Money*, Denton and Morris praise it as "the first public statue in the nation honoring a gambler, and in otherwise gaudy, statue-laden Las Vegas, the only sculpture of a real-life character instead of mythological gods and monsters" (37).

39. Hopkins, "Benny Binion," 66–67.

40. I capitalize Cowboy Church in this section because Copenhaver incorporated his specific church with that name. Lowercase letters are used throughout the book when I am speaking about cowboy church more generally.

41. Peter Applebome, "Church Just Like Home to Cowboys," *New York Times*, 27 Apr. 1987.

42. Eccles. 1:9: "What has been will be again, what has been done will be done again; there is nothing new under the sun" (NIV).

43. Barker, "Plus ça Change . . ."; see also Barker, "What Are We Studying?"

44. As of 2016, this church still exists in that space as Ranchman's Cowboy Church.

45. Karin Miller, "Nashville Cowboy Church's Simple Message, Style Resonate," *Mobile Reporter*, 3 January 2004. That church is now called the Nashville Cowboy Church and it meets in a theater; it seems to have a large tourist appeal.

46. Except where noted, all information in this section is based on Miller, interview with author, and the church document "Cowboy Church of Henrietta."

47. According to pastor Larry Miller, the Iowa Park church eventually moved to its own building.

48. Copenhaver, interview with author; Spence, interview with author.

49. Miller, personal communication.

50. See Barker, "Plus ça Change . . ."

51. Information about this church is based on Russ Weaver, interview with author; Russ Weaver, interview with Jake McAdams, transcript; and site visit to Shepherd's Valley church by author.

52. On the day I visited, the montage also included an advertisement for an upcoming series about the Bible that would be shown on the History Channel. The *Cowboy Church* program, discussed further in chapter 6, sometimes includes Weaver's sermons.

53. Information in this paragraph is based on Paul and Donna Lutz, interview with author.

54. Personally, I found him to be intelligent and focused with a dry sense of humor. The "White Whale" is a reference to *Moby Dick*.

55. Except where noted, information in this section is based on Ron and Jane Nolen, interview with author.

56. Morgan, interview with author.

57. This is also true of the Nolens. In a single interview with them, they indicated several different pivotal moments.

58. Core Group meeting minutes from 1999 and 2000, as reprinted in "The Beginnings."

59. "The Beginnings."

60. Morgan, interview with author.

61. Morgan, interview with author.

62. Nolen, personal communication.

63. It does not appear that the TFCC was ever a formal suborganization of the BGCT. The IRS website indicates that the TFCC obtained tax-exempt status in June 2006, at the time Ron Nolen left the Convention to become its full time director.

64. Horn and Morgan, "A Brief History"; Morgan, personal communication.

65. Horn and Morgan, "A Brief History."

66. "Cowboy Church Board Removes Nolen from Leadership Post," *Baptist Standard*, 6 October 2010; Nolen, personal communication.

67. As AFCC executive director Todd Mitchell conveyed to me, legally the TFCC still exists, though it is only on paper. The AFCC operates under its aegis.

68. Horn and Morgan, "A Brief History."

69. Anonymous personal communication 004.

70. Anonymous interview 005.

71. Morgan, personal communication.

72. Morrow, interview with author.

73. Pressley, interview transcripts.

74. Copenhaver, interview with author. As a point of clarity, the historical record disputes several aspects of this version. For example, Rutherford's dissertation on Pentecostal evangelist David du Plessis shows that the earliest reported versions of the prophecy indicated the revival would be led by Pentecostals. See Rutherford, "From Prosecutor to Defender," 147–50. Copenhaver is the only pastor who ever told me that three groups would be part of the great revival; other pastors only seemed to be aware of cowboys in the prophecy.

75. Something I found particularly interesting was how this story became distorted even further. For example, Copenhaver's name came up in another interview, and it became evident that my interviewee had heard a version of this story but thought it was Copenhaver himself who had claimed to have raised people from the dead. As a result, this person was skeptical of him. I tried to clarify but was not sure I changed the interviewee's impression.

76. Nolen, interview with author.

77. Smith, *Apostle, Cowboy Style*, 156. This version is so different that one might question whether he is referring to another prophecy altogether. However, the historical record indicates that, at most, Wigglesworth only uttered one prophecy; more likely, he never uttered one at all.

78. Cartwright, *The Real Smith Wigglesworth*, 12.

79. For examples see Rutherford, "From Prosecutor to Defender," esp. chap. 5; and Cartwright, *The Real Smith Wigglesworth*, 153–59.

80. Rutherford, "From Prosecutor to Defender," 174, indicates that the messages of du Plessis were prone to situational changes.

81. It is also possible that McLeish read the same book Nolen recalled, and that that book is the source of the cowboy detail. I scoured many small old paperbacks about Wigglesworth in search of this factoid but did not find it. My attempts to locate McLeish were also unsuccessful.

CHAPTER 4

1. Verna Reid, personal communication.

2. Nolen, interview with author.

3. Coe, interview with author.

4. Nolen, interview with author.

5. Ron and Jane Nolen, "Ranchhouse School."

6. Nolen, interview with author.

7. Morgan, interview with author.

8. Todd Mitchell, personal communication. I refer to the event interchangeably as a school and a clinic.

9. At one school I did receive a booklet that contained more detailed information. At a second school they ran out of the booklets, and at the third I did not see any booklets at all.

10. In my experience, men significantly outnumbered women at the clinics.

11. In the spirit of full disclosure: I traveled to Colorado and Texas to attend CCU, and in both cases the Church waived my registration fee.

12. They interchangeably refer to it as a model, a method, and a methodology.

13. Michael Meeks, interview with author.

14. For an excellent discussion of this issue, see Gregg, *Sparks from the Anvil*.

15. In our interview, Nolen recalled that the low barrier language he used came specifically from the book *Natural Church Development* by Christian Schwarz; however when I read Schwarz it became clear to me that Nolen had misremembered. The low barrier language is actually found in books by George Hunter and Rick Warren, rather than in Schwarz.

16. For examples, see L. Anderson, *A Church*; Pritchard, *Willow Creek Seeker Services*; Schuller, *Your Church*; Towns, Vaughan, and Seifert, *Complete Book*, esp.

chap. 16. Schuller discusses eleven "growth-restricting obstacles" to churches; however, the only correlations with the low barrier method relate to preaching positive sermons and avoiding controversial subjects from the pulpit. Schuller, *Your Church*, 37–47, 135–41.

17. Strobel, *Inside the Mind*, 166.

18. Nolen, interview with author. These statements about the church as an organism echo ideas found in Schwarz, *Natural Church Development*.

19. Schwarz, *Natural Church Development*, 28–29.

20. Because of a perception that deacons often become power-hungry tyrants, the AFCC cowboy church model has eliminated this position.

21. I also encountered a few cowboy churches that were theologically closer to fundamentalism. For defining evangelicalism and fundamentalism, I use the markers widely accepted within Religious Studies as set forth by both David Bebbington and Mark Noll. For further discussion, see essays in Noll, Bebbington, and Rawlyk, *Evangelicalism*.

22. Anonymous interview 001.

23. Hill, interview with author.

24. Anonymous interview 003.

25. My small, non-American car was always the oddball in the church parking lot. As pastor Mike Morrow joked, my car was the type that should just pull up alongside his truck to nurse.

26. Randy Reasoner, interview with author.

27. I attended services at four cowboy churches that met in traditional church spaces: three in Oklahoma, and one in Texas.

28. Goldberger, "The Gospel." For further discussion about the ideology of megachurch architecture, including deviations from a utilitarian approach, see Loveland and Wheeler, *From Meetinghouse to Megachurch*, esp. chaps. 7–8.

29. For an extended discussion of cowboy church as a "suburban movement," see McAdams, "Can I Get a Yee-Haw," 133–46.

30. Shane Winters, interview with author.

31. Scott McAfee, interview with author. There are many other potential ways to explore the meaning(s) of the physical space of the cowboy church milieu. For instance, if we consider their ideas about spatial simplicity in relation to prosperity gospel theology, we might find an enlightening class analysis related to the space. Or, a consideration of how white privilege plays into this deliberate construction of space might yield an interesting racial analysis of the movement. The physical space is an avenue ripe for further exploration.

32. Morgan, interview with author.

33. Lutz, interview with author.

34. Spurger, interview with author.

35. As stated at Cowboy Church Clinic, 23 May 2015.

36. Jason Taylor, interview with author.

37. Author's rendition of a joke told by pastor Glen Null at Cowboy Church Clinic, 23 May 2015.
38. Spurger, interview with author.
39. Meeks, interview with author.
40. Nolen, interview with author.
41. Morgan, interview with author.
42. As stated at Cowboy Church University, 1 September 2012.
43. Anonymous interview 006.
44. Hill, interview with author.
45. Anonymous interview 001.
46. Meeks, interview with author.
47. In contrast, in "Can I Get a Yee-Haw," 111–27, McAdams finds cowboy churches to be highly politicized environments in which conservative politics are front and center, and he classifies the members as "part of the New Christian Right."
48. Jake Shue, personal communication.
49. Although I never saw a copy, I was told that an early edition of *The Way for Cowboys* contained profiles of some Christian rodeoers who subsequently lost their faith.
50. Harvey, interview with author.
51. Weatherby, *Gospel of Matthew*, i.
52. "Long X Ranch," Save the Cowboy, http://www.savethecowboy.org/longxranch.
53. Taylor, interview with author.
54. Morgan, interview with author.
55. Robert McDonald, interview with author.
56. Mitchell, interview with author.
57. Morrow, interview with author.
58. As I learned in seminars, formal arena events require significant knowledge and organization in a wide variety of areas. For instance, legal release forms, both for youth and adults, are always necessary; public health notices for horses must be posted; if prize money is part of the event, the church has to issue 1099s; the church needs appropriate liability insurance; relatively tame animals should be obtained for rough stock events so that people can actually ride and have a good time. The list of necessary considerations goes on and on. Some leaders spoke against the idea of making money from the arena.
59. Meeks, interview with author.
60. A "play day" with horses is exactly what it sounds like: casual, unstructured time for people to ride their horses in the arena.
61. Anonymous interview 001.
62. Morrow, interview with author.
63. Ibid.
64. Miller, interview with author.
65. Lutz, interview with author.

66. Miller, interview with author.
67. Ginger Hayes, interview with author.
68. Whitaker, interview with author.
69. Although some pastors consider sporadic attendance to be a problem relating to people being new Christians, it is possible that it simply reflects the hectic nature of life in the twenty-first century, and/or modern trends in commitment to voluntary associations.
70. Wiley, personal communication.
71. Nolen, interview with author.
72. Coe, interview with author. The CCU training manual indicates that cowboy churches can anticipate an average income of eight to twelve dollars per week per person.
73. As stated at Ranchhouse School, 29 Mar. 2014.
74. Winters, interview with author.
75. Jason and Christie Taylor, interview with author.
76. Barker, "What Are We Studying?," 94–95.
77. Morrow, interview with author.
78. Winters, interview with author.
79. Miller, interview with author.
80. As stated at Ranchhouse School, 29 Mar. 2014.
81. Nolen, interview with author.
82. Mitchell, interview with author, and personal communication.
83. Reid, personal communication. Verna "Bunny" Reid, the wife of pastor Henry Reid, serves as copastor of their church in Joshua, Texas, where she preaches twice a month.
84. Morgan, interview with author.
85. Ibid.
86. This is also a gendered issue. Later in the session, the same pastor warned those present to never "shun anyone who walks in the door, even if they're wearing a suit and tie." This was met with a round of "amen" from audience members, demonstrating their willingness to accept men on any terms, but not women.
87. When I later asked this pastor about the sources of influence on his moral teachings, he briskly and confidently answered, "I know what's moral and what's not moral." Anonymous interview 008.
88. Morrow, as stated at Cowboy Church Clinic, 23 May 2015, and interview with author.
89. Miller, interview with author.
90. Nolen, interview with author.
91. Coe, interview with author.
92. Among the exceptions in this comparison, the most obvious one is charismata.
93. Strobel, *Inside the Mind*, 28.

94. For further discussion of the spectrum of new paradigm churches, see Miller, *Reinventing American Protestantism*; and Eskridge, *God's Forever Family*, esp. chap. 10.

CHAPTER 5

1. As stated at Ranchhouse School, 29 March 2014; italics mine.
2. As stated at Cowboy Church Clinic, 23 May 2015.
3. Summary and quotes are from Cowboy Church University, 1 September 2012 and 25 April 2014.
4. Meeks interview with author; Morrow interview with author; Coe interview with author; as spoken at CCU, 1 September 2012.
5. Bartkowski, *Remaking the Godly Marriage*, 62.
6. Ladd and Mathisen, *Muscular Christianity*, chap. 5; Putney, *Muscular Christianity*, 3–8.
7. Others might argue that it is not a third wave, but rather an extended second wave.
8. Cole, "Promising," 119, 120.
9. Moczygemba's thesis, "Rounding Up Christian Cowboys," also attests to exceptions in which women hold leadership positions, 82–84.
10. Anonymous interview 001.
11. Copenhaver, interview with author. The issue of male headship became particularly heated in 1998 when the Southern Baptist Convention added explicit formal language affirming it. For history about ideas of male headship in the SBC, see Flowers, *Into the Pulpit*, and among American evangelicals more generally, see Stasson, "The Politicization."
12. Comments from CCU attendees on 25 April 2014 and 2 September 2012; McDonald, interview with author.
13. Reasoner, interview with author.
14. Morgan, interview with author.
15. Mitchell, personal communication.
16. Anonymous interview 008.
17. Anonymous interview 009.
18. Morrow, interview with author.
19. Taylor, interview with author. Technically, Taylor quoted scripture to me, rather than naming the books.
20. For further commentary on the Pastorals, see Dewey, "1 Timothy"; Ehrman, *The New Testament*, chaps. 25 and 26; Fiore, *The Pastoral Epistles*; and Wagener, "Pastoral Epistles."
21. Anonymous interview 007. Although I had completely forgotten this exchange, the transcript shows that at the time I told the pastor I thought it was a problematic comparison. I am not aware of Jesus saying such a thing, but the apostle

Paul makes a point somewhat like this in 1 Cor. 7:21–24. There are similar admonitions in Col. 3 and Eph. 6, though most critical scholars classify both books as pseudepigrapha. My thanks to Jill Hicks-Keeton for these references.

22. Coe, interview with author; Morrow, interview with author; Morgan, interview with author.

23. As spoken at CCU, 25 April 2014; italics mine.

24. As spoken at Ranchhouse School, 24 August 2013; as spoken at CCU, 1 September 2012.

25. As spoken at CCU, 1 September 2012.

26. As spoken at CCU, 26 April 2014.

27. Morrow, *Why Men Hate*, 3–17, 140, 151–52.

28. Many of the sources Morrow uses are controversial from an academic stand-point. For example, the Barna Group, a research firm with an explicitly religious mission, has been known to change its definitions and terminology in apparent attempts to suit outcome purposes. Podles's *The Church Impotent* traces the feminization of Christianity back to the Middle Ages, but has been criticized by scholars for containing numerous historical inaccuracies. And many disregard the extreme conservative perspective taken by Dobson, founder of Focus on the Family and a prolific writer of Christian self-help books.

29. Morrow, interview with author.

30. Anonymous interview 005.

31. Low, "The Truth." I am indebted to the work of Jake McAdams for the footnote that led to Low's article.

32. Haug, Compton, and Courbage, *Demographic Characteristics*, 154–55.

33. The standard international FFS question set asked about the religious identity and involvement of the interviewee and the interviewee's partner, but not about respondents' parents' religion; thus, questions about parental religion must have been additions made on the Swiss version. I was unable to obtain the Swiss FFS survey, but general documents related to the FFS can be found at unece.org, the website of the United Nations Economic Commission for Europe.

34. Haug, Compton, and Courbage, *Demographic Characteristics*, chap. 4; Nicolet and Tresch, "Changing Religiosity," 76–77.

35. Suziedelis and Potvin, "Sex Differences"; Nelsen, "Religious Identification"; Salisbury, "Religious Identity."

36. Kieren and Munro, "Following the Leaders"; Mattis et al., "Factors Influencing"; Clark, Worthington, and Danser, "Transmission."

37. For maternal influence, see Nelsen, "Religious Transmission"; Copen and Silverstein, "Transmission"; Nelsen, "Religious Identification"; and Bao et al., "Perceived Parental Acceptance." For equal parental influence, see Hoge and Petrillo, "Determinants"; Willits and Crider, "Church Attendance"; Ploch and Hastings, "Effects"; Baker-Sperry, "Passing on the Faith"; and Zhai et al., "Parental Divorce." Also relevant to this question is the Pew Research Center

study, "One-in-Five U.S. Adults Were Raised in Interfaith Homes," released on the Pew Forum website 26 October 2016, http://www.pewforum.org/2016/10/26/one-in-five-u-s-adults-were-raised-in-interfaith-homes/.

38. Barna Group, *Churchless*, 37. In some liberal Protestant churches, the gender disparity is much greater, but theological differences make these ill-suited as points of comparison to the cowboy church.

39. I do not believe I saw any service where men outnumbered women. Admittedly, if the space was so large that it would fit many hundreds of people, it was more difficult to count.

40. Laird, *Ordained Women*, 11–13; Perabeau, "Church of the Nazarene," 147–58, 209–10.

41. McDonald, interview with author.

42. As discussed at CCU, 2 September 2012 and 25 April 2014.

43. Information in this section based on Hayes, interview with author and Hayes, personal communication.

44. Coe, interview with author.

45. Winters, interview with author; Morrow, interview with author; Taylor, interview with author.

46. Cowgirl Get Together history is based on Michelle Carson, personal communication and Carson, interview with author. The other women involved in the founding of the event were Debbie Chapman and Vivian Hardgrave.

47. Approximately twenty additional forms were disqualified: some had been filled out by minors, others were incomplete, et cetera.

48. Seven percent left this question blank. Less than 3 percent of total respondents indicated they had a graduate degree.

49. Slightly less than 1 percent wrote in that women should be able to serve as elders but not as pastors.

50. Italics mine. My favorite response was the woman whose reason for opposing female pastors simply said, "I'm Baptist!" as though that explains everything. And perhaps it does.

51. In 2016, follow-up interviews were attempted with every woman who had voluntarily left an email address on her form. Only a small number responded.

52. Women age seventy-plus trended in the opposite direction, agreeing that women should be able to pastor; however, the raw number of respondents in that bracket was not large enough to be statistically significant.

53. This and the following paragraph are based on Harvey, interview with author; and Harvey, personal communication.

54. "Our Thanks Goes Out To . . ." *Christian Ranchman* v. 2 n. 2 1975.

55. Hillhouse, *Horses, Hoofbeats, and Halos*, 39–41, 46–49.

56. Ibid., 76.

57. Qtd. in Hillhouse, *Horses, Hoofbeats, and Halos*, 73.

58. Information in this section based on Alphen, personal communication.

59. This and the following paragraph are based on Miller, interview with author.
60. Bartkowski, *Remaking the Godly Marriage*, 99.

CHAPTER 6

1. He was not "critically" injured, but that was how it appeared to me at the time. Newsom recovered from his injuries—a concussion, facial lacerations, and a torn MCL, according to the PBR website—and returned to working as a bull-fighter within a few weeks.
2. McDannell, *Material Christianity*, chap. 8.
3. PBR history in this section is primarily based on Custer, personal communication; see also Wooden and Ehringer, *Rodeo in America*, 237–38; and Woerner, *Cowboy Up!*, 242–54. Custer referred to the salary as an appearance fee, adding that no one becomes wealthy from it.
4. Sullivan, *A Ministry of Presence*, 176.
5. L. D. Russell, *Godspeed*, 72–73; Lambert, *Spirituality, Inc.*, 125–30.
6. Information in this section is based on Carl Crisswell, personal communication.
7. O'Dell, "Denton Offutt of Kentucky," 173, 174.
8. Ibid., 195–207.
9. Johnson, *Healing Shine*, 312, 208.
10. Although I am not certain what I expected to see/hear, I did expect Christianity to be more explicitly a part of the training itself. Partly this was because in 2012 I attended one of Lew Sterrett's horse clinics as an observer, during which he spoke with me individually about biblical ideas connected with horse training principles.
11. As spoken by Todd Pierce at "Born Wild, Created to be Free," 3 Mar. 2013, Sulphur Springs, Texas.
12. Statements from Mike Lee and Elsie Frost as spoken at "Born Wild, Created to be Free," 3 March 2013.
13. In news reports, Riggs stated that he came up with the idea two days prior to leaving and initially planned to go alone, but others voluntarily joined him on the journey.
14. My thanks to Carl Crisswell for pointing out some of the horse racing distinctions that I was not aware of.
15. My assertion about the nature of these scandals is based on information people have told me, typically off the record, in combination with database searches of public records.
16. Spurger, interview with author.
17. For extensive discussion of these and other religious movement types, see Hadden, "Religious Movements."
18. Eskridge, *God's Forever Family*, 273.
19. Miller, *Reinventing American Protestantism*, 20, 67.

20. Eskridge, *God's Forever Family*, 275.
21. For example, see Loveland and Wheeler, *From Meetinghouse to Megachurch*, chap. 7.
22. A theoretical model for success is laid out in a short article by Stark, "Why Religious Movements"; see also Stark, "How New Religions." Although Stark would characterize cowboy church as a sect, rather than a NRM, this does not alter how its potential for success or failure would be measured using his model.
23. Coe, interview with author.
24. James, *Cow-Boy Life in Texas*, 28.

Bibliography

INTERVIEWS AND PERSONAL COMMUNICATIONS WITH AUTHOR

Anonymous 001. Interview with author. Oklahoma, 2012.
Anonymous 002. Interview with author. Oklahoma, 2012.
Anonymous 003. Interview with author. Oklahoma, 2012.
Anonymous 004. Personal communication with author. Texas, 2013.
Anonymous 005. Interview with author. Texas, 2013.
Anonymous 006. Interview with author. Oklahoma, 2012.
Anonymous 007. Interview with author. Texas, 2014.
Anonymous 008. Interview with author. Oklahoma, 2012.
Anonymous 009. Personal communication with author. Oklahoma, 2012.
Alphen, Lee. Personal communication with author. March 2016.
Carson, Michelle. Interview with author via telephone. May 2016.
Carson, Michelle. Personal communication with author. December 2013.
Coe, Jon. Interview with author. Texas, May 2015.
Copenhaver, Jeff. Personal communication with author. May 2015.
Copenhaver, Jeff and Sherry. Interview with author. Texas, June 2014.
Crisswell, Carl. Personal communication with author. Oklahoma, May 2016.
Custer, Cody. Personal communication with author. Oklahoma, January 2016.
Harvey, Dave. Interview with author. Texas, March 2013.
Harvey, Dave. Personal communication with author. Texas, July 2014.
Hayes, Ginger. Interview with author via telephone. June 2014.
Hayes, Ginger. Personal communication with author. Colorado, September 2012.
Hill, Terry and Evelyn. Interview with author. Oklahoma, May 2012.
Lutz, Paul and Donna. Interview with author. Oklahoma, March 2012.
McAfee, Scott. Interview with author. Oklahoma, June 2012.
McDonald, Robert. Interview with author. Texas, April 2014.
Mecks, Michael E. Interview with author. Oklahoma, February 2012.
Miller, Larry. Interview with author. Texas, September 2013.
Miller, Larry. Personal communication with author. April 2015.

Mitchell, Todd. Interview with author. Texas, August 2013.

Mitchell, Todd. Personal communication with author. Texas, May 2015.

Morgan, Gary. Interview with author. Texas, April 2013.

Morgan, Gary. Personal communication with author. May 2015.

Morrow, Mike. Interview with author. Texas, August 2013.

Nolen, Ron. Personal communication with author. May 2015.

Nolen, Ron and Jane. Interview with author. Texas, June 2014.

O'Daniel, Dan. Personal communication with author. Oklahoma, October 2012.

Reasoner, Randy. Interview with author. Oklahoma, May 2012.

Reid, Verna "Bunny." Personal communication with author. Texas, April 2013.

Schricker, Lynne. Personal communication with author. September 2014.

Shue, Jake. Personal communication with author. Colorado, September 2012.

Spence, Sam Ed. Interview with author. Texas, July 2014.

Spurger, George "Sonny" and Cindy. Interview with author. Texas, March 2013.

Taylor, Jason and Christie. Interview with author. Texas, January 2014.

Thomas, Ezard Charles "Chap." Personal communication with author. July 2016.

Walker, Lynn. Personal communication with author. Oklahoma, July 2012.

Weaver, Russ. Interview with author. Texas, March 2013.

Whitaker, K. D. Tucker. Interview with author. Texas, March 2012.

Wiley, Stacy. Personal communication with author. Texas, January 2014.

Winters, Shane. Interview with author. Texas, April 2013.

Womack, Steve. Personal communication with author. July 2016.

OTHER INTERVIEWS (NOT WITH AUTHOR)

Hamblen, Stuart. Interview by John W. Rumble. Transcript. 30 May 1986. Country Music Foundation Oral History Project, Country Music Hall of Fame and Museum, Nashville, Tennessee.

Hamblen, Stuart, and Suzy Hamblen. Interview by Douglas B. Green. Transcript. Circa 1974. Country Music Foundation Oral History Project, Country Music Hall of Fame and Museum, Nashville, Tennessee.

Pressley, Ted. Interviews by Becca Doe Cox (Schilinski). Transcripts. Texas, January and March 1999. Transcripts held privately by Becca Cox Schilinski.

Weaver, Russ. Interview by Jake McAdams. Transcript. Texas, July 2013. Transcript held by the East Texas Research Center, R. W. Steen Library, Stephen F. Austin State University.

SPECIAL COLLECTIONS AND MIXED-MEDIA SOURCES

"American Fellowship of Cowboy Churches." Seminar workbook, 2013.

"The Beginnings of the Cowboy Church of Ellis County." Booklet from church archives, n.d.

Copenhaver, Jeff. Personal papers. Privately held.

Cowboy Authentic. Television program, RFD-TV. 2013–2014.

Cowboy Church. Television program, RFD-TV. 2007–2016.

"Cowboy Church of Henrietta, 1993–2013." Booklet from church archives, 2013.

"Cowboy Church University: Making Christ-like Disciples in the Western Heritage Culture." Seminar workbooks, 2009, 2012, and 2014.

Cowboys for Christ archives. Privately maintained by president Dave Harvey of Cowboys for Christ.

FUMC-CS. Archives of the First United Methodist Church of Colorado Springs, CO. Privately maintained by the church.

Hamblen, Stuart. *The Cowboy Church.* LP. Waco, TX: Word Records, n.d.

Hart, John A., with others. *History of Pioneer Days in Texas and Oklahoma.* N.p.: n.p., n.d. Western History Collection, University of Oklahoma.

Horn, Greg, and Gary Morgan. "A Brief History of the BGCT and the TFCC/AFCC." Unpublished manuscript, 2013. Print copy.

Nolen, Ron, and Jane Nolen, comps. "Ranchhouse School of Cowboy Church Planting Manual/Workbook." Seminar booklet, 2004.

Pew Research Center. *Religious Landscape Study,* 2014, http://www.pewforum.org/religious-landscape-study/.

Rocky Mountain Conference of the United Methodist Church Collection. Margaret E. Scheve Archives, Iliff School of Theology, Denver, CO.

WPA Federal Writers' Project Collection. Manuscript Division, Library of Congress, http://www.loc.gov/collections/federal-writers-project.

BOOKS, ARTICLES, AND DISSERTATIONS

Abbott, E. C., and Helena Huntington Smith. *We Pointed Them North: Recollections of a Cowpuncher.* Norman: University of Oklahoma Press, 1939.

Adams, Ramon Frederick. *The Old-Time Cowhand.* New York: MacMillan, 1961.

Aihoshi, Terri Cundy. "'The Best Place to Be': 'Keepin' Cowboy' Through Narratives of Place, Experience, and Identity." Master's thesis, York University (Ontario), 1992.

Anderson, John W. *From the Plains to the Pulpit.* Rev. ed. Goose Creek, TX: J. W. Anderson & Sons, 1922.

Anderson, Leith. *A Church for the 21st Century.* Minneapolis: Bethany House, 1992.

Baker-Sperry, Lori. "Passing on the Faith: The Father's Role in Religious Transmission." In "Religion in America," special issue, *Sociological Focus* 34, no. 2 (2001): 185–98.

Bao, Wan-Ning, Les B. Whitbeck, Danny R. Hoyt, and Rand D. Conger. "Perceived Parental Acceptance as a Moderator of Religious Transmission among Adolescent Boys and Girls." *Journal of Marriage and Family* 61, no. 2 (1999): 362–74.

Barker, Eileen. "Plus ça Change . . ." *Social Compass* 42, no. 2 (1995): 165–80.

Barker, Eileen. "What Are We Studying? A Sociological Case for Keeping the 'Nova.'" *Nova Religio* 8, no. 1 (2004): 88–102.

Barna Group, with eds. George Barna and David Kinnaman. *Churchless: Understanding Today's Unchurched and How to Connect with Them*. Austin: Tyndale Momentum, 2014.

Bartis, Peter Thomas. "A History of the Archive of Folk Song at the Library of Congress: The First Fifty Years." PhD diss., University of Pennsylvania, 1982.

Bartkowski, John P. *Remaking the Godly Marriage: Gender Negotiations in Evangelical Families*. New Brunswick, NJ: Rutgers University Press, 2001.

Bebbington, David. *Evangelicalism in Modern Britain: A History from the 1730s to the 1980s*. London: Unwin Hyman, 1989.

Bendixsen, Casper G. "Pastoralist Ethic and a 'Spirit' of Traditionalism: Livestock, Land, and Kin in the US West." PhD diss., Rice University, 2014.

Bennett, David Leo. "Bloys Camp Meeting: Cultural Center of Camaraderie, Community, and Faith in the American Southwest." PhD diss., University of New Mexico, 2004.

Blazer, Annie. *Playing for God: Evangelical Women and the Unintended Consequences of Sports Ministry*. New York: New York University Press, 2015.

Brady, Cyrus. *Recollections of a Missionary in the Great West*. New York: Scribner's, 1900.

Carlson, Paul H. "Cowboys and Sheepherders." In *The Cowboy Way: An Exploration of History and Culture*, edited by Paul H. Carlson, 109–18. Lubbock: Texas Tech University Press, 2000.

Carlson, Paul H. "Myth and the Modern Cowboy." In *The Cowboy Way: An Exploration of History and Culture*, edited by Paul H. Carlson, 1–10. Lubbock: Texas Tech University Press, 2000.

Cartwright, Desmond. *The Real Smith Wigglesworth: The Life and Faith of the Legendary Evangelist*. Grand Rapids, MI: Chosen Books, 2003.

Clark, Cynthia A., Everett L. Worthington Jr., and Donald B. Danser. "The Transmission of Religious Beliefs and Practices from Parents to Firstborn Early Adolescent Sons." *Journal of Marriage and Family* 50, no. 2 (1988): 463–72.

Clayton, Lawrence, Jim Hoy, and Jerald Underwood. *Vaqueros, Cowboys, and Buckaroos*. Austin: University of Texas Press, 2001.

Clayton, Lawrence Ray. "John A. Lomax's *Cowboy Songs and Other Frontier Ballads*: A Critical Study." PhD diss., Texas Tech University, 1974.

Cole, Robert A. "Promising to Be a Man: Promise Keepers and the Organizational Constitution of Masculinity." In *The Promise Keepers: Essays on Masculinity and Christianity*, edited by Dane S. Claussen, 113–32. Jefferson, NC: McFarland, 2000.

Copen, Casey, and Merril Silverstein. "Transmission of Religious Beliefs across Generations: Do Grandparents Matter?" *Journal of Comparative Family Studies* 38, no. 4 (2007): 497–510.

Cragun, Ryan T., and Joseph H. Hammer. "'One Person's Apostate Is Another Person's Convert': What Terminology Tells Us About Pro-Religious Hegemony in the Sociology of Religion." *Humanity and Society* 35, nos. 1–2 (2011): 149–75.

Cranfill, James B. *Dr. J. B. Cranfill's Chronicle: A Story of Life in Texas.* New York: F. H. Revell Co., 1916.

Denton, Sally, and Roger Morris. *The Money and the Power: The Making of Las Vegas and Its Hold on America, 1947–2000.* New York: Alfred A. Knopf, 2001.

Dewey, Joanna. "1 Timothy." In *The Women's Bible Commentary,* edited by Carol A. Newsom and Sharon H. Ringe, 353–58. Louisville, KY: Westminster / John Knox, 1992.

Dorson, Richard M. *American Folklore & the Historian.* Chicago: University of Chicago Press, 1971.

Dunn, Joseph. *Sharing the Victory: The Twenty-Five Years of the Fellowship of Christian Athletes.* New York: Quick Fox, 1980.

Ehrman, Bart D. *The New Testament: A Historical Introduction to the Early Christian Writings.* 5th ed. New York: Oxford University Press, 2012.

Eilers, Leonard. *Breaking Into the Movies.* Burbank, CA: printed by author, 1938.

Erickson, John R. *The Modern Cowboy.* 2nd ed. Denton: University of North Texas Press, 2004.

Eskridge, Larry. *God's Forever Family: The Jesus People Movement in America.* New York: Oxford University Press, 2013.

Evans, Joe M. *Bloys Cowboy Camp Meeting.* El Paso, TX: Guynes Printing Co., 1959.

Evans, Joe M. *The Cowboys' Hitchin' Post.* El Paso, TX, n.p, ca. 1946–1947.

Evans, Norman. *Muddy Shoes: A Ministry in the Mud and Dirt of the Horse Tracks.* N.p.: Xulon Press, 2004.

Fenster, Mark. "Preparing the Audience, Informing the Performers: John A. Lomax and Cowboy Songs and Other Frontier Ballads." *American Music* 7, no. 3 (1989): 260–77.

Fife, Austin, and Alta Fife. *Heaven on Horseback: Revivalist Songs and Verse in the Cowboy Idiom.* Logan, UT: Utah State University Press, 1970.

Fiore, Benjamin. *The Pastoral Epistles: First Timothy, Second Timothy, Titus.* Edited by Daniel J. Harrington. Collegeville, MN: Liturgical Press, 2007.

Flowers, Elizabeth H. *Into the Pulpit: Southern Baptist Women and Power since World War II.* Chapel Hill: University of North Carolina Press, 2012.

Forbis, William H., and the editors of Time-Life Books. *The Cowboys.* New York: Time-Life Books, 1973.

Fredriksson, Kristine. *American Rodeo: From Buffalo Bill to Big Business.* College Station: Texas A&M University Press, 1985.

Fry, Phillip L., and James Ward Lee. *Texas Country Singers.* Fort Worth: Texas Christian University Press, 2008.

Fussell, Betty. *Raising Steaks: The Life and Times of American Beef.* Orlando: Harcourt, 2008.

George-Warren, Holly. *Public Cowboy No. 1: The Life and Times of Gene Autry.* New York: Oxford University Press, 2007.

Goldberger, Paul. "The Gospel of Church Architecture, Revised." *New York Times,* 20 April 1995.

Graves, H. A., comp. *Reminiscences and Events in the Ministerial Life of Rev. John Wesley DeVilbiss.* Galveston, TX: W. A. Shaw & Co., 1886.

Gregg, Robert. *Sparks from the Anvil of Oppression: Philadelphia's African Methodists and Southern Migrants, 1890–1940.* Philadelphia: Temple University Press, 1993.

Hadden, Jeffrey K. "Religious Movements." In *Encyclopedia of Sociology,* 2nd ed, edited by Edgar F. Borgatta and Rhonda J. V. Montgomery, 2364–76. New York: MacMillan Reference, 2001.

Haley, James E. *The XIT Ranch of Texas and the Early Days of the Llano Estacado.* Rev. ed. Norman: University of Oklahoma Press, 1953.

Hall, Ralph J. *The Main Trail.* San Antonio, TX: The Naylor Co., 1971.

Hassrick, Peter H. *Remington, Russell and the Language of Western Art.* Washington, DC: Trust for Museum Exhibitions, 2000.

Haug, Werner, Paul Compton, and Youssef Courbage, eds. *The Demographic Characteristics of National Minorities in Certain European States.* Vol. 2. Strasbourg: Council of Europe Publishing, 2000.

Hillhouse, John C., Jr. *Horses, Hoofbeats and Halos: The History of Race Track Chaplaincy of America, Inc. 1969–1999.* Graceville, FL: Hargrave Press, 1999.

Hine, Robert V. *The American West: An Interpretive History.* Boston: Little, Brown and Co., 1973.

Hoge, Dean R., and Gregory H. Petrillo. "Determinants of Church Participation and Attitudes among High School Youth." *Journal for the Scientific Study of Religion* 17, no. 4 (1978): 359–79.

Homann, Ronnie Dean. "Contemporary Cowboy Culture and the Rise of American Postmodern Solidarity." PhD diss., University of North Texas, 2006.

Hopkins, A. D. "Benny Binion: He Who Has the Gold Makes the Rules." In *The Players: The Men Who Made Las Vegas,* edited by Jack E. Sheehan, 48–67. Reno: University of Nevada Press, 1997.

Hunter, George G., III. *Church for the Unchurched.* Nashville: Abingdon Press, 1996.

Hurley, Jimmie. "Christian Cowboys." *The Western Horseman,* December 1974, 8–10 and 97.

James, Will S. *Cow-Boy Life in Texas, or 27 Years a Mavrick.* Chicago: Donohue & Co., 1893.

Johnson, Michael. *Healing Shine: A Spiritual Assignment . . . .* Campbell, TX: Season of Harvest Publications, 2007.

Jordan, Philip D. "The Pistol Packin' Cowboy." In *The Cowboy: Six-Shooters, Songs, and Sex,* edited by Charles W. Harris and Buck Rainey, 57–83. Norman, OK: University of Oklahoma Press, 1976.

Kellogg, Jay C. *The Broncho Buster Busted, and Other Messages.* Tacoma, WA: Whole Gospel Crusaders of America, Inc., 1932.

Kieren, Dianne K., and Brenda Munro. "Following the Leaders: Parents' Influence on Adolescent Religious Activity." *Journal for the Scientific Study of Religion* 26, no. 2 (1987): 249–55.

Ladd, Tony, and James A. Mathisen. *Muscular Christianity: Evangelical Protestants and the Development of American Sport.* Grand Rapids, MI: Baker Books, 1999.

Laird, Rebecca. *Ordained Women in the Church of the Nazarene.* Kansas City, MO: Nazarene Publishing House, 1993.

Lambert, Lake, III. *Spirituality, Inc.: Religion in the American Workplace.* New York: New York University Press, 2009.

Landis, Kevin. *The Cowboy Steward: The Cowboy Way to the Christian Life.* New York: iUniverse, 2006.

Lawrence, Elizabeth Atwood. *Rodeo: An Anthropologist Looks at the Wild and the Tame.* Knoxville: University of Tennessee Press, 1982.

LeCompte, Mary Lou. *Cowgirls of the Rodeo: Pioneer Professional Athletes.* Urbana: University of Illinois Press, 1993.

Lim, Chaeyoon, Carol Ann MacGregor, and Robert D. Putnam. "Secular and Liminal: Discovering Heterogeneity among Religious Nones." *Journal for the Scientific Study of Religion* 49, no. 4 (2010): 596–618.

Limerick, Patricia Nelson. *The Legacy of Conquest: The Unbroken Past of the American West.* New York: W. W. Norton, 1987.

Logsdon, Guy. "The Cowboy's Bawdy Music." In *The Cowboy: Six-Shooters, Songs, and Sex,* edited by Charles W. Harris and Buck Rainey, 127–38. Norman, OK: University of Oklahoma Press, 1976.

Logsdon, Guy, comp. *"The Whorehouse Bells Were Ringing" and Other Songs Cowboys Sing.* Urbana: University of Illinois Press, 1989.

Lomax, John A., comp. *Cowboy Songs and Other Frontier Ballads.* Reprint of the 1919 rev. edition. New York: MacMillan, 1931.

Lomax, John A., comp. *Songs of the Cattle Trail and Cow Camp.* 1919. Reprint, New York: Macmillan, 1927.

Loveland, Anne C., and Otis B. Wheeler. *From Meetinghouse to Megachurch: A Material and Cultural History.* Columbia: University of Missouri Press, 2003.

Low, Robbie. "The Truth about Men & Church." *Touchstone: A Journal of Mere Christianity* (June 2003), http://www.touchstonemag.com/archives/article.php?id=16-05-024-v.

Marler, Penny Long, and C. Kirk Hadaway. "Toward a Typology of Protestant 'Marginal Members.'" *Review of Religious Research* 35, no. 1 (1993): 34–54.

Mattis, Jacqueline S., Kiu Eubanks, Alix A. Zapata, Nyasha Grayman, Max Belkin, N'Jeri K. Mitchell, and Sharon Cooper. "Factors Influencing Religious Non-Attendance among African American Men: A Multimethod Analysis." *Review of Religious Research* 45, no. 4 (2004): 386–403.

McAdams, Jake R. "Can I Get a Yee-Haw and an Amen: Collecting and Interpreting Oral Histories of Texas Cowboy Churches." Master's thesis, Stephen F. Austin State University, 2013.

McCaffrey, Raymond. "God Does Not Wear Wranglers." *Colorado Springs Gazette,* 1 August 1998.

McCoy, Joseph G. *Historic Sketches of the Cattle Trade of the West and Southwest.* Kansas City, MO: Ramsey, Millett, and Hudson, 1874.

McDannell, Colleen. *Material Christianity: Religion and Popular Culture in America.* New Haven, CT: Yale University Press, 1995.

McGill, Jerry C., James R. Hall, W. Randall Ratliff, and Raymond F. Moss. "Personality Characteristics of Professional Rodeo Cowboys." *Journal of Sport Behavior* 9, no. 4 (1986): 143–51.

McGillis, Roderick. *He Was Some Kind of a Man: Masculinities in the B Western.* Waterloo: Wilfred Laurier University Press, 2009.

Meinig, D. W. "American Wests: Preface to a Geographical Interpretation." *Annals of the Association of American Geographers* 62, no. 2 (1972): 159–84.

Messner, Michael A. *Politics of Masculinities: Men in Movements.* Thousand Oaks, CA: Sage Publications, 1997.

Miller, Donald E. *Reinventing American Protestantism: Christianity in the New Millennium.* Berkeley: University of California Press, 1997.

Moczygemba, Sarah. "Rounding Up Christian Cowboys: Myth, Masculinity and Identity in Two Texas Congregations." Master's thesis, University of Florida, 2013.

Moore, Jacqueline M. *Cow Boys and Cattle Men: Class and Masculinities on the Texas Frontier, 1865–1900.* New York: New York University Press, 2010.

Morrell, Zenos N. *Flowers and Fruits from the Wilderness.* 3rd ed. St. Louis, MO: Commerical Print Co., 1882.

Moses, L. G. *Wild West Shows and the Images of American Indians, 1883–1933.* Albuquerque: University of New Mexico Press, 1996.

Murrow, David. *Why Men Hate Going to Church.* Nashville: Thomas Nelson Publishers, 2005.

Nelsen, Hart M. "The Religious Identification of Children of Interfaith Marriages." *Review of Religious Research* 32, no. 2 (1990): 122–34.

Nelsen, Hart M. "Religious Transmission versus Religious Formation: Preadolescent-Parent Interaction." *The Sociological Quarterly* 21, no. 2 (1980): 207–18.

Nicolet, Sarah, and Anke Tresch. "Changing Religiosity, Changing Politics?: The Influence of 'Belonging' and 'Believing' on Political Attitudes in Switzerland." *Politics and Religion* 2, no. 1 (2009): 76–99.

Noll, Mark A., David W. Bebbington, and George A. Rawlyk, eds. *Evangelicalism: Comparative Studies of Popular Protestantism in North America, the British Isles, and Beyond, 1700–1990.* New York: Oxford University Press, 1994.

O'Dell, Gary A. "Denton Offutt of Kentucky: America's First 'Horse Whisperer'?" *The Register of the Kentucky Historical Society* 108, no. 3 (2010): 173–211.

Oxford Encyclopedia of Food and Drink in America. Edited by Andrew F. Smith. New York: Oxford University Press, 2004.

Parisot, P. F. *The Reminiscences of a Texas Missionary.* San Antonio: Johnson Brothers Printing, 1899.

Perabeau, Charles L. "The Church of the Nazarene in the U.S.: Race, Gender, and Class in the Struggle with Pentecostalism and Aspirations Toward Respectability, 1895–1985." PhD diss., Drew University, 2011.

Perry, Everett L., Ruth T. Doyle, James H. Davis, and John E. Dyble. "Toward a Typology of Unchurched Protestants." In "The Unchurched American: A Second Look," supplement, *Review of Religious Research* 21, no. 4 (1980): 388–404.

Ploch, Donald R., and Donald W. Hastings. "Effects of Parental Church Attendance, Current Family Status, and Religious Salience on Church Attendance." *Review of Religious Research* 39, no. 4 (1998): 309–20.

Podles, Leon J. *The Church Impotent: The Feminization of Christianity.* Dallas: Spence Publishing, 1999.

Porterfield, Nolan. *Last Cavalier: The Life and Times of John A. Lomax.* Urbana: University of Illinois, 1996.

Potter, Claire Bond, and Renee C. Romano. *Doing Recent History: On Privacy, Copyright, Video Games, Institutional Review Boards, Activist Scholarship, and History that Talks Back.* Athens: University of Georgia Press, 2012.

Pritchard, G. A. *Willow Creek Seeker Services: Evaluating a New Way of Doing Church.* Grand Rapids, MI: Baker Books, 1996.

Putney, Clifford. *Muscular Christianity: Manhood and Sports in Protestant America, 1880–1920.* Cambridge, MA: Harvard University Press, 2001.

Rainey, Buck. "The Reel Cowboy." In *The Cowboy: Six-Shooters, Songs, and Sex,* edited by Charles W. Harris and Buck Rainey, 17–55. Norman: University of Oklahoma Press, 1976.

Rister, Carl Coke. *Southern Plainsmen.* Norman: University of Oklahoma Press, 1938.

Rollins, Philip A. *The Cowboy: His Characteristics, His Equipment, and His Part in the Development of the West.* 1922. Reprint, New York: Scribner's, 1926.

Roozen, David. A. "Church Dropouts: Changing Patterns of Disengagement and Re-entry." In "The Unchurched American: A Second Look," supplement, *Review of Religious Research* 21, no. 4 (1980): 427–50.

Russell, Don. "The Cowboy: From Black Hat to White." In *The Cowboy: Six-Shooters, Songs, and Sex,* edited by Charles W. Harris and Buck Rainey, 5–15. Norman: University of Oklahoma Press, 1976.

Russell, L. D. *Godspeed: Racing Is My Religion.* New York: Continuum, 2007.

Rutherford, Brinton L. "From Prosecutor to Defender: An Intellectual History of David J. du Plessis, Drawn from the Stories of his Testimony." PhD diss., Fuller Theological Seminary, 2000.

Salisbury, W. Seward. "Religious Identity and Religious Behavior of the Sons and Daughters of Religious Intermarriage." *Review of Religious Research* 11, no. 2 (1970): 128–35.

Savage, William W., Jr. *The Cowboy Hero: His Image in American History & Culture.* Norman: University of Oklahoma Press, 1979.

Savage, William W., ed. *Cowboy Life: Reconstructing an American Myth.* Rev. ed. Niwot, CO: University Press of Colorado, 1993. PDF e-book.

Schwarz, Christian A. *Natural Church Development: A Guide to Eight Essential Qualities of Healthy Churches.* St. Charles, IL: ChurchSmart Resources, 1996.

Schuller, Robert H. *Your Church Has Real Possibilities!* Glendale, CA: G/L Publications, 1974.

Sheler, Jeffrey L. *Believers: A Journey into Evangelical America.* New York: Viking, 2006.

Skaggs, Jimmy M. *The Cattle-Trailing Industry Between Supply and Demand, 1866–1890.* 1973. Reprint, Norman: University of Oklahoma Press, 1991.

Slatta, Richard W. *The Cowboy Encyclopedia.* Santa Barbara: ABC-CLIO, 1994.

Slatta, Richard W. *Cowboys of the Americas.* New Haven, CT: Yale University Press, 1990.

Smith, Glenn. *Apostle, Cowboy Style.* Post, TX: International Western World Outreach Center, 1994.

Spencer, Davalyn. "Christian Cowboys." *The Western Horseman,* January 1992, 69–70.

St. John, Bob. *On Down the Road: The World of the Rodeo Cowboy.* Englewood Cliffs, NJ: Prentice-Hall, 1977.

Stanfield, Peter. *Horse Opera: The Strange History of the 1930s Singing Cowboy.* Urbana: University of Illinois Press, 2002.

Stark, Rodney. "How New Religions Succeed: A Theoretical Model." In *The Future of New Religious Movements,* edited by David G. Bromley and Phillip E. Hammond, 11–29. Macon, GA: Mercer University Press, 1987.

Stark, Rodney. "Why Religious Movements Succeed or Fail: A Revised General Model." *Journal of Contemporary Religion* 11, no. 2 (1996): 133–46.

Stasson, Anneke. "The Politicization of Family Life: How Headship Became Essential to Evangelical Identity in the Late Twentieth Century." *Religion and American Culture* 24, no. 1 (2014): 100–138.

Steiner, Michael C., and David M. Wrobel. "Many Wests: Discovering a Dynamic Western Regionalism." In *Many Wests: Place, Culture, & Regional Identity,* edited by David M. Wrobel and Michael C. Steiner, 1–30. Lawrence, KS: University Press of Kansas, 1997.

Strobel, Lee. *Inside the Mind of Unchurched Harry & Mary.* Grand Rapids, MI: Zondervan, 1993.

Sullivan, Winnifred Fallers. *A Ministry of Presence: Chaplaincy, Spiritual Care, and the Law.* Chicago: University of Chicago Press, 2014.

Suziedelis, Antanas, and Raymond H. Potvin. "Sex Differences in Factors Affecting Religiousness among Catholic Adolescents." *Journal for the Scientific Study of Religion* 20, no. 1 (1981): 38–51.

Swanson, Doug J. *Blood Aces: The Wild Ride of Benny Binion, the Texas Gangster Who Created Vegas Poker*. New York: Viking, 2014.

Sweeney, J. Gray. "Racism, Nationalism, and Nostalgia in Cowboy Art." *Oxford Art Journal* 15, no. 1 (1992): 67–80.

Szasz, Ferenc Morton. *The Protestant Clergy in the Great Plains and Mountain West, 1865–1915*. Rev. ed. Lincoln: University of Nebraska Press, 2004.

Szasz, Ferenc Morton. *Religion in the Modern American West*. Tuscon: University of Arizona Press, 2000.

Tamney, Joseph B., Shawn Powell, and Stephen Johnson. "Innovation Theory and Religious Nones." *Journal for the Scientific Study of Religion* 28, no. 2 (1989): 216–29.

Taylor, Lonn, and Ingrid Maar. *The American Cowboy*. New York: Harper & Row, 1983.

Thor, James. "Realities of Rodeo." In "Extreme Medicine," edited by Charles Young, Faith McLellan, and Virginia Barbour, special issue, *The Lancet* 362 (December 2003): S52–53.

Thorp, N. Howard "Jack." *Songs of the Cowboys*. 1908. Reprint, Cambridge: Applewood Books, 1989.

Tinsley, Jim Bob. *He Was Singin' This Song*. Orlando: University of Central Florida Press, 1981.

Towns, Elmer L., John N. Vaughan, and David J. Seifert. *The Complete Book of Church Growth*. 2nd ed. Wheaton, IL: Tyndale House, 1989.

Wagener, Ulrike. "Pastoral Epistles: A Tamed Paul—Domesticated Women." In *Feminist Biblical Interpretation*, translated by Everett R. Kalin and edited by Luise Schottroff and Marie-Theres Wacker, 830–47. Grand Rapids, MI: Eerdmans, 2012.

Warner, R. Stephen. "Work in Progress toward a New Paradigm for the Sociological Study of Religion in the United States." *American Journal of Sociology* 98, no. 5 (1993): 1044–93.

Warren, Rick. *The Purpose Driven Church: Growth without Compromising Your Message & Mission*. Grand Rapids, MI: Zondervan, 1995.

Weatherby, Kevin. *Gospel of Matthew: Simplified Cowboy Version*. N.p.: printed by author, 2013.

Wedel, Kip Anthony. "Permission to Dissent: Civil Religion and the Radio Western, 1933–60." *Religion and American Culture* 22, no. 1 (2012): 31–52.

Westermeier, Clifford P. "The Cowboy and Religion." *The Historical Bulletin*, January 1950, 31–37.

Westermeier, Clifford P. *Trailing the Cowboy: His Life and Lore as Told by Frontier Journalists*. Caldwell, ID: Caxton Printers, 1955.

Williams, Justin. "Historicizing the Breakbeat: Hip-Hop's Origins and Authenticity." *Lied und populäre Kultur/Song and Popular Culture* 56 (2011): 133–67.

Williams, Katy Frances. "The Land-Grant Mission and the Cowboy Church: Diffusing University Community Engagement." Master's thesis, Texas A&M University, 2011.

Williford, John W., Jr. "Ethereal Cowboy Way: An Ethnographic Study of Cowboy Churches Today." PhD diss., Regent University, 2011.

Willits, Fern K., and Donald M. Crider. "Church Attendance and Traditional Religious Beliefs in Adolescence and Young Adulthood: A Panel Study." *Review of Religious Research* 31, no. 1 (1989): 68–81.

Woerner, Gail Hughbanks. *Cowboy Up! The History of Bull Riding.* Austin, TX: Eakin Press, 2001.

Wooden, Wayne S., and Gavin Ehringer. *Rodeo in America: Wranglers, Roughstock, & Paydirt.* Lawrence: University Press of Kansas, 1996.

Zhai, Jiexia Elisa, Christopher G. Ellison, Norval D. Glenn, and Elizabeth Marquardt. "Parental Divorce and Religious Involvement among Young Adults." *Sociology of Religion* 68, no. 2 (2007): 125–44.

Index